# FUNDAMENTALS OF FEDERAL CONTRACT LAW

# FUNDAMENTALS OF FEDERAL CONTRACT LAW

Eugene W. Massengale

QUORUM BOOKS
Westport, Connecticut • London

**Library of Congress Cataloging-in-Publication Data**

Massengale, Eugene W. (Eugene William).
Fundamentals of federal contract law / Eugene W. Massengale.
p. cm.
Includes bibliographical references and index.
ISBN 0-89930-604-7 (lib. bdg. : alk. paper)
1. Public contracts—United States. I. Title.
KF849.M365 1991
342.73'023—dc20
[347.30223] 90-40700

British Library Cataloguing in Publication Data is available.



Library of Congress Catalog Card Number: 90-40700
ISBN: 0-89930-604-7

First published in 1991

Quorum Books, 88 Post Road West, Westport, CT 06881
An imprint of Greenwood Publishing Group, Inc.

Printed in the United States of America

The paper used in this book complies with the Permanent Paper Standard issued by the National Information Standards Organization (Z39.48-1984).

10 9 8 7 6 5 4 3 2

# Contents

# Acknowledgments

This book has evolved over a long period of time during which I performed as a contracts manager in both government and industry and, more recently, as a lecturer in the subject area of government contract law and procurement principles. While I owe thanks to many people who have been instrumental in helping me develop an understanding of the fundamentals of federal procurement policies and procedures over the years, two stand out above all others. I owe a special debt of gratitude to Dr. George A. Zimmar, whose belief in the book made it happen. I also wish to thank Elizabeth, who, though her patience grew thin on more than one occasion, stood by with encouragement and assistance when it counted the most.

# FUNDAMENTALS
# OF
# FEDERAL CONTRACT
# LAW

# 1

# Common Law and Constitutional Bases of Federal Acquisition

## INTRODUCTION

The U.S. government is the world's single largest purchaser of goods and services. The civil and military departments of the executive branch annually award billions of dollars in contracts to the private sector for material ranging from paper clips to complex weapons systems and space vehicles, and for a variety of services from garbage collection to exotic research and development programs. These acquisitions are accomplished through an intricate procurement process that has evolved since 1775 from a few unrelated statutory fragments and the common law of contracts. The federal acquisition system is today governed by a body of law, commonly referred to as government contract law, that is based on the Constitution, federal statutes, executive orders, federal court decisions, rulings of Boards of Contract Appeals, and Comptroller General decisions. The system is implemented regulatorily through the Federal Acquisition Regulation (FAR), which has the force and effect of law. Government contract law, therefore, can best be viewed as a special blend of federal law and commercial contract law, with the overriding public interest dominating transactions between private parties and the sovereign power.

## THE COMMON LAW AND FEDERAL CONTRACTS

A major portion of the applicable law governing federal procurement is derived from the common law of contracts. Though the legal elements of government and commercial contracts are essentially the same, with similar rules of construction, there are certain fundamental differences that directly affect the parties to a government contract. These arise from the dual character of the United States as both a sovereign power and a party to a contract, from statutory and constitutional requirements implemented through the FAR, from the limited procedural means by which government obligations and liabilities are enforced, and from the fact that the government can only enter into contracts with private parties through its authorized agents.

### Choice-of-Law Considerations in Federal Acquisitions

The Constitution provides that "The Congress shall have Power to dispose of and make all needful Rules and Regulations respecting the Territory or other Property belonging to the United States. . . ." Art. IV, § 3, cl. 2. The Congress also has the power to "make all Laws which shall be necessary and proper for carrying into Execution . . . all other Powers vested by this Constitution in the Government of the United States, or in any Department or Officer thereof." Art. 1, § 8, cl. 18. Further, "[t]his Constitution, and the Laws of the United States which shall be made in Pursuance thereof . . . shall be the supreme Law of the Land. . . ." Art. VI, Cl. 2.

Every acquisition, holding, or disposition of property by the federal government depends on proper exercise of a constitutional grant of power. Acquisition policies established under federal authority may not be defeated or limited by state law. The purpose of the supremacy clause of the Constitution is to avoid the disparities, confusion, and conflicts that would follow if the government's general authority were subject to local controls. The validity and construction of contracts through which the United States is exercising its constitutional functions, their effects on the rights and obligations of the parties, and the titles or liens that they create or permit all present questions of federal law not controlled by the law of any state. *United States v. Allegheny County,* 322 U.S. 174 (1944); *Armstrong v. United States,* 144 Ct. Cl. 441, 169 F. Supp. 259 (1959).

The right of the United States to make purchases is derived from the Constitution. A petitioner's right to make sales to the United States was not given by a state and does not depend on state law. It results from the authority of the national government under the Constitution to choose its own means and sources of supply. *United States v. Department of Revenue of State of Illinois,* 202 F. Supp. 757 (N. D. Ill.), *aff'd per curiam,* 371 U.S. 21 (1962). In the absence of an applicable act of Congress, it is for the federal courts to fashion the governing rule of law according to their own standards. In so doing, the courts may adopt a state rule and apply it as federal common law. Such an application is within the general principles embodied in the supremacy clause of the Constitution and establishes a uniform rule to be applied to federal contracts. *Clearfield Trust Co. v. United States,* 318 U.S. 363 (1943). Choice-of-law considerations, therefore, do not arise with respect to government contracts awarded, performed, and paid within the United States, its territories, and its possessions.

Contracts between the United States and foreign firms, on the other hand, inevitably raise choice-of-law questions in the event of a dispute between the parties. Continued expansion of international commerce, at the government level, has generated new interest in the implications of international law relating to government contracts. However, inconsistencies and lack of clear knowledge abound when the United States acquires supplies, services, or construction from foreign firms. Where the parties select the law of a particular nation for the purpose of interpreting and enforcing contractual obligations at the time of contracting, it is generally accepted that such election will be applied unless there are contrary, overriding public policy considerations. If the parties have not made an election as to the law to be applied in the resolution of a dispute, the federal courts and Boards of Contract Appeals will generally apply U.S. law in reaching choice-of-law decisions. In so doing, one of four U.S. choice-of-law theories will be considered:

1. The place of making the contract—*lex loci contractus*
2. The place of performance or payment of the contract—*lex loci solutionis*
3. The intent of the parties
4. The center of gravity of the contract.

Whether a contract between the United States and a foreign firm is governed by the common law or the civil law can be crucial to its interpretation and enforcement. In the common law countries, the literal wording of a contract is given strict interpretation, and common law courts require strict compliance. Each civil law nation has established codes that embrace the various rules and principles of the law of that nation. Notwithstanding the existence of such a code, there is generally considerable flexibility in the application of code statements to contracts, and precedent has little of the importance it enjoys under the common law.

One of the principal differences between the common law and the civil law, as such systems apply to contracts, lies in the treatment given to certain circumstances that, under both systems, are described as constituting *force majeure*. Under the common law, *force majeure* is a superior, irresistible force that impedes performance of a contract; in short, it is a fire, flood, drought, epidemic, strike, or the like that causes an excusable delay. Generally, contracts performed in common law jurisdictions only provide for a time extension for delays attributable to *force majeure*, whereas contracts performed in civil law jurisdictions usually provide for compensation to the party who is delayed in addition to a time extension. In order to establish *force majeure* in civil law jurisdictions, the causative event must have been unforeseeable at the time of contract execution. The causative event must render contract performance absolutely impossible; the event must arise independently of the will of the party who relies on it and not be subject to his subsequent control.

Contracts between the government and private foreign contractors may be awarded, performed, and paid either in the United States or abroad. In determining whether U.S. federal common law or foreign law should apply, the Armed Services Board of Contract Appeals has applied traditional conflict-of-law rules in arriving at a decision. Under such rules, the law of the nation in which the contract is executed or performed, in which payment is to take place, or in which there is a center of gravity has been applied by the Board. By and large, the Board appears to have based its decisions on the principle that the law of the place of contract performance should be controlling in the event of a dispute between the parties, unless the parties have expressly elected a specific forum.

The first instance in which a choice-of-law question was raised before the Board was in *Joc. A. Vonk's Handelmaaschapij, N.V.*, ASBCA No. 621 (1950), where the Board said:

> The contracts are silent as to what law should govern the rights of the parties. In determining disputes arising out of Government contracts made and performed in the United States, the Board follows the general Federal law rather than that of any particular state. *United States v. Allegheny County,* 322 U.S. 174 (1944). The Federal court decisions have, through the years, applied certain principles of conflict of laws that have become part of the Federal law. The Federal court decisions that have applied such principles to contract actions have shown a confusion of opinion. 2 *Beale, Conflict of Laws,* sec. 332.9 (1935). One rule that appears to be quite firmly imbedded in the Federal law at this time is that as to matters of performance with regard to non-Government contracts the law of the place of performance governs. *Scudder v. Union National Bank,* 91 U.S. 406, 23 L. Ed. 245 (1875); *Zimmerman v. Sutherland,* 274 U.S. 253 (1926); *Kessler v. Armstrong Cork Co.,* 158 F. 744 (CCA-2 1907); 2 *Beale, Conflict of Laws,* secs. 346.5, 346.8 (1935). There is no apparent reason why the same rule should not apply to the performance of Government contracts outside the United States. See *United States v. Guaranty Trust Co.,* 393 U.S. 340 (1934). In such a case there would be no basis for considering the application of the supremacy clause of the Constitution which was the deciding factor in *United States v. Allegheny County, supra.* See *Clearfield Trust Co. v. United States,* 318 U.S. 363 (1943). The facts presented to the Board do not show where the contract was made. The place of acceptance could have been either in Germany or the Netherlands. However, the place of performance was unquestionably in Germany. The proper conclusion, therefore, is that the law of Germany should apply.

But, in the absence of evidence of German law, the Board held that it could not presume German law to be the same as the federal law since

German law had its origin in the civil law, whereas U.S. law grew out of the common law.

The Board followed *Vonk's, supra,* in *Philippine Sawmill Co.,* ASBCA No. 569 (1951), holding that Philippine law governed because the "instant contract was entered into and performed entirely within the area of the Philippines." Moreover, the Comptroller General recognized that while foreign law and customs may apply to a government contract, they do not take precedence over specific contract terms or specific statutory provisions. *Fuji Motors Corp.,* ASBCA No. 2117, 58-1 BCA 1817. *See also Nikko Kensetsu Co.,* ASBCA Nos. 5758 & 5955, 61-1 BCA 5038.

The Board has also applied the center-of-gravity theory in deciding choice-of-law questions. Under German law, the center of gravity of the contractual transaction would control the choice of law to be applied where the contract itself does not make an express election of law to govern under the Disputes clause of the contract. Under this approach, the law governing the transaction would be that of the place of performance—that is, the Federal Republic of Germany. Under German law, thus applied, all of the documents would be read as one contract, and reformation would not be required. But the Board was reluctant to accept the contractor's affidavits as conclusive evidence of how the various documents and testimony before it might be interpreted under German law. Without accepting at full value the contractor's evidence concerning German law, it disposed of the motion before it by applying principles of law that would have controlled had the contract been performed in the United States. *Schiffart und Kohler-Agentur,* ASBCA No. 10219, 65-2 BCA 5038.

Similarly, *Gourmet Enterprises,* ASBCA No. 16543, 73-2 BCA 10,064, involved purchase orders issued by American military personnel located in Vietnam to a seller located in Hong Kong. The first question to be resolved was that of the law to be applied. Here, the Board said:

> The basic modern rule of the choice of law in respect of contracts with multinational contacts is that in the first place the intent of the parties governs. Absent such intent or proof thereof, modern decisions adopt the approach of looking for the most significant connections of the transaction with a particular legal system or, as it is expressed, a "center of gravity" approach, and search for that national law with which the transaction has its closest and most real connection. Clearly, this law is not the law of the Republic of VietNam with which the transaction has no substantial connection. For its only connection with that country is the fortuitous circumstance that the buyer, Da Nang NCO Open Mess, was located there. Its legal existence and its activities were governed by American law, including the statutes, rules and regulations of the Federal common law, applicable to Government contracts. This law (which is also the law of the forum) has here the closest contact with the transaction since the purchase orders were furnished to appellant and it was to deliver the . . . [goods] at the NCO Open Mess, the place of the buyer's business. On the other hand, contact with English law, which is applied in Hong Kong, is

much more tenuous since it is only the law of appellant's (the seller's) domicile and the contracts were neither entered or to be performed there.

In *Gessellschaft Fuer Fertigunstechnik u. Machinen bau AG (FM)*, ASBCA No. 24816, 81-1 BCA 14,924, the Board held that the threshold problem in adjudicating a foreign-law question, after deciding that the issue should in fact be governed by foreign law, is determining what body of law to apply: Is the reference to the substantive law that X would apply to a nonconflict set of facts, or is it the whole law of X, including X's conflict rules as X would apply to the facts before the court? Leflor, *American Conflicts Law* (rev. ed. 1968). The "Doctrine of Renvoi" refers to the situation where the "court in resorting to a foreign law adopts the rules of the foreign law as to conflict of laws, which rules may in turn refer the court back to the law of the forum." *Black's Law Dictionary* 1167 (5th ed. 1979). In the United States, the courts have nearly always disposed of the matter as a procedural question, applying the choice-of-law rules of the forum. This results in reference only to the substantive law of the selected jurisdiction, and not to its conflict law. The Armed Services Board has always followed this practice, as well as federal law rather than that of any particular state. In *Juan Gonzales Villaba*, ASBCA No. 11942, 68-1 BCA 6885, the Armed Services Board continued to insist that foreign law be proved by evidence. Although there was no evidence in the record as to the law of Spain, the place of performance, the Board nevertheless examined those sections, as well as other sections, of the Civil Code of Spain to which the contractor had directed its attention and found nothing therein to contravene U.S. federal law. As to the contractor's specific charge that the competent authority to adjudicate the case was the Spanish court, under article 1256 of the Civil Code, the Board said:

> It is sufficient answer that the Disputes clause in this contract provides . . . that upon appeal the decision of the Secretary or his duly authorized representative for the determination of appeals (which this Board is) shall be final and conclusive to the extent permitted by law. It is well established that in courts of law, foreign law must be proved by evidence. *Cuba Railroad Co. v. Crosby*, 222 U.S. 473 (1912); *Restatement: Conflict of Laws*, sec. 621 (1934).

Thus, in *Marubeni-Iida Co.*, ASBCA No. 16937, 72-1 BCA 9408, the Board held:

> The law of this forum respecting conflict of laws requires us to follow the general civil law of Japan, as the place of performance, with respect to the discharge of the duty of performance, provided the civil law be proved as a fact. Also the civil law of Japan as the place of contracting, or as the place of performance, or as the law of both places, would also, if proved, govern interpretation of the contract, subject to limitations in favor of the forum respecting proof.

Subsequently, the Board adopted the Federal Rules of Civil Procedure. Rule 44.1 provides that:

> A party who intends to raise an issue concerning the law of a foreign country shall give notice by pleadings or other reasonable written notice. The court, in determining foreign law, may consider any relevant material or source, including testimony, whether or not submitted by a party or admissible under the Federal Rules of Evidence. The court's determination shall be treated as a ruling on a question of law.

In *Mai-To-Hghiem, d/b/a Hang T.S.C. V.N.*, ASBCA No. 16813, 73-2 BCA 10,347, the Board ruled that the determination of foreign law was to be treated as a ruling on a question of law. And in *Kei Kodasha Hanbei, K.K.*, ASBCA No. 16800, 73-1 BCA 9982, the Board accepted the testimony of a government witness, a distinguished and experienced practitioner before the Japanese courts in civil and contractual matters, to determine the foreign law applicable to the contract.

Where the parties have made a foreign law inapplicable as a condition precedent to entering into a contract, the Board has upheld the intent of the parties. It is well established that two parties can stipulate that the contract will be controlled by the law of a particular state where that state bears a reasonable relationship to the transaction, *Consolidated Jewelers v. Standard Financial Corp.*, 325 F.2d 31 (6th Cir. 1963), and where the fundamental policy of the forum is not vitiated, *B.M. Heede, Inc. v. West India Machinery & Supply Co.*, 272 F. Supp. 236 (S.D.N.Y. 1967). *See also Siegelman v. Cunard White Star*, 221 F.2d 195 (2d Cir. 1955); *Depositors Trust Co. v. Hudson General Corp.*, 485 F. Supp. 13 (E.D.N.Y. 1980); *Business Incentives Co. v. Sony Corp. of America*, 397 F. Supp. 63 (S.D.N.Y. 1975).

The power of the parties to select the jurisdiction whose law they intend to control their obligations, rights, and duties under the contract is subject to certain limitations. Thus, a stipulation by which the parties select the law to govern the contract is valid and will be given effect only if it is not contrary to the public policy of the forum or to the law or public policy of the state whose law would govern in the absence of an effective choice of law by the parties, or if it is not in violation of a statute of the forum enacted for the protection of its citizens—and then only if the selection is made in good faith and with no purpose of evading the law of the place where the contract was made or the otherwise applicatory law. Moreover, the parties' power to choose the governing law is frequently delimited by further qualifications that the contract be properly referable to the state selected and that such state have a direct, real, substantial, or significant relationship, or at least a reasonable relationship, to or connection with the transaction or subject matter of the contract. Am. Jur. 2d *Conflict of Laws § 78*.

Where the contract explicitly provided that it is "mutually agreed that the rights and liabilities imposed by this contract shall be determined by the express terms of the contract and not by Italian laws," the Armed Services Board held:

> Although a contract entered into and performed in a foreign country is governed by the laws of that country, in this case the parties made the nonapplicability of Italian laws a condition precedent to the contract. They reinforced this divorcement of the contract from Italian law by the inclusion of a special provision to that effect.

Since the contractor waived an Italian law beneficial to its financial interests, which was not shown to contravene either a public policy or an Italian law, the contract was enforced as written and as accepted by the contractor. *S.p.A. Giola & C.*, ASBCA No. 22554, 79-1 BCA 13,608.

Where the parties stipulated that the contract was to be construed and that the rights and obligations thereunder were to be governed by the law of the District of Columbia, as interpreted by the federal courts, regardless of the place of execution or performance, the question before the Board was whether it may, or must, give full literal reach to that provision. The Board held that its research did not reveal any precedent causing it to believe that the law of the District of Columbia, as interpreted by the federal courts, would require it to reach any conclusion different from the one it would reach by applying the normal federal common law of contracts:

> In the absence of a conflicting intention on the part of two contracting parties, we are satisfied that what they had in mind by their choice of law language was to have their disputes, if any, resolved by the normal applicable law applied in the Federal courts in resolving disputes involving a Federal contract.

*Honolore Brown*, ASBCA No. 23492, 83-1 BCA 16,305.

## Common Law Rights of the Government as a Party to a Contract

When the United States becomes a party to a commercial transaction, it incurs all the responsibilities of a private person under the same circumstances. *Cooke v. United States*, 91 U.S. 389 (1875). The government's contractual liability must be decided in the same manner as that of a private party in the same circumstances. *Krupp v. Federal Housing Administration*, 285 F.2d 833 (1st Cir. 1961). In the domain of commerce, the government and the contractor are on equal footing and subject to the same laws that govern individuals. Both must turn square corners in their dealings with each other. *Truong Xuan Truc v. United States*, 212 Ct. Cl. 51 (1976).

While this is generally true, some reservations must be made. First, the courts have consistently held that some common law rules are incompatible with the special needs of the government and therefore are inapplicable to its contracts. Second, the government is the controlling authority, and it could, within constitutional limitations, subordinate or supersede the common law of contracts in the public interest. For example, under the common law of contracts, a party is not entitled to recover any profits earned by the other party. Notwithstanding this fact, during the conduct of World War II, Congress authorized the government to recover excess profits realized, through profiteering, by passage of the Renegotiation Act. The Supreme Court upheld the constitutionality of the Act as providing the necessary authorization for the recovery of excess profits through renegotiation. *Lichter v. United States,* 334 U.S. 742 (1948); *Monolith Portland Midwest Co. v. Reconstruction Finance Corp.,* 282 F.2d 439 (4th Cir. 1960). During the Korean War, the Renegotiation Act of 1951 was enacted to provide for the renegotiation of certain contracts made by the United States for the purpose of national defense so as to eliminate excess profits therefrom. The Act provided the necessary authorization to recover excess profits realized during that war through renegotiation, *Litton Industries of Maryland v. Renegotiation Board,* 298 F.2d 156 (4th Cir. 1962), and the Act applied to subcontractors, *Cooper-McDonald, Inc. v. United States,* 214 Ct. C1. 481 (1977).

With respect to commercial transactions, a party cannot cancel a contract, absent a breach, without compensating the other party for his loss of anticipatory profits. Under the Act of June 15, 1917, 40 Stat. 182, Congress empowered the President to "modify, suspend, cancel, or requisition any existing or future contract for the building or purchase of ships or materials." This was a temporary measure, which was to terminate six months after the signing of a final peace treaty between the United States and Germany. Under the Act, whenever the government elected to cancel, modify, suspend, or requisition any contract, just compensation was required to be made therefor as determined by the President. In fixing just compensation, the court may consider the value of the contract at the time of cancellation, not what it would have produced by way of profits if it had been fully performed. *Russell Motor Car Co. v. United States,* 251 U.S. 514 (1923). A petitioner was not entitled to anticipated profits as compensation for the cancellation of its contracts, but only to the value of the contract at the date of cancellation. *DeLaval Steam Turbine Co. v. United States,* 284 U.S. 61 (1931). The right to recover for anticipated profits arises only if the termination of the contract by the government is wrongful and constitutes a breach. *G.L. Christian & Assocs. v. United States,* 160 Ct. Cl. 1, 312 F.2d 418 (1963).

For the most part, the government has not elected to assert its sovereign prerogatives, and the common law of contracts thus remains a significant and vital part of its contract law. Hence, government contracts, as with contracts between private parties, are generally subject to the common law rules of offer and acceptance, mutuality of consideration, mistake, misrepresentation, nondisclosure of material facts, impossibility, fraud, unconscionability, illegality, implied warranty of mutual cooperation, implied warranty of specifications, interpretation and construction, breach of contract, and measure of damages. In these respects, the government, if at fault, generally fares no better than private parties do under the common law.

## Sovereign Act Immunity

The United States is not liable to a contractor for its sovereign acts under the theory that it should not be held responsible for damages when it acts for the good of the public as a whole. Sovereign acts may include wartime rationing, the establishment of priorities for the allocation of goods and material between the public and private sectors, and special embargoes imposed on materials imported from a particular nation-state in furtherance of national policy.

From the time the United States first surrendered its sovereign immunity and consented to being sued in actions *ex contractu*, contractors commenced bringing suit against it to recover damages based on government acts that increased their cost of performance. The Court of Claims was called on to draw a distinction between acts of the government constituting breach of contract, for which the government was liable in damages, and acts of the government increasing the contractor's cost of performance, which did not subject the government to liability for monetary damages. From these cases, the Court of Claims developed the doctrine of sovereign act immunity under which the government as a contractor could not be held answerable for its public acts as a sovereign. *See Empire Gas Engineering Co.*, ASBCA No. 7190, 1962 BCA 3323.

The two characters that the government possesses as a contractor and as a sovereign cannot be fused. Nor can the United States, while sued in the one character, be made liable in damages for its acts done in the other. Whatever acts the government may do, be they legislative or executive, they cannot be deemed specially to alter, obstruct, or violate the particular contracts into which it enters with private persons. Though a contract between the government and an individual cannot be affected specially by a general law, the United States as a contractor cannot be held liable directly or indirectly for the public acts of the United States as a sovereign. *Alfred H. Jones v. United States*, 1 Ct. Cl. 383 (1865). *Accord Horowitz v. United States*, 267 U.S. 458 (1925); *Bateson-Stolte, Inc. v. United States*, 158 Ct. Cl. 455, 305 F.2d 386 (1982); *Correlated Development Corp. v. United States*, 214 Ct. Cl. 106, 556 F.2d 515 (1977).

The United States cannot be held to any liability except such as flows from its acts and defaults as a party to a contract with the plaintiff. As a consequence, any liability that attaches to the government must result from its acts or omissions in its purely contractual capacity and cannot be culled from its general and public acts as a sovereign. Therefore, the United States does not incur any liability by reason of its issuing priority orders that forbade the use of certain materials called for in the specifications of the contract. It issued those priority orders for the purpose of mobilizing the economy for war, and such issuance was an act of a general and public character, affecting all persons situated similarly to the plaintiff. *Aragona Constr. Co. v. United States,* 165 Ct. Cl. 382 (1964).

But the doctrine of "public and general" sovereign acts laid down in *Alfred H. Jones v. United States* and *Horowitz v. United States, supra,* does not relieve the government of liability when it has specially undertaken to perform the very act from which it later seeks to be excused. When the United States enters into a contract, it should carry out its terms in good faith and invoke its great powers of a sovereign act when and only when and to the extent necessary to carry out its essential government functions. To come within the rule for immunity for a sovereign act, the action taken must be in the public interest and have a general rather than a specific or local application, and it must not be unduly oppressive on individuals. *Air Terminal Services v. United States,* 165 Ct. Cl. 525, 330 F.2d 974 (1964).

## CONSTITUTIONAL BASES OF FEDERAL ACQUISITION

The authority of the United States to acquire goods or services is not found in any express provision of the Constitution. But it nevertheless has a capacity to contract, a capacity incidental to the general rights of sovereignty. The United States, being a body politic, may, within the sphere of the constitutional powers confided to it and through the instrumentalities to which those powers are confided, enter into contracts that are not prohibited by law and are appropriate to the just exercise of those powers. To adopt a different principle would be to deny the United States the ordinary rights of sovereignty. *United States v. Tingey,* 30 U.S. (S. Pet.) 115 (1831).

The United States is a government and consequently a body politic and corporate, capable of attaining the objects for which it was created. This great corporation was created by the American people and endowed by them with great powers for important purposes. Its powers are unquestionably limited, but within those limits, it is as perfect a government as any other, having all the faculties and properties belonging to a government with a perfect right to use them in order to accomplish the objects of its institutions. One of the means by which these objects are to be accomplished is the contract, and its contracts may be made in the name of the United States. *United States v. Maurice,* 26 F. Cas. 1211 (C.C.D. Va. 1823). But the abstract powers of the United States to contract must be carefully distinguished from the authority of the government's procuring agencies to enter into a contract that may be, and quite often is, restricted by Congress.

### Appropriations

Though the Constitution does not specifically address the acquisition of goods and services, two of its provisions are especially relevant. Article 1, section 8, clause 1 provides that Congress shall have the power to "lay and collect Taxes, Duties, Imposts, and Excises, to pay the Debts and provide for the common Defence and general Welfare of the United States. . . ." Article 1, section 9, clause 7 provides that "[n]o Money shall be drawn from the Treasury, but in Consequence of Appropriations made by law. . . ." Sections 8 and 9 of article 1 are the fundamental authorities by which Congress exercises control over the federal acquisition process. Congress has not only the power to appropriate funds, but also the power to regulate the manner in which these funds are accounted for and expended.

Accordingly, no officer, however high—not even the President, much less a Secretary of Treasury or a Treasurer—is empowered to pay debts of the United States generally, when presented to them. The difficulty in the way is the want of an appropriation by Congress. It is a well-known constitutional provision that no money can be taken or drawn from the Treasury except under an appropriation by Congress. *Reeside v. Walker,* 52 U.S. (11 How.) 272 (1850).

It is no defense that Congress fails to appropriate the entire amounts due, while it leaves unrepealed the law that established a program. The United States can no more discharge its contracts by part performance than an individual person can. Congress may fail to appropriate, in whole or in part, the money required for payment of a public creditor and thus leave the public officers without authority to draw the money from the Treasury for that purpose, but the indebtedness of the government does not generally depend on appropriations. The constitutional provision in article 1, section 9 is a mere limitation and restriction on the executive officers of the Treasury Department and does not prevent Congress, the lawmaking power, from involving the government in contracts to pay money to any extent. When such contracts are made, the parties that acquire rights to compensation thereunder must wait until an appropriation is made before they can receive their money, but the rights on their part and the obligations on the part of the United States remain unchanged. Failing to obtain direct appropriations for their benefit, public creditors may sue in the Court of Claims and thus obtain payment out of any money appropriated for the payment and satisfaction of private claims. *Mitchell v. United States,* 18 Ct. Cl. 281 (1883).

Moreover, absent the most explicit of statutory language, a congressional limitation on expenditures should not be read as excluding recovery for circumstances over which the contractor could have no control and which were not his fault. It is difficult to conclude that Congress intended that a contractor would remain without a remedy for over-limitation expenses for additional work caused by errors or defects in the government's plans and specifications or required by changed conditions encountered in the performance of the work. Maximum contract provisions do not ordinarily control where contractors suffer additional costs because of the government's fault. *Ross Constr. Corp. v. United States,* 183 Ct. Cl. 694, 392 F.2d 984 (1968). *Accord Foster Constr. C.A. v. United States,* 193 Ct. Cl. 587 (1970); *Raymond Constructors of Africa v. United States,* 188 Ct. Cl. 147 (1969).

Appropriations include funds and authorizations to create obligations by contract in advance of appropriations and any other funds available for obligation or expenditure. 31 U.S.C. § 2. A specific appropriation is a particular act of Congress for a specific purpose. For example, a specific appropriation of $63,000 was made for books and periodicals for the Supreme Court, to be purchased by the Librarian of the Supreme Court under the direction of the Chief Justice. Judiciary Appropriations Act, Pub. L. No 93-433 (1975). Where an alleged liability rests wholly on the authority of an appropriation, they must stand and fall together, so that when the latter is exhausted, the former is at an end, to be revived, if at all, only by subsequent legislation by Congress. *Shipman v. United States,* 18 Ct. Cl. 138 (1883). A specific appropriation remains available until exhausted and is to be used in preference to a general appropriation when the former is available.

General appropriations are made for a group of objects necessary for the performance of a broad function (e.g., personnel funds; operations and maintenance funds; procurement–high dollar value funds; research, development, test, and evaluation funds; and construction funds). Operations and maintenance appropriations are typically authorized to cover expenses not otherwise provided for that are necessary for the operation and maintenance of an agency or service. *See* Department of Defense Appropriations Act of 1984, Pub. L. No. 98-212, 97 Stat. 1421, 1423 (1983). This particular category of funds has been described as a "murky world which does not easily lend itself to clearcut conclusions." Comp. Gen. B-213137 (1984).

There are, however, statutory restrictions applicable to the expenditure of general funds. Sums appropriated for the various branches of expenditures must be applied solely to the objects for which they are authorized, except as otherwise provided by law. The Comptroller General has identified three tests to be considered in determining whether an expense is necessary or incidental to the proper execution of the object of an appropriation. First, the expenditure must be reasonably related to the purposes for which the appropriation was made. 42 Comp. Gen. 226, 228 (1962). Second, the expenditure must not be prohibited by law. 38 Comp. 782, 785 (1959). Third, the expenditure must not fall specifically within the scope of some other category of appropriations. *Id.* This last requirement applies even if the more appropriate funding source is exhausted and therefore unavailable. Comp. Gen. B-139510 (1959).

Case-by-case decisions as to which appropriation may be used for a particular purpose are left to agency discretion, and so long as such determinations are made in conformity with these rules, they generally have not been questioned by the Comptroller General. See 18 Comp. Gen. 298 (1938). In certain cases, either of two appropriations may reasonably be construed as available for an expenditure not specifically mentioned under either appropriation. In such cases, it is within the discretion of the agency to determine which appropriation is to be used, but once the determination has been made, it cannot later be changed. *See* 59 Comp. Gen. 518 (1980).

In 41 U.S.C. § 12, it is provided that no contract shall be entered into for the erection, repair, or furnishing of any public building, or for any public improvement, that will bind the government to pay a larger sum of money than the amount in the Treasury appropriated for that specific purpose. This provision is applicable to all executive departments. *Sutton v. United States,* 256 U.S. 575, 579 (1921). The Comptroller General has interpreted 41 U.S.C. § 12 as requiring that funding for construction projects be specifically authorized by Congress. Other, more general funds, such as operations and maintenance appropriations, are generally not available for such projects. *See* Comp. Gen. B-165289 (1968); 42 Comp. Gen. 212 (1962). In addition to the restrictive language of 41 U.S.C. § 12, such activities clearly fall within the scope of appropriations provided by Congress for such purposes.

Utilizing funds for any purpose other than for the bona fide needs for which they were appropriated is prohibited by 31 U.S.C. § 1301(a). The general rule for lawfully obligating a fiscal year appropriation is that the supplies or services are intended to serve a bona fide need of the fiscal year in which the need arose or to replace stock used in such fiscal year. 37 Comp. Gen. 60 (1957); 21 Comp. Gen. 1159 (1941). Except as otherwise provided by law, all balances of appropriations contained in the annual appropriations bills and made specifically for the service of any fiscal year shall be applied only to the payment of expenses properly incurred during that year or to the fulfillment of contracts properly made within that year. 31 U.S.C. § 712(a).

Thus, where a contract is entered into in one fiscal year and services are not required until the next fiscal year, the appropriation current at the time the services are to be performed is charged. Comp. Gen. B-174226 (1972); Comp. Gen. B-123964 (1962); Comp. Gen B-114619 (1955). But if the services rendered under the contract are a single undertaking determinable at the time of contract execution, as to both the services to be rendered and the price to be paid, then the contract is considered entire or nonseverable, and the appropriation charged at the date of obligation is the proper statute to charge for the bona fide need of that fiscal year. 23 Comp. Gen. 370 (1943). When amounts for increases in cost reimbursement contracts exceed the original contract ceiling price and are not based on an antecedent liability enforceable by the contractor, the increase may be charged to funds available when a contract price increase is granted by the Contracting Officer. 61 Comp. Gen. 609 (1982).

Since the government cannot foresee increases in contract expenditures at the time the contract is made, it is not forced to reserve funds for contingencies. The Comptroller General has consistently recognized that the government may not be obligated to pay uncertain or unlimited contingent liabilities since it can never be said that sufficient funds have been appropriated to cover such contingencies. Comp. Gen. B-186313 (1976); Comp. Gen. A-95749 (1938); 16 Comp. Gen. 803 (1937). If the government is liable upon the happening of a remote event, it will result in an obligation at the time of decision by the Contracting Officer. 42 Comp. Gen. 708 (1963).

When a contract is terminated for default, funds obligated for the defaulted contract generally remain available to finance the reprocurement contract, whether awarded in the same or the following fiscal year. Even if the default termination is converted to a termination for convenience after award of the reprocurement contract, deobligation is not required. Comp. Gen. B-198074 (1981).

## Anti-Deficiency Act

Congress, in making appropriations, has the power and the authority to designate not only the purpose of appropriation, but also the terms and conditions under which the executive departments of the government may expend public monies. *Manlove & Spaulding Mfg. Co. v. Douglas Aircraft Co.*, 154 F.2d 419 (9th Cir. 1946). It likewise has the power under the Constitution to enact criminal sanctions to assure that such monies are, in fact, expended in accordance with the wishes of the legislature. The Anti-Deficiency Act is both a statute that expresses the legislature's frustration with executive agency practices of ignoring the limitations placed on expenditures and a punitive statute that expresses the desire of Congress that those who ignore its edicts be dealt with. The Act is the principal statutory authority by which Congress assures itself that expenditures of appropriated funds by the executive branch are kept within the levels established by appropriations and related statutes. In so doing, Congress is meeting its obligations under article 1, sections 8 and 9 of the Constitution, and no executive branch agency has the power or authority to obligate or expend public funds until Congress has fulfilled its duty.

In 1870, Congress sought to curb the pervasive practice of creating obligations without appropriations by the passage of the Act of July 2, 1870, 16 Stat. 251, which became known as the Anti-Deficiency Act. Following several amendments, the Act is today codified at 31 U.S.C. § 1341(a), which provides that:

> (1) An officer or employee of the United States Government or of the District of Columbia government may not—
> (A) make or authorize an expenditure or obligation exceeding an amount available in an appropriation or fund for the expenditure or obligation; or
> (B) involve either government in a contract or obligation for the payment of money before an appropriation is made unless authorized by law.

The Act does not prohibit award of a conditional contract where the government's liability is contingent on the availability of funds. 39 Comp. Gen. 340 (1959). Accordingly, the Contracting Officer may initiate a contracting action chargeable to funds of the new fiscal year before such funds are available, provided that the contract is contingent on the availability of new fiscal year funds. This authority may be used only for operation and maintenance and for continuing services (e.g., rentals, utilities, and supply items not financed by stock funds) (1) which are necessary for normal operations and (2) for which Congress previously had consistently appropriated funds, unless specific statutory authority exists permitting applicability to other requirements. FAR § 32.703-2. An Availability of Funds clause must be included in the solicitation instrument, as well as in the resultant contract. FAR § 32.705-1. FAR clauses provide that funds are not presently available for the procurement and that the government's liability is contingent on their being made available. Under these provisions, legal liability on the part of the government does not arise unless and until funds are available and notice of such availability is issued to the contractor in writing by the Contracting Officer.

Though this authority permits the executive agencies to place contracts in anticipation of appropriations, its limitations are well established in relation to multiyear contracts dependent on annual appropriations. The Armed Services Board of Contract Appeals has consistently denied claims resulting from suspension of work because the contract was subject to a funds limitation and the required funds did not become available. Under the circumstances, the contractor was chargeable with knowledge of the Contracting Officer's lack of authority to obligate the government in the absence of appropriated funding. This result comes from the general rule binding one to notice of limitations on a government agent's authority. *John E. Burke Engineering & Constr,* ASBCA No. 8182, 1963 BCA 3713. Similarly, a contract funded with fiscal year appropriations and having multiple yearly renewal options that provided for payment by the government of separate charges for failure to exercise a renewal option was illegal as violative of federal statutes prohibiting obligation of funds beyond the appropriation period because the charges represented the price of future years' requirements. 55 Comp. Gen. 142 (1976).

A cost overrun resulting from a modification of overhead rates under a cost-plus-fixed-fee contract for consulting services was chargeable to the

# 2

# Statutory and Regulatory Bases of Federal Acquisition

## INTRODUCTION

Acquisition at the federal level is accomplished under the specific authority of a number of statutes that have application to both the procuring agencies and their contractors. These not only provide the authority to make contracts on behalf of the United States, but also prescribe the conditions and circumstances that must be met prior to contract execution. Specific authority of the acquiring agency is set forth therein, as are limitations that must be adhered to in the execution of that authority. These statutes have been implemented through the Federal Acquisition Regulation (FAR) and agency supplements thereto, which provide specific authority for the Contracting Officer to enter into, administer, and terminate contracts.

## STATUTORY BASES OF FEDERAL ACQUISITION

### Historical Background

Since the beginning of this nation, Congress has expressed its belief that the only effective method of preventing fraud and abuse in government acquisitions is by means of a competitive, open bid system.

The Civil Sundries Appropriations Act was passed on March 2, 1861, and was relied on by the United States during the American Civil War. Following further amendments in 1874 and 1878, the Act became known as section 3709 of the Revised Statutes. Section 3709 stressed the use of the formally advertised method of acquisition, but did permit procurement by negotiation under certain circumstances. The Act was suspended during

World War II under provisions of the First War Powers Act, but was reinstated immediately following the end of that war.

The use of the formally advertised method of procurement mandated by section 3709 was unsuccessfully challenged in the courts during its existence, but it was consistently held that where a statute mandates a specific method of contracting or requires the inclusion of a particular clause in a contract, the resultant contract is not binding on the United States if it is not in accord with the statute. Thus, where a statute requires for the government's benefit that its contracts be made after public advertising, this rule applies. Section 3709 was not enacted for the protection of sellers and conferred no enforceable rights on prospective bidders. The United States needs the protection of publicity, form, and affidavit to prevent possible fraud on it by others. Like private individuals and businesses, the government enjoys the unrestricted power to produce its own supplies, to determine those with whom it will deal, and to fix the terms and conditions on which it will make needed purchases. Acting through its agents, as it must of necessity, the government may for the purpose of keeping its own house in order lay down guideposts by which its agents are to proceed in the acquisition of supplies or services and which create duties to the government alone. It has done so in the various procurement statutes. *Perkins v. Lukens Steel Co.,* 310 U.S. 113 (1940).

## The Armed Services Procurement Act of 1947

The end of World War II necessitated the return to prewar authority for the acquisition of goods and services by executive agencies. This return mandated the use of formal advertising by and large, which had proven ineffective in the face of a national emergency. In the light of concern in both Congress and the executive branch over the ability of nation to maintain a strong defense posture in the face of a growing split with the Soviet Union, and the perceived potential of the federal procurement system as a tool for the implementation of socioeconomic policies, the Armed Services Act was passed in 1947.

The Armed Services Procurement Act of 1947, 10 U.S.C. §§ 2301–2314, applies to purchases, and contracts to purchase, by the Department of Defense, the National Aeronautics and Space Administration, and the Coast Guard. It is applicable to purchases of all property, less real property in being, and all services for which payment is to be made from appropriated funds. 10 U.S.C. § 2305(a) & (b).

In promulgating the Act, Congress established a policy that all services and property (including weapons systems and associated items) for the Department of Defense be acquired through the use of any contract type, except for cost-plus-percentage-of-cost contracts, including multiyear contracts, that would promote the interests of the United States. Congress also mandated that such contracts, when practicable, provide for the purchase of property at times and in quantities that would result in reduced costs to the government and provide incentives to contractors to improve productivity through investment in capital facilities, equipment, and advanced technology. Furthermore, Congress required that a fair proportion of the purchases and contracts made under the Act be placed with small business concerns. 10 U.S.C. § 2301(a) & (b).

Congressional preference for the sealed bid method of acquisition was reflected in 10 U.S.C § 2304(a), which provided in part:

> Purchases of and contracts for property or services covered by this chapter shall be made by formal advertising, and shall be awarded on a competitive bid basis to the lowest responsible bidder, in all cases in which the use of the method is feasible and practicable under the existing conditions and circumstances.

When formal advertising was used, Congress ordered that the advertisement be made a sufficient time before the purchase or contract and that the specifications and invitations for bids permit such full and free competition as is consistent with the procurement of the property or services by the agency concerned. Moreover, if the specification in an invitation for bids did not include the necessary descriptive language and attachments, or if those attachments were not accessible to all competent and reliable bidders, the invitation was invalid, and no award could be made. 10 U.S.C. § 2305(a) & (b).

If the use of formal advertising was not feasible or practicable, the head of a procuring agency, subject to the requirements for determinations and findings in 10 U.S.C § 2310, could authorize negotiations if the facts and circumstances of the procurement met the requirements of one of the exceptions to formal advertising cited in 10 U.S.C. § 2304(a)(1) through (17).

In all negotiated procurements in excess of $25,000, in which rates or prices were not fixed by law or regulation and in which time of delivery permitted, proposals, including price, had to be solicited from the maximum number of qualified sources consistent with the nature and requirements of the supplies or services to be procured. Written or oral discussions were required with all responsible offerors who submitted proposals within a competitive range, price, and other factors considered. However, the requirement with respect to written or oral discussions need not be applied to procurements where it could be clearly demonstrated, from the existence of adequate competition or accurate prior cost experience with the product, that acceptance of an initial proposal without discussion could result in fair and reasonable prices and where the request for proposals notified all offerors of the possibility that award might be made without discussion. 10 U.S.C. § 2304(g).

## The Federal Property and Administrative Services Act of 1949

The Federal Property and Administrative Services Act of 1949, 41 U.S.C §§ 251–260, is concerned with procurement policies and procedures, and specifies the legal requirements applicable to formally advertised and negotiated methods of acquisition with respect to the civil agencies of the executive branch. With the exception of a few minor changes relative to civil agency requirements, this title follows in structure, and is substantially identical to, the Armed Services Procurement Act.

## The Competition in Contracting Act

The Competition in Contracting Act, Pub. L. No. 98-369, 98 Stat. 494 (1984), is the single most important procurement act to be enacted by Congress since passage of the Armed Services Procurement Act and the Federal Property and Administrative Services Act. The Competition in Contracting Act (CICA), among other changes that will be discussed in succeeding chapters, abolished traditional congressional bias toward formal advertising to permit the executive agencies to use the competitive procedure, or the combination of competitive procedures, that is most suitable under the circumstances of the procurement. Under CICA, the negotiated method of acquisition has been placed on the same footing as the sealed bid method.

With the passage of CICA, Congress abandoned its traditional preference for procurement by formal advertising. Competitive procurement, whether by sealed bids or competitive proposals (e.g., negotiation), has become the preferred method. CICA amended the Armed Services Procurement Act and the Federal Property and Administrative Services Act to abolish the circumstances permitting negotiation in lieu of formal advertising, but stresses that the head of a procuring agency conducting a procurement for property or services shall *obtain full and open competition through the use of competitive procedures.*

In determining the appropriate competitive procedures to be used under the circumstances of the procurement, the head of the procuring agency is required to solicit sealed bids if (1) time permits the solicitation, submission, and evaluation of sealed bids; (2) the award will be made on the basis of price and other price-related factors; (3) it is not necessary to conduct discussions with the responding sources about their bids; and (4) there is a reasonable expectation of receiving more than one sealed bid. 10 U.S.C. § 2304(a)(2); 41 U.S.C. § 303(a)(2).

The heads of procuring agencies may exclude a particular source of supply for property or services if it is determined that to do so would (1) increase or maintain competition and probably result in reduced overall costs for such procurement, or for any anticipated procurement, of property or services; (2) be in the interest of national defense in having a facility (or a producer, manufacturer, or other supplier) available for furnishing the property or service in the case of a national emergency or industrial mobilization; or (3) be in the interest of national defense in establishing or maintaining an essential engineering, research, or development capability to be provided by an educational or other nonprofit institution or a federally funded research and development center. 10 U.S.C. § 2304(b)(1); 41 U.S.C. § 303(b)(1).

The single most important change made by CICA lies in the statutory provisions restricting sole source procurements previously authorized by both the Armed Services Procurement Act and the Federal Property and Administrative Services Act. In recent years, because of growing reliance on, and suspected abuses of, prior statutory authority, sole source procurements have received increasingly close scrutiny by the executive, judicial, and legislative branches.

The propriety of sole source awards, particularly those justified on the basis of the technical and administrative superiority of a sole source contractor, has been addressed many times by the Comptroller General in connection with negotiated procurements under statutes and regulations that mandate competition. The Comptroller General ruled in *Electronic Systems U.S.A.*, Comp. Gen. B-200947 (1981), that, under the Federal Procurement Regulation, procurements must be conducted on a competitive basis to the maximum practical extent. Procurement on a noncompetitive basis is authorized when the legitimate needs of the government so require (e.g., when the minimum needs of the procuring agency can be met only with items or services that are unique; when time is of the essence and only one known source can meet the agency's need within the required time frame; when it is necessary to ensure compatibility between the procurement and the existing equipment; or when the award would result in unacceptable technical risks). *Northern Marine Technology*, Comp. Gen. B-191151 (1978); *Kent Watkins & Assocs.*, Comp. Gen. B-191078 (1978). Because of the requirement for maximum practicable competition, the agency's decision is subject to scrutiny and therefore must be supported by adequate legal justification. *Kent Watkins & Assocs., supra.* A decision to procure on a sole source basis will not be disturbed when the agency's written findings and determinations of the need to negotiate on a noncompetitive basis are supported by the record. *Precision Dynamics Corp.*, 54 Comp. Gen. 1114 (1975).

Where the record did not support the conclusion that competitive procurement was precluded, the Comptroller General intervened. For example, the Federal Communications Commission (FCC) attempted to justify a sole source acquisition on the basis that one firm was best qualified to install phase protection circuitry and an energy management system in an FCC laboratory because it was well acquainted with the electrical features and design of the existing equipment and therefore would require less time and expense to install the system. The FCC also stated that it was reasonable to have one contractor maintain the sole responsibility for the functioning of the system. In the Comptroller General's view, these statements did not constitute adequate justification for conducting a noncompetitive procurement. A company's prior experience with the procuring agency that may facilitate the company's performance of the required service and enable it to better anticipate problems in the implementation of the system is not a legally adequate justification to support a sole source procurement.

The fact that a particular contractor may be able to perform the services with greater ease than any other contractor does not justify a noncompetitive procurement to the exclusion of others. *Systems Group Assocs.*, Comp. Gen. B-195392 (1980); *Kent Watkins & Assocs., supra.* Neither does the possibility of incurring additional costs by employing the services of another contractor constitute adequate justification, for a sole source award may not be justified on the basis of costs to be incurred as a result of a change in contractors. Instead, this cost factor may be considered in the evaluation of proposals submitted by competitors of the incumbent. *Systems Group Assocs., supra.* The FCC's indication that its decision was based in part on the urgency of the need for the system was likewise an unacceptable justification in the absence of a definite required time frame and evidence that there was only one known source. *Las Vegas Communications*, Comp. Gen. B-195966 (1980). In fact, there was no indication that the FCC made any effort to determine the existence of other commercial sources or the feasibility of a competitive procurement prior to conducting the procurement. *Electronic Systems U.S.A.*, Comp. Gen. B-200947 (1981).

Decisions to procure on a sole source basis have in the past been affirmed by the Comptroller General, unless there was no rational basis for them. The party challenging the decision had a heavy burden of proof of irrationality. The flexibility the Comptroller General has always allowed procurement officers in defining their own needs thus was never extended to their approval of sole source procurements where the facts show the company selected was not the only one competent to perform the contract. Implicit in that firm principle is an assumption that a procurement officer has not discharged his obligation if, before competition could have begun, he preemptorily selects the "best" company. If there is more than one merely competent firm, then a hard look at the competition may substantially improve the results obtained by the government.

The public interest in competition is not vindicated until a procurement officer invites and evaluates proposals from firms that are capable of performing the work. If, in that process, market forces lead a technically competent firm to make an offer ultimately unfavorable to itself, the procurement officer may decide with competing offers before him whether the bargain will be so difficult for the offeror to meet that the government's interests will be jeopardized. But, particularly in a negotiated procurement, the essence of the procurement process is that competing offerors must at some point make independent business judgments and stick by them. It is the very difference between one offeror's judgment and that of another that allows the Contracting Officer to choose the proposal most advantageous to the government. *Kentron Hawaii v. Warner,* 480 F.2d 1166 (D.C. Cir. 1973); *Aero Corp v. Department of the Navy,* 540 F. Supp. 180 (D.C. Cir. 1982).

The procurement law's preference for competition places on the procurement officer the duty of investigating competition until he has a rational basis for believing that only one source would be capable of performing the contract or contracts he intends to offer. Unless and until a procurement officer makes a rational determination that a single firm is the only possible source for every phase of a procurement, the procurement statutes and regulations require that a Contracting Officer position himself to solicit by competitive bid all feasible contracts within the overall procurement. *Aero Corp., supra.*

In a memorandum to the heads of departments and agencies entitled "Competition in Federal Procurement," President Reagan said on August 11, 1985:

> Competition is fundamental to our free enterprise system. It is the single most important source of innovation, efficiency, and growth in our economy. Yet, far too often the benefits of competition are excluded from the Federal procurement process—a process which now results in expenditures of over $160 billion annually. Numerous examples of waste and exhorbitant costs due to the lack of competition have been detailed by the Congress and the press in recent months.

Against this backdrop of concerns, Congress severely restricted the use of sole source procurement authority when it enacted the Competition in Contracting Act. Under CICA, an agency may use procedures other than competitive procedures when

1. The property or services needed by the agency are available from only one responsible source, and no other type of property or services will satisfy the needs of the agency;
2. The agency's need for the property or services is of such an unusual or compelling urgency that the United States would be seriously injured unless the agency is permitted to limit the number of sources from which it solicits bids or proposals;
3. It is necessary to award the contract to a particular source in order to (a) maintain a facility, producer, manufacturer, or other supplier available for furnishing property or services in case of a national emergency or to achieve industrial mobilization or (b) establish and maintain an essential engineering, research, or development capability to be provided by an educational or other nonprofit institution or a federally funded research and development center;

4. The terms of an international agreement or a treaty between the United States and a foreign government or international organization, or the written directions of a foreign government reimbursing the agency for the cost of the procurement or the property or services for such government, have the effect of requiring the use of procedures other than competitive procedures;
5. A statute expressly authorizes or requires that the procurement be made through another agency or from a specified source, or the agency's need is for a brand-name commercial for authorized resale;
6. The disclosure of the agency's needs would compromise the national security, unless the agency is permitted to limit the number of sources from which it solicits bids or proposals; or
7. The head of an agency determines that it is necessary in the public interest to use procedures other than competitive procedures in the particular procurement concerned and notifies Congress in writing of such determination not less than 30 days before award of the contract. 10 U.S.C. § 2304(c); 41 U.S.C. § 303(c).

When using other than competitive procedures, the Contracting Officer is required to justify the use of such procedures in writing and to certify that the justification is accurate and complete. Moreover, the head of the agency may not award a contract under these procedures until the required approvals have been obtained.

Under no circumstances may the head of an agency enter into a contract for property or services using procedures other than competitive procurements on the basis of the lack of advance planning or concerns related to the amount of funds available to the agency for procurement functions. Nor may it obtain supplies or services from another agency, unless such agency is in full compliance with the requirements of CICA.

CICA also amended the Office of Federal Procurement Policy Act to require that the head of each executive agency appoint an Advocate for Competition. The Advocate is statutorily responsible for challenging barriers to and promoting full and open competition in the acquisition of supplies and services by the agency, to include challenges to unnecessarily restrictive statements of need.

## The Truth in Negotiations Act

Congress enacted the Truth in Negotiations Act, Pub. L. No. 87-653, in response to growing concerns with respect to the excess profits being realized by defense contractors. The congressional intent was to improve the government's chance of obtaining fair and reasonable prices in negotiated procurements by requiring contractors to fully disclose the basis for their cost proposals. The purpose of the Act is to avoid excessive contract costs that result when a contractor has in its possession accurate, current, and complete cost or pricing information and the government does not possess the same data.

Codified at 10 U.S.C. § 2306(f) and 41 U.S.C. § 304(d), the Act requires prime contractors and subcontractors to submit cost or pricing data and to certify that such data are accurate, complete, and current, under the following circumstances:

- Prior to the award of any prime contract using procedures other than sealed bid procedures, if the contract price is expected to exceed $100,000
- Prior to pricing any contract change or modification, if the price adjustment is expected to exceed $100,000 or such lesser amount as may be prescribed by the agency head
- Prior to the award of a subcontract at any tier, when the prime contractor and each higher-tier subcontractor have been required to furnish such a certificate, if the price of such subcontract is expected to exceed $100,000
- Prior to pricing any contract change or modification to a subcontract subject to the foregoing requirements, if the price adjustment is expected to exceed $100,000 or such lesser amount as may be prescribed by the agency head

The Act also requires that any contract, or change or modification thereto, under which a certificate is required shall include a provision that the price to the government, including profit or fee, shall be adjusted to exclude any significant sums by which it may be determined by the agency head that such price was increased because the contractor or any subcontractor required to furnish such a certificate furnished cost or pricing data that, as of a date to be agreed on by the parties (which date shall be as close to the date of agreement on the price as is practicable) were inaccurate, incomplete, or not current. For the purpose of evaluating the accuracy, completeness, and currency of data submitted as a consequence of the Act, any authorized representative of the agency who is an employee of the United States shall have the right, until the expiration of three years after final payment under the contract or subcontract, to examine all books, records, documents, and other data of the contractor or subcontractor related to the proposal for the contract, the discussions conducted on the proposal, pricing, or performance of the contract or subcontract.

The Truth in Negotiations Act does not require the submission of cost or pricing data when the price negotiated is based on adequate price competition, the established catalog or market price of commercial items sold in substantial quantities to the general public, or prices set by law or regulation. FAR § 15.804-3(a).

Adequate price competition is deemed to exist if offers are solicited and two or more responsible offerors that can satisfy the government's requirements submit priced offers responsive to the solicitation's expressed requirements, and if those offerors compete independently for a contract to be awarded to the responsible offeror submitting the lowest evaluated price. FAR § 15.804-3(b). Whether there is in fact adequate competition is a matter of judgment on the part of the Contracting Officer, taking into consideration the extent to which each of the stated bases has been met. If all conditions have been met, adequate price competition is presumed to exist, unless the Contracting Officer finds that the solicitation was made under conditions (1) where one or more known and qualified offerors are unreasonably denied an opportunity to compete, (2) where the low offeror has such a decided advantage over other competitors that it is practically immune to the stimulus of competition, or (3) where there is a finding, supported by a statement of the facts and approved at a level above the Contracting Officer, that the lowest price is unreasonable. FAR § 15.804-3(b).

Price competition may also be based on price analysis, if such analysis clearly demonstrates that the proposed price is reasonable in comparison with current or recent prices for the same or substantially the same items that were purchased in comparable quantities and under terms and conditions for contracts that resulted from adequate price competition.

A proposal is likewise exempt from the requirements of certified cost or pricing data if the prices are, or are based on, established catalog or market prices of commercial items sold in substantial quantities to the general public. FAR § 15.804-3(c). The application of this exception also requires analysis and judgment on a case-by-case basis, where each element of the exception must be considered. In order for the exemption to apply, a price must meet all of the conditions set forth, and the terms of the proposed purchase (i.e., quantity and delivery requirements) should be sufficiently similar to those of commercial sales that the catalog or market price will be fair and reasonable.

A catalog price is a price included in a catalog, price list, or schedule maintained by the manufacturer or vendor that is either published or otherwise available for inspection by customers and that sets forth prices at which sales currently are, or were last, made to a significant number of buyers constituting the general public. An established market price is a current price, established in the usual and ordinary course of trade between buyers and sellers free to bargain, that can be substantiated from sources independent of the manufacturer or the vendor. The term "commercial items" includes both supplies and services. The test is that they must be of a kind regularly sold for other than government purposes and also sold or offered in the course of normal business affairs. The facts or circumstances must support a reasonable conclusion that the quantities regularly sold are sufficient to constitute a real commercial market. The general public is defined as a significant number of buyers, other than the government or affiliates of the offeror.

When negotiated prices are based on established catalog or market prices and price differences can be identified and justified without resort to cost analysis, the determination to apply the exception is discretionary and requires the exercise of sound judgment by the Contracting Officer. Where a decision that the "based on" concept applies has been reached after an extensive and careful review of the factual matters involved, there has been a proper exercise of the discretion, and certified cost or pricing data must be furnished by the contractor or subcontractor. Exemptions are permissive, not mandatory, permitting the exercise of discretion and judgment on the part of procurement personnel. 49 Comp. Gen. 216, B-167823 (1969). Although requirements for cost data need not be applied to contracts where the price negotiated is based on established catalog or market prices, the statutory language envisions no mandatory exemptions from cost disclosures. Nor is such a mandate found in pertinent procurement regulations. *Sperry Flight Systems v. United States*, 212 Ct. Cl. 329, 548 F.2d 915 (1977).

Cost or pricing data, by definition, consist of all the facts existing up to the time of agreement on price that prudent buyers and sellers would reasonably expect to have an effect on the negotiation of final price. The definition includes more than historical accounting data. Rather, it includes labor rates, current and projected indirect cost structures, hours expended on related effort, prices and quotations from vendors or subcontractors, and other costs incurred or expected to be incurred for which firm quotations have been received. Also typically included are nonrecurring costs; changes in the offeror's procurement methods, or procurement or production volumes; and unit cost trends, such as those deriving from labor efficiencies. In short, cost or pricing data consist of all the facts that can reasonably be expected to contribute to sound estimates of future costs and that, being factual, can readily be verified by the Contracting Officer. FAR § 15.801.

Facts do not include judgments, though they do include the facts forming the basis for those judgments. An offeror must nevertheless disclose that a judgment was made with respect to the preparation of his proposal. Although there is no liability for erroneous judgments, the distinction between facts, to which the Certificate of Current Cost or Pricing Data apply, and judgments is difficult to make within statutory disclosure requirements.

This leads to one of the most difficult questions an offeror submitting a proposal to the government must resolve: What is the extent of disclosure to be made, and what data must be made available to the government in order to comply with the statute and implementing regulations?

The Truth in Negotiations Act imposes a duty on government contractors to disclose cost and pricing information that is accurate, complete, and current. The Act grants to the government the right to adjust the contract price when the price is increased because the contractor did not fulfill his duty. The duty is imposed on government contractors by statute and therefore cannot be waived by a government agent. The purpose of the Act is to avoid excessive contract costs that result from a contractor's having in his possession current information when the government does not possess the same data. If a contractor possesses data that is relevant to negotiations with the government and he neither physically delivers the data to the government auditor nor makes the government aware of the information's significance, then he has not fulfilled his duty under the Act. *M–R–S Mfg. Co. v. United States,* 203 Ct. Cl. 551, 492 F.2d 835 (1974).

An offeror's failure to disclose that he had parts in stock that might be used during contract performance constituted a breach of the Price Reduction for Defective Cost or Pricing Data clause of the contract because an offeror must disclose all facts that prudent buyers or sellers could expect to significantly impact price negotiations. The test of reasonableness is an objective, not a subjective, test. The possibility that parts in stock might be used in the performance of the contract was not so remote that the offeror could properly withhold disclosure. The duty of disclosure extends not only to quotes a contractor knows he will use, but also to quotes he may use. A prospective contractor does not meet his disclosure obligation by merely handing over data. It is also necessary that the government's representative be advised of the bearing that such information has on the price proposal. *Hardie-Tynes Mfg. Co.,* ASBCA No. 20367, 76-1 BCA 11,827.

In *Aerojet General,* ASBCA No. 12873, 69-1 BCA 7585, it was held that a vendor quotation on a rocket motor component, which offered a quality different from that sought and which was conditioned on a 30-day acceptance limit and a production schedule that was unacceptable to the prime contractor, was nevertheless cost or pricing data that should have been disclosed during negotiations. The contractor must disclose that judgments were made. The concealment or misrepresentation of such judgments makes his data incomplete or inaccurate, and he will be held liable.

The Truth in Negotiations Act is aimed at cases where costs are known, but information concerning them is withheld. Thus, a contractor's failure to disclose that he was considering a bid from a lens supplier that was significantly lower than the price quoted was cause to eliminate the quoted price from the overall offer and to direct the parties to renegotiate the offer based on the omitted information. *Cutler Hammer, Inc.,* ASBCA No. 10900, 67-1 BCA 6432; *aff'd, Cutler Hammer, Inc. v. United States,* 189 Ct. Cl. 76, 416 F.2d 1306 (1969).

The offeror can argue about the relevance and cyclical nature of disclosed information, but he has an obligation to disclose it. He cannot unilaterally decide what can be disclosed and what cannot. *Singer Company, Librascope Division v. United States,* 217 Ct. Cl. 225, 576 F.2d 905 (1978). This is particularly true where the government has analyzed the data and the contractor then receives reduced quotations from his suppliers. If there is a logical nexus between the nondisclosed pricing data and the possibility of a lower negotiated contract price, then the data are to be considered significant and subject to disclosure. *Sylvania Electric Products v. United States,* 202 Ct. Cl. 16, 479 F.2d 1342 (1973).

Subcontractors are also subject to the Truth in Negotiations Act, with the same dollar thresholds and exceptions as are applied to prime contractors. Moreover, subcontractor cost or pricing data must be accurate, complete, and current as of the same data specified in the prime contractor's certificate. The prime contractor is responsible for updating a prospective subcontractor's data, and failure on the part of the prime contractor to submit subcontractor cost or pricing data may be cause for disqualifying the prime from further consideration for contract award. These statutory and regulatory requirements raise two significant issues, however.

First, from the prime contractor's perspective, it is clear that the intent of the Act and its implementing regulations is to hold the prime contractor liable for a price reduction if he fails to submit subcontractor cost or pricing data, as well as for defective pricing data submitted by the subcontractor. In *Lockheed Aircraft Corp.,* ASBCA No. 10453, 67-1 BCA 6356, Lockheed's subcontractor failed to advise Air Force auditors verifying cost or pricing data used as a basis for negotiation of the existence of purchase orders for materials to be used in the performance of the subcontract. It was held that this justified the government's claim against Lockheed for the difference between the original negotiated price and the price supported by data ultimately developed. Although audit personnel were offered access to all records of the subcontractor, they were not informed of the existence of current purchase orders relating to the items being procured by the government. Therefore, failure to disclose significant and reasonably available cost data having an effect on the negotiations constituted a basis for recovery by the government.

On appeal, the Court of Claims held the prime contractor liable even though the defective subcontractor data had been submitted directly to the government and Lockheed had neither seen nor examined it. Prime contractor liability was dictated by the Price Reduction clause in the prime contract, which covered all defective data relating to the contract price with the government, and Lockheed could initiate civil action to recover from its subcontractor based on the defective pricing clauses incorporated into the prime contract. When subcontractor data have been submitted to the government prior to the negotiation of the prime contract price, whether required or not, the prime contractor is subject to a price reduction for defective cost or pricing data as if they had been the prime contractor's data. *Lockheed Aircraft Corp. v. United States,* 193 Ct. Cl. 86, 431 F.2d 801 (1970).

The second issue raised by the requirement for the submission of subcontractor cost or pricing data, from the subcontractor's perspective, is the detail of disclosure that must be made to a prime contractor. This is particularly troublesome in those cases where the prime contractor may be in competition with its subcontractors. The Truth in Negotiations Act is applicable to subcontractors and requires the submission of certified cost or pricing data to the prime contractor on nonexempt subcontracts in excess of $100,000. Moreover, the Comptroller General has ruled that a subcontractor cannot properly refuse the demands of the prime contractor and the government for certified cost or pricing data in connection with its subcontract. 49 Comp. Gen. 216 (B-167823) (1969). The FAR permits the Contracting Officer to "make other arrangements," including direct submission to the acquiring agency by the subcontractor in those cases where the subcontractor refuses to submit such data directly to the prime. FAR §§ 15.804-6(i)(5), 15.805-5(k). However, direct submission does not excuse the prime contractor from liability for defective cost or pricing data submitted by its subcontractors.

## The Small Business Act

In amending the Small Business Act on July 18, 1958, Congress declared that the essence of the U.S. economic system of private enterprise is free competition. Only through full and unrestricted competition can free markets, free entry into business, and opportunities for the expression and growth of personal initiative and individual judgment be assured. The preservation and expansion of such competition are basic not only to the economic well-being but also to the security of the nation. Such security and well-being cannot be realized unless the actual and potential capacities of small business are encouraged and developed. It is the express policy of Congress that the government should aid, counsel, assist, and protect, insofar as possible, the interests of small business concerns in order to preserve free competitive enterprise, by ensuring that a fair share of the total purchases and contracts for property and services required by the government is placed with small business concerns.

This policy has the dual purpose of ensuring the continued existence of small business firms and hence a healthy competitive environment and of ensuring a broad base of capable suppliers and service organizations in the event a future national emergency requires expansion of the nation's productive capacity. To achieve these purposes, the Small Business Act, Pub. L. No. 85-536, provides that preferential treatment must be accorded to small business concerns in the award of government contracts. Public Law No. 95-507 further amended the Act to ensure that small firms owned and controlled by socially and economically disadvantaged persons are given an opportunity to participate in the nation's free enterprise system.

By definition, a small business concern is deemed to be one that is independently owned and operated and that is not dominant in its field of operations. In order to qualify as a small concern in the field of operations for which it intends to submit a proposal or bid, a firm must be within the size standards established by the Small Business Administration (SBA), which has been granted final authority to determine matters of small business size for procurement purposes. 15 U.S.C. § 634(b).

A firm is not considered to be dominant in its field of operations if it does not exercise a controlling or major influence in a type of business endeavor in which a number of concerns are primarily engaged. In determining whether dominance exists, the SBA gives consideration to number of employees, dollar volume of annual sales, and percentage of the market held by the company. The last basis was first used in 1966 when a determination was issued that manufacturers of automobile tires would be considered small if they had less than 5 percent of the domestic market for those products. 31 Fed. Reg. 14544 (1966). Under this determination, American Motors Corporation, a firm with over 28,000 employees and sales of more than $1.7 billion, was considered to be a small business firm.

The Contracting Officer is required to accept as conclusive an offeror's representation that his is a small business concern, within one of the size standards prescribed by FAR § 19.102, unless another offeror or interested party challenges the representation or the Contracting Officer has reason to challenge it. FAR § 19.301(b). Such a representation will be effective, notwithstanding that a question concerning its validity may be raised, unless and until the SBA finds that the bidder is not a small business concern. The SBA is empowered to issue documentation certifying that the holder is a small business concern when requested to do so by either a Contracting Officer or a competing firm protesting the representation, and such certification is conclusive.

Under the Act, the SBA establishes size standards for various industries and rules on the size status of individual companies when their status is questioned. Its size standard regulations are conclusive upon the Comptroller General and the procuring agencies of the executive branch. 41 Comp. Gen. 649 (1962). The SBA has established a Size Appeals Board to consider appeals of initial determinations as to the size of given companies. When the Size Appeals Board applies its own rules and follows long-established practices in finding that a contractor meets applicable size requirements, its findings are conclusive. *Allen M. Campbell Co. v. Lloyd Wood Constr. Co.*, 446 F.2d 261 (5th Cir. 1971).

Under the provisions of section 8(b)(7) of the Small Business Act, the SBA is statutorily authorized to certify the competency of any small business concern as to all elements of responsibility, as prescribed by section 9.104-1 of the FAR. This includes, but is not limited to, capability, competence, capacity, integrity, preseverance, and tenacity. If the Contracting Officer determines to reject the low bid or offer of a small business concern on the basis of nonresponsibility, he is required to delay contract award and refer the matter to the local SBA office having authority to process the referral. The SBA is required, within 15 working days, to inform the small concern of the Contracting Officer's determination and offer it an opportunity to apply for a Certificate of Competency. Upon timely receipt of an application from a small firm, the SBA will either issue a Certificate of Competency or confirm the Contracting Officer's determination of nonresponsibility. If a Certificate of Competency is issued, and concurred in by the SBA Central Office, it is conclusive upon the contracting agency.

Small business concerns are eligible to participate in procurements reserved exclusively or partially for small firms. Government purchasing agencies are required to reserve procurements that can be performed solely by small firms for competition among small business concerns or to set aside a portion of divisible procurements for small business participation. Small business concerns competing for awards under the set-aside portion of a solicitation must submit a proposal for the nonset-aside portion in order to be eligible for subsequent consideration. Negotiations will be conducted only with those small firms that submit a proposal for the nonreserved portion of a procurement even though that portion may ultimately be awarded to a large business.

Congress has not established quotas in order to stimulate small business participation in federal acquisition programs. Nevertheless, it is interesting to note that the Public Works Employment Act of 1977 requires, absent an administrative waiver, that at least 10 percent of the federal funds granted for local public works be used by the state or local grantee to procure supplies or services from businesses owned by minorities. The legality of this statutory quota was upheld by the Supreme Court in *Fullilove v. Klutznik*, 448 U.S. 448 (1980), where the Court said, "Considered in the context of many years of Governmental efforts to remedy past racial and ethnic discrimination, the court found it difficult to imagine any purpose for the program other than to remedy such discrimination."

It was in this spirit that Congress enacted Public Law No. 95-507 to amend section 8(a) of the Small Business Act to provide means by which to promote the competitive viability of socially and economically disadvantaged concerns. For the purposes of the Act, the term "socially and economically disadvantaged small business concern" means any small business firm (1) that is at least 51 percent owned by one or more socially and economically disadvantaged individuals or, in the case of any publicly owned business, that has at least 51 percent of its stock owned by one or more socially and economically disadvantaged individuals; and (2) whose management and daily business operations are controlled by one or more such individuals. Socially disadvantaged individuals are defined as those who have been subjected to racial, ethnic, or cultural bias because of their identity as a member of a group without regard to their individual qualities. Economically disadvantaged is defined as those socially disadvantaged individuals whose ability to compete in the free enterprise system has been impaired due to diminished capital and credit opportunities as compared to others in the same business who are not socially disadvantaged.

Business owners who certify that they are members of named groups (Black Americans, Hispanic Americans, Native Americans, Asian-Pacific Americans) are to be considered socially and economically disadvantaged. With respect to a subcontract relationship with a small concern, contractors acting in good faith may rely on written representations by their subcontractors regarding their status as either a small business concern or a small business concern owned and controlled by socially and economically disadvantaged individuals.

Public Law No. 95-507 requires that solicitations for bids or offers to perform a contract or contract modification that individually is expected to exceed $500,000 ($1 million in the case of construction) and that has subcontracting possibilities include a requirement for the apparently successful bidder or offeror to submit a subcontract plan to the government. Under either the negotiated or the sealed bidding method of acquisition, an acceptable plan must be submitted to the Contracting Officer within prescribed time frames, or the offeror shall be ineligible for award of the contract. Small business concerns are exempt from this requirement. But to qualify for the exemption, a firm must demonstrate that it would have been eligible to participate in a set-aside procurement had the acquisition been reserved for small business. FAR § 19.702.

With respect to those contracts or modifications meeting the criteria, the FAR mandates that no contract will be awarded unless and until an acceptable subcontract plan, as defined by FAR § 19.704, has been submitted to and accepted by the Contracting Officer and that such plan will be incorporated into and made a material part of the contract. An acceptable plan must provide the maximum practicable opportunity for small businesses and small disadvantaged businesses to participate in the performance of the contract. The most important aspect of the plan is the percentage goals (expressed in terms of percentages of total planned subcontract dollars) for the utilization of such concerns. For the purposes of this requirement, a firm may include all purchases that contribute to the performance of the contract, including a proportionate share of products, services, or supplies, the cost of which is normally allocated as an indirect cost to the contract. The FAR prohibits negotiating a goal upward if it is apparent that a higher goal would significantly increase the government's cost or seriously impede the attainment of acquisition objectives. FAR § 19.705-4(c).

In determining whether a plan is acceptable, procuring agencies are required to consider the contractor's "make or buy" program or policy to ensure that it does not conflict with the proposed subcontracting plan and is in the government's interest. FAR § 19.705-4(d)(2). While this appears to be inconsistent with the spirit and intent of Public Law No. 95-507 because it authorizes submission of a negative plan and may ultimately be amended by new legislation, it is not the present policy of Congress or the executive branch to reverse a contractor's justifiable make-or-buy decision.

Any contractor or eligible subcontractor failing to comply in good faith with the requirements of the subcontracting plan will be considered to be in material breach of the contract or subcontract. FAR § 19.702(c). If such a breach occurs, the Contracting Officer is required to review the existing facts to determine which available remedy is in the best interests of the government. Such remedies presumably include termination of the contract for default pursuant to the appropriate termination clause set forth in FAR § 52.249, reduction in the contract price, negotiation of a revised subcontract plan, or such other measures as the Contracting Officer may deem appropriate, to include the imposition of liquidated damages.

The Contracting Officer may use various approaches in the development of small and small disadvantaged business subcontracting initiatives. These approaches may take many forms, from a fully qualified schedule of payments based on actual subcontract achievement to an award fee employing subjective criteria. However, the incentive should not reward the contractor for results other than those that are directly attributable to the contractor's efforts under the incentive subcontracting program. FAR § 19.708(c)(2).

When using other than sealed bidding competitive procurement procedures, the Contracting Officer may insert a clause in the solicitation instrument and contract substantially the same as the clause at section 52.219-10 of the FAR, Incentive Subcontracting Program for Small and Small Disadvantaged Business Concerns. The clause may be used only when a subcontracting plan is required, the Contracting Officer determines that a monetary incentive is necessary to increase subcontracting opportunities for small and small disadvantaged businesses, and the incentive is commensurate with the efficient and economical performance of the contract. FAR § 19.708(c)(1). Section 52.219-10 of the FAR provides that, to the extent that the contractor exceeds his subcontract plan goals, he will receive a negotiated percentage not to exceed 10 percent of the total amount of such excesses, unless it is determined that such excesses were not due to the efforts of the contractor. Thus, where subcontractor cost overruns occur, where the actual subcontract amount exceeds that estimated in the subcontracting plan and such actual amount was known to the contractor at the time the plan was negotiated, or where planned subcontracts were not disclosed in the subcontract plan during contract negotiation, recovery of the incentive would be prohibited.

## Labor Surplus Area Program

It is also the policy of the United States to alleviate, through the federal acquisition mechanism, unemployment in those sections of the nation classified by the Department of Labor as areas of concentrated unemployment or underemployment or as areas of labor surplus. Section 20.102 of the FAR provides that the government shall award appropriate contracts to labor surplus area concerns and encourage prime contractors to place subcontracts with concerns located in labor surplus areas. With the exception of contracts funded by Military Construction Appropriation Acts, part 20 of the FAR does not apply to the Department of Defense (DoD) because DoD is prohibited from paying price differentials in contracts awarded for purposes of relieving economic dislocations. 10 U.S.C. § 2392; FAR § 20.201-2.

To be eligible for award under a labor surplus area set-aside, a firm must agree to perform a substantial portion of the production or manufacturing or provide a substantial portion of the services in a labor surplus area. A "substantial portion" has been interpreted as meaning that performance costs incurred in the labor surplus area are in excess of 50 percent of the contract price. FAR § 20.201.

### The Buy American Act

The Buy American Act, Pub. L. No. 428, 41 U.S.C. § 10, was enacted during the Great Depression in 1933 to give preferential treatment to U.S. producers and manufacturers in the case of purchases of materials and supplies by federal agencies and establishments, as well as to construction contractors. The Act provides that, notwithstanding any other provision of law, and unless the head of the department or independent agency determines the requirement to be inconsistent with the public interest or the cost to be unreasonable, only such articles, materials, or supplies as have been manufactured in the United States from articles, materials, or supplies mined, produced, or manufactured, as the case may be, in the United States shall be acquired for public use. The same restriction applies to construction contracts with respect to articles, materials, or supplies used in the project. The Act does not apply to supplies, materials, or articles purchased for use outside the United States. Through Executive Order 10,582, December 17, 1954, the President has determined that materials are to be considered of foreign origin if the cost of the foreign products used constitutes 50 percent or more of all the products used in such materials or supplies.

In implementing the Act, the executive branch established the policy that bids and proposals will be evaluated so as to give preference to domestic bids, except that bids or proposals offering certain supplies mined, produced, or manufactured in certain foreign countries shall be evaluated on a parity with domestic bids and proposals. FAR § 25.103. The offered price of a domestic end product is considered unreasonable when the lowest acceptable bid or offer exceeds the lowest acceptable foreign bid or offer, inclusive of duty, by more than 6 percent if the domestic bid or offer is from a large business concern that is not a labor surplus concern or by more than

12 percent if the bid or offer is from either a small business concern or a labor surplus concern.

The broad implications of the Act have generated considerable litigation as to what constitutes foreign products within the meaning of the Act. For example, a contractor's use of domestically processed foreign-made steel tubing in manufacturing construction material was in violation of the Act because the cost of the components of the construction material, the tubing, constituted more than 50 percent of the cost of all products used. The contractor contended that the resulting construction was domestic because the cost of the tubing was less than half the value of the finished product. The Comptroller General ruled that it is the cost of the components of the construction material, rather than the final completed cost of such construction material, that must be considered in applying the 50 percent rule. Comp. Gen. B-166613 (1969). The total cost of the end product, what it would sell for minus profit, is irrelevant since it includes noncomponent costs. Labor and other overhead costs and packaging, testing, and evaluation costs incurred in manufacturing the end product are not included as part of the total costs of all the components used to make the end product, but are included in determining what the component itself cost. Comp. Gen. B-1666405 (1969).

If an end product is assembled outside the United States from domestic components, it is not a domestic product even though substantially all of the costs of the product are incurred domestically. 52 Comp. Gen. 13 (1972).

The prohibitions of the Act do not apply in those situations where the supplies or materials are not mined, produced, or manufactured in the United States in sufficient and reasonably available commercial quantities of a satisfactory quality. FAR § 25.108. Accordingly, it was not a violation of the Act to purchase cork board from foreign sources since cork is not an item that is native to, or grown in, the United States. Comp. Gen. B-84306 (1949).

The Department of Defense and the National Aeronautics and Space Administration have determined that it is inconsistent with the public's interest to apply the restrictions of the Act to the acquisitions for public use of certain supplies mined, produced, or manufactured in certain foreign countries. FAR § 25.103. Since Canada has long been one of those "certain" foreign countries to which the prohibitions do not apply, a domestic labor surplus area bidder did not have preference over a Canadian bidder that had submitted a lower bid. Since it was clearly the intent of the Armed Services Procurement Regulations to exclude all Canadian purchases from the application of the Buy American Act and from the restrictions of section 3(c) of Executive Order 10,582, an award to a Canadian firm was not only proper but also required under the military competitive statute (10 U.S.C. § 2305). Comp. Gen. B-150183 (1963).

## REGULATORY BASES OF FEDERAL ACQUISITION

### The Office of Federal Procurement Policy

The Office of Federal Procurement Policy (OFPP), established by Public Law No. 93-400 (1974), as subsequently amended, is charged with promoting economy, efficiency, and effectiveness in the acquisition of goods and services by and for the executive branch. Situated in the Office of Management and Budget, OFPP provides overall direction of the acquisition systems of the executive branch. In carrying out this mandate, OFPP was given broad powers to prescribe governmentwide procurement policies in a single set of regulations. These regulations are to be followed by executive agencies in the procurement of property (other than real property in being); the procurement of services (including research and development); and the construction, alteration, repair, or maintenance of real property.

In promulgating the Office of Federal Procurement Policy Act, Congress consistently stressed a policy of economy, efficiency, and effectiveness in the acquisition of property and services by

- Promoting full and open competition
- Establishing policies, procedures, and practices that will provide the government with property and services of the requisite quality, within the time needed, and at the lowest reasonable cost
- Promoting the development of simplified, uniform procurement processes
- Promoting the participation of small business concerns
- Supporting the development of a competent, professional work force
- Eliminating fraud and waste in the procurement process
- Eliminating redundant administrative requirements placed on contractor and federal procurement officials
- Promoting fair dealings and equitable relationships with the private sector
- Ensuring that payment is made in a timely manner and only for value received
- Requiring, to the extent practicable, the use of commercial products to meet the government's needs
- Requiring that personal services be obtained in accordance with applicable personnel procedures and not by contract
- Ensuring the development of procurement policies that will accommodate emergencies and wartime as well as peacetime requirements
- Promoting, whenever feasible, the use of specifications that describe needs in terms of the functions to be performed or the performance required

Public Law No. 96-83 amended the Office of Federal Procurement Policy Act to require the Administrator of OFPP to develop and submit a proposal to Congress for a Uniform Procurement System, to include a full description of the system (e.g., uniform policies, regulations, procedures, and forms), projected costs and benefits, and short- and long-term plans for implementing the system. Moreover, and for the first time in our nation's history, Congress defined procurement in Public Law No. 96-83 as a system that "includes all stages of the process of acquiring property or services, beginning with the process for determining a need for property and services and ending with contract completion and close-out."

### The Federal Acquisition Regulation

OFPP issued the Federal Acquisition Regulation (FAR) on September 9, 1983, to become effective April 1, 1984, pursuant to the authority of Public Law No. 93-400, as amended by Public Law No. 96-83. The FAR was established for the codification of uniform policies and procedures for the acquisition of supplies and services by all executive branch departments and agencies. The Regulation is prepared, issued, and maintained, and the Federal Acquisition Regulation System prescribed, jointly by the Secretary of Defense, the Administrator of General Services, and the Administrator of the National Aeronautics and Space Administration under their several statutory authorities. The FAR System does not include internal agency guidance, but it does authorize procuring agencies to supplement the FAR, provided that such supplements are limited to additional policies and solicitation or contract provisions required to satisfy specific departmental needs.

# 3

# Authority of Government Agents

## INTRODUCTION

The U.S. government is a vast enterprise and, of necessity, must fulfill its diverse obligations and carry out its varied functions through duly appointed agents. Forced as it is to conduct its affairs with private parties through its agents, the government has adopted certain rules, both statutorily and regulatorily, prescribing the authority and limitations of its agents in order to protect the public interest. In interpreting these rules, the courts have established limits on government liability that are applied when a government agent acts without, or exceeds, express authority granted by statute or regulation. With respect to contracts, only the Contracting Officer has authority to enter into, administer, or terminate contracts on behalf of the government. Contracting Officers can only bind the government to the extent of the authority delegated to them, and the United States is not bound contractually by acts of Contracting Officers, or their representatives, who clearly exceed the scope of their authority. Nor is the government bound by the acts of unauthorized agents.

## GOOD FAITH RELATIONSHIP BETWEEN THE PARTIES

As in business transactions between commercial parties, the United States seeks to establish a good faith relationship with its contractors. The government's objective is to employ qualified contractors capable of delivering required goods or services that meet its specifications, are delivered on time, and are provided at fair and reasonable prices. Because it is neither feasible nor desirable for the government to attempt to supervise every aspect of contract performance, it places a great deal of trust in its contractors.

The good faith concept traces its origin to both the law of equity and the law of contracts. Good faith has been variously defined as

1. That state of mind denoting honesty of purpose, freedom from intention to defraud, and, generally speaking, faithfulness to one's duty or obligation, *Effron v. Kalmanovitz,* 249 Cal. App. 2d 187 (1967);
2. Honesty of intention and freedom from knowledge or circumstances that ought to put the holder on inquiry, *Siano v. Helvering,* 13 F. Supp. 776 (D. N.J. 1936); or
3. An honest intention to abstain from taking an unconscientious advantage of another, even through the technicalities of law, together with an absence of all information, notice, or benefit or belief of facts that render transactions unconscientious, *Natural Gas Co. v. Allen,* 248 Ky. 646 (1933). The Uniform Commercial Code, on the other hand, defines good faith as honesty in fact in the conduct or transaction involved. U.C.C. § 1-201(19).

During preliminary negotiations or other steps taken by the parties to reach a mutually agreeable contractual relationship and during subsequent contract performance, the good faith concept should be uppermost in the minds of both parties. Both the government and the contractor exchange promises and make representations and inducements to be met during contract performance. Thus, the relationship between the government and its contractors from the inception of the contract, whether let by sealed bidding or competitive negotiation, involves an exchange of representations and promises, estimates, and disclosures, each of which must be offered with a view that its accuracy will someday be known. The fine line between ethical hard bargaining and unethical sharp practices is of critical importance. Not all of the ethical ground rules are written, nor is it possible to formulate the daily application of such rules to the negotiation and administration of government contracts and subcontracts. A good faith relationship between the parties, founded on honesty and fairness in an ever-changing acquisition environment, is all the more essential during this period when the public and Congress appear to doubt the ability of the government and its private contractors to carry out their roles effectively and honestly in the federal acquisition process.

## AUTHORITY OF AN AGENT TO ENTER INTO A CONTRACT

The authority of an officer to enter into a contract binding the United States must be found in some legally enacted provision of law. Lack of contracting authority in a government agent renders unenforceable against the United States a contract made by such agent, whether that contract is express or implied in fact. *Narva Harris Constr. Corp. v. United States,* 216 Ct. Cl. 238, 574 F.2d 508 (1978); *New York Mail & Newspaper Trans. Co. v. United States,* 139 Ct. Cl. 751, 154 F. Supp. 271 (1957). The basic statutory authority enabling duly appointed Contracting Officers to enter into, administer, or terminate contracts for, and on behalf of, the government is the Armed Services Procurement Act of 1947, 10 U.S.C. § 2301 *et seq.*, and the Federal Property and Administrative Services Act of 1949, 41 U.S.C. § 251–260, as amended by the Competition in Contracting Act, Pub. L. No. 98-369, 98 Stat. 494 (1984). The FAR implements these statutory authorities and provides that contracts may be entered into and signed on behalf of the government only by Contracting Officers, FAR § 1.601, but only to the extent of the authority delegated to them, FAR § 1.602-1(a). Moreover, no contract shall be entered into unless the Contracting Officer ensures that all requirements of law, executive orders, and regulations have been met and all other applicable procedures, including clearances and approvals, followed. FAR § 1.602-1(b).

It is a well-recognized principle of procurement law that the Contracting Officer, as an agent of the executive department, has only that authority actually conferred by statute or regulation. If, by ignoring statutory and regulatory requirements, the Contracting Officer exceeds such actual authority, the government is not estopped to deny the limitations of that authority. *Federal Crop Insurance Corp. v. Merrill,* 332 U.S. 380 (1947); *Prestex Inc. v. United States,* 162 Ct. Cl. 620, 320 F.2d 367 (1963); 16 Comp. Gen. 329 (1936). No officer or agent of the government can act beyond the limits of his authority. *Fansteel Metallurgical Corp. v. United States,* 145 Ct. Cl. 496, 499, 172 F. Supp. 268, 270 (1959). Moreover, neglect of duty on the part of officers of the government is no defense to a suit by it to enforce a public right or protect a public interest. *Utah Power & Light Co. v. United States,* 243 U.S. 409 (1917); *United States v. Gudewicz,* 45 F. Supp. 787 (E.D.N.Y. 1942). The general authority to make contracts normally includes the power to choose with whom and on what terms the contracts will be made. When Congress in an act grants authority to contract, that authority is no less than the general authority, unless Congress has placed some limit on it. *Arizona v. California,* 373 U.S. 546 (1963).

The courts have historically construed the role and authority of the Contracting Officer more broadly than the Boards of Contract Appeals have. In recognition of the important role the Contracting Officer plays in the operation of government contracts, the courts have liberally interpreted his authority to enter into and administer contracts. *Arthur Verneri Co. v. United States,* 180 Ct. Cl. 920, 381 F.2d 748 (1967). The Contracting Officer in a sense is a party to the contract, not only representing, but also speaking for the impersonality of the government. *United States v. Mason & Hanger Co.,* 260 U.S. 323 (1922). Consequently, the authority of the Contracting Officer has been construed to include the power to settle claims arising under the contract. *United States v. Corliss Steam Engine Co.*, 91 U.S. 321 (1875).

In general, an officer authorized to make a contract for the United States has the implied authority thereafter to modify the provisions of that contract, particularly where it is in the interests of the United States to do so. *Whitman v. United States*, 124 Ct. Cl. 464, 110 F. Supp. 444 (1953); *Branch Banking & Trust Co. v. United States*, 120 Ct. Cl. 72, 98 F. Supp. 657, *cert. denied*, 342 U.S. 893 (1951). Thus, it has been held that the Contracting Officer may change a contract term requiring delivery on a certain date by accepting deliveries made well beyond the specific date set forth in the contract. *Copco Steel & Engineering Co. v. United States*, 69 Ct. Cl. 601, 341 F.2d 590 (1965). And in a contract involving the leasing of prisoners of war to a private contractor for 50 cents an hour, the Fifth Circuit rejected the argument that the Contracting Officer lacked the authority to reduce the contract price to 37.5 cents per hour. *United States v. Adams Packing Ass'n*, 197 F.2d 33 (5th Cir.), *cert. denied*, 344 U.S. 865 (1952).

The Boards of Contract Appeals, on the other hand, have been considerably more conservative in construing the authority of the Contracting Officer. The Armed Services Board has held that the mere fact that the contract authorizes the Contracting Officer to take an action that binds the government does not mean that the Contracting Officer may act without regard to the limitations of his authority or without regard to restrictions imposed by regulation or law. For example, the Changes articles provide that change within the general scope of the contract may be ordered by the Contracting Officer, and, if ordered, the contractor is obligated to comply. The standard form contract does not state that the Contracting Officer may not order the change, unless he has authority to do so and funds are available. This is, of course, primarily a matter between the Contracting Officer and the government, but the fact that there is some limitation on the Contracting Officer's authority is well known. The decision to order or not to order a change is a discretionary administrative decision not entailing any fact finding and not coming within the Disputes clause. However, in issuing or deciding not to issue the change order, the Contracting Officer must act in accordance with the requirements of applicable law, regulations, and the specific instructions of his higher authority. The contractor cannot appeal from this administrative decision, nor does a contractor have ground for complaint, if the Contracting Officer's initial decision to order a change that would be profitable to the contractor is frustrated by the refusal of the funding authority to allot the necessary funds or by the determination of a higher authority that the change is not in the best interests of the government, or is otherwise frustrated by regulations or higher authority. *General Electric Co.*, ASBCA No. 11,990, 67-2 BCA 6565.

## GOVERNMENT NOT BOUND BY DOCTRINE OF APPARENT AUTHORITY

To bind the government, the officer purporting to act on its behalf must have actual authority to do so. *Penn-Ohio Steel Corp. v. United States,* 173 Ct. Cl. 1064, 354 F.2d 254 (1965). The government is bound by actions of its officers only when they are acting within the scope of their authority. *Carrier Corp. v. United States,* 164 Ct. Cl. 666, 328 F.2d 328 (1964).

Unlike commercial parties, the government is not bound by the common law rule of apparent authority, which makes the principal responsible for the acts of its agents, even though the agent exceeds his authority, in those cases where the principal has clothed the agent with the appearance of unlimited authority. The government or public authority is not bound in such a case where private parties are bound by the acts and declarations of their agents, even where the act or declaration was made or done without any authority, unless it manifestly appears that the agent was acting within the scope of his authority or was employed in his capacity as a public agent to do the act or make the declaration for the government. Unauthorized acts committed by an officer in the service of the United States do not render the government liable even though the acts were apparently for the public benefit. *Whiteside v. United States,* 93 U.S. 247 (1876). The government is too vast, and its operations too varied and intricate, to put it to the risk of losing that which it holds for the nation as a whole because of the oversight of subordinate officials. *Montana Power Co. v. Federal Power Comm'n,* 185 F.2d 491, 497 (D.C. Cir.), *cert. denied,* 340 U.S. 947 (1950).

Individuals as well as courts must take notice of the extent of authority conferred by law on a person acting in an official capacity, and the rule applies in such a case that ignorance of the law furnishes no excuse for any mistake or wrongful act. It is better that an individual should occasionally suffer from the mistakes of public officers or agents than to adopt a rule that, through improper combination or collusion, might be turned to the detriment and injury of the public. *Whiteside, supra.*

If, by ignoring statutory authority and regulatory requirements, the Contracting Officer exceeds his actual authority, the government is not estopped to deny the limitations on his authority even though the private contractor may have relied on the Contracting Officer's apparent authority to his detriment. *Sutton v. United States,* 256 U.S. 575 (1921); *Pine River Logging Co. v. United States,* 189 U.S. 279 (1902); *Filor v. United States,* 76 U.S. 45 (1869).

The contractor is charged with notice of all statutory and regulatory limitations. Whatever the form in which the government functions, anyone entering into an arrangement with the government takes the risk of having accurately ascertained that he who purports to act for the government stays within the bounds of his authority. *Wilbur National Bank v. United States,*

294 U.S. 120 (1935). The scope of this authority may be explicitly defined by Congress or be limited by delegated legislation, properly exercised through the rule-making power. And this is so even though the agent himself may have been unaware of the limitation on his authority. *Federal Crop Insurance Corp. v. Merrill, supra.* Thus, one who purports to contract with the United States assumes the risk that the official with whom he deals is clothed with actual authority to enter into the contract alleged, and the United States will not be estopped to deny the acts of its agents who have acted beyond the scope of their actual authority. *Putnam Mills Corp. v. United States,* 202 Ct. Cl. 1, 478 F.2d 1334 (1973).

The Armed Services Board drew a distinction between commercial and governmental contracts when it said that if it were deciding a dispute between two private parties, rather than between a private party and the government, it would not hesitate to hold that the Contracting Officer had apparent authority to bind his principal and that the latter was, by the actions of his agent, bound by the agreements made. But where one of the parties is the government, the doctrine of apparent authority cannot be invoked against it. *Chalker & Lund Co. v. United States,* 123 Ct. Cl. 381 (1952); *Johnson, Drake, and Piper, Inc.,* ASBCA Nos. 9824 & 10,199, 65-2 BCA 4868.

Following this line of reasoning, the Board has ruled that a purveyor of alarm clock radios could not recover the purchase price of 700 such radios that he had tendered pursuant to two government purchase orders because the officer who issued the orders did not have authority to execute contracts for more than $500 without prior approval. It was indisputable that the custodian of the DaNang Non-Commissioned Officer's Mess was not authorized by the bylaws of the Mess to enter into transactions with the contractor, on which his claim was based. Each purchase order exceeded $500 in value and required approval of the Board of Directors of the NCO Open Mess and the Commander, I Corps Advisory Group. Neither was obtained, and the transaction was therefore beyond the custodian's powers. Under U.S. federal law, such a transaction is absolutely invalid when the party exceeding his authority is a federal government official, and the reliance of the other party to the transaction on the apparent authority of the government official does not restore its validity. *Gourmet Enterprises,* ASBCA No. 16543, 73-2 BCA 10,064.

The same rules apply to implied-in-fact contracts between the government and a private party. When it is asserted that an agent of the government has the authority to bind it to an arrangement or agreement, such authority is a strict prerequisite of an implied-in-fact contract with the United States. The claimant for money damages for breach of an implied-in-fact contract must show that the officer who supposedly made the contract had the authority to obligate public funds. If no showing is made that the officer had the requisite authority to bind the government, the government is not estopped to deny the unauthorized acts or promises of that officer. *Robert G. Phelps v. United States,* 5 Cl. Ct. 740 (1984).

While the courts and Boards of Contract Appeals adhere strictly to the rule that the government will not be estopped to deny the unauthorized acts of its agents, they liberally apply the theory of apparent authority when dealing with a government contractor's agent. It is now commonplace that, except where formality is expressly required, apparent authority to do an act on behalf of a principal may be created by written or spoken words or other conduct of the principal that, if reasonably interpreted, causes a third person to believe that the principal consents to have the act done on his behalf by the person purporting to act for him. Although the federal government still stands on the stricter requirement of actual authority for its agents, the agents of government contractors are governed by the usual rules. *American Anchor & Chain Corp. v. United States,* 166 Ct. Cl. 1 (1964).

## GOVERNMENT ESTOPPED UNDER CERTAIN CIRCUMSTANCES

Similarly, the United States is neither bound nor estopped by acts of its officers or agents in entering into an arrangement or agreement to do or cause to be done what the law does not sanction or permit. *Utah Power & Light Co. v. United States, supra.* This is true even where it might be said that there are grounds for estoppel. *Shephard Engineering Co. v. United States,* 289 F.2d 681 (8th Cir. 1961).

The doctrine of estoppel is an equitable one, which adjusts the relative rights of the parties based on considerations of justice and good conscience. *United States v. Georgia-Pacific Co.,* 421 F.2d 92 (9th Cir. 1970). Estoppel is a concept that prohibits a party from escaping liability for his statements, actions, or inactions if they have been relied on by the other party. *Universal Painting Corp.,* ASBCA No. 20536, 77-1 BCA 12,355. Thus, if one party relies to his detriment on the words or deeds of another party, the acting party will not be permitted to deny the validity of his acts or the lack of authority to undertake such acts.

Since agents of the government must find authority in a statute to bind the United States to a contractual relationship, failure to comply with statutory requirements would result in an unauthorized act by the agent. Hence, in *Singer Co., Librascope Division,* ASBCA No. 17604, 75-2 BCA 11, 401; *aff'd,* 217 Ct. Cl. 225, 576 F.2d 905 (1978), where the contractor submitted cost or pricing data to the government, pursuant to the requirements of the Truth in Negotiations Act, 10 U.S.C. § 2306(f), that the Contracting Officer knew was not current, the government was not estopped from obtaining a price reduction. The Armed Services Board held:

No government representative had authority to waive the statutory requirement of disclosure of accurate, complete and current data. We need not further discuss the application of estoppel since it fails at a threshold question. We note parenthetically that a far different case would exist had appellant fully disclosed its data in relation to its proposal and the government then, for whatever reason, failed to make use of the data in the negotiation process.

*Muncie Gear Works,* ASBCA No. 18184, 75-2 BCA 11,380; *Levinson Steel Co.,* ASBCA No. 16520, 73-2 BCA 10,116.

The growth of government and concomitant increases in its functions, powers, and contacts with private parties have made many courts reluctant to deny the defense of equitable estoppel in appropriate situations. The government, in its caretaker role for all the public, should not be bound by the unauthorized or unlawful acts of its representatives. On the other hand, it is hardly in the public's interest for the government to deal dishonestly or in an unconscientious manner. This is especially imperative in a time when few individuals and corporations, if any, can escape numerous dealings with the government and its agents. While it is said that the government can be estopped in its proprietary role, but not in its sovereign role, the authorities are not clear as to which activities are embraced by each role. In its proprietary role, the government is acting as a private concern would; in its sovereign role, the government is carrying out its unique government functions for the benefit of the whole public. *United States v. Georgia-Pacific Co., supra.*

The courts generally hold that two threshold conditions must be satisfied before an estoppel may be found against the government: first, the government must be acting in its proprietary, rather than in its sovereign, capacity; and second, the government's representative, whose acts form the basis for the estoppel, must have been acting within the scope of his authority. *United States v. Georgia-Pacific Co., supra.* And then, before one may assert the doctrine against the government, the Court of Claims has held that it is necessary for that party to show that the party against whom an equitable estoppel is set up acquiesced in the transaction in such a manner as to change the relationship of the parties and make its repudiation of the proceedings contrary to equity and good conscience. *Emeco Industries v. United States,* 202 Ct. Cl. 1006, 485 F.2d 652 (1973).

Four elements must be present to set up an estoppel against the government: (1) the party to be estopped must know the facts, (2) he must intend that his conduct shall be acted on or must so act that the party asserting the estoppel has a right to believe it is so intended, (3) the latter must be ignorant of the true facts, and (4) he must rely on the former's conduct to his injury. *Emeco Industries v. United States, supra; United States v. Georgia-Pacific* Co., *supra; American Electronic Laboratories v. United States,* CAFC No. 85-780, 33 CCF 73,973 (1985); *Hughes Aircraft Corp.,* 83-1 BCA 81, 156.

When the official is acting within his delegated authority, and his actions are not prohibited by statute, an estoppel will be found even though the action is based on a mistaken interpretation of the government's obligations. *Broad Avenue Laundry & Tailoring v. United States,* 231 Ct. Cl. 1, 681 F.2d 747 (1982); *Portmann v. United States,* 674 F.2d 1155 (7th Cir. 1982).

## ABUSE OF AUTHORITY BY CONTRACTING OFFICER

As an agent of the government, the Contracting Officer is expected to exercise authority delegated in accordance with law and regulation and, in administering contracts awarded, in consonance with the terms and conditions of such contracts. The powers thus delegated are broad indeed, but there are nevertheless limitations on the Contracting Officer that must be adhered to. If these limitations are exceeded, the courts and Boards of Contract Appeals will find that the Contracting Officer has abused discretionary powers or has acted arbitrarily and capriciously.

In *Roby Hillside Drilling,* ASBCA No. 20178, 76-2 BCA 11,982, the Armed Services Board held that the contractor was entitled to additional compensation for extra work involved in drilling a water well and for the cost of lost equipment because the government's direction was an unreasonable exercise of discretion constituting a change. The contractor drilled to 250 feet and then requested permission to case the hole. The government's representative, without visiting the site or examining any cutting samples, ordered the contractor to drill an additional 25 feet. He refused the contractor's request to case the well and then drill deeper, if necessary. Because of the delay attendant on drilling the extra footage, clay swelling was encountered. As a consequence, much of the drilling equipment became trapped and was lost in the hole. Had the government accepted the contractor's recommendation that the well be cased, a satisfactory well could have been produced, and no equipment would have been lost. The government's direction to appellant to drill an additional 25 feet in the face of the known dangerous condition of the initial well hole, and the presence of a water-bearing formation at 230 feet, was an unreasonable exercise of discretion and constituted a change under the contract. As a consequence of what the Board found to have been arbitrary action on the government's part, the contractor was entitled, under the Changes clause of the contract, to an equitable adjustment of the contract price.

In *New York Shipbuilding Corp.,* ASBCA No. 10819, 67-1 BCA 6242, it was recognized that when the parties entered into the contract, even if the contractor had an adequate number of qualified personnel, vendor engineering services should be provided by and at the expense of the government. To this end, the contract's specifications were modified at the time it was executed to provide that the services would be provided at "Government expense" under the only circumstances originally specified for the furnishing of such services, which was "if in the opinion of the Supervisor, they are necessary." That the furnishing of these engineering services was not intended to be left to the uncontrolled judgment and discretion of each local supervisor was evidenced by instructions from higher authority, which set forth standards under which the government would furnish such services to shipbuilders. The builder contracted directly for the services in accordance with the Navy's policies and practices remaining in effect without substantial change when the government failed to discharge its duties under the contract in a timely and proper manner.

When the contract provided for the furnishing of vendor engineering services at government expense, it contemplated that the government would at its expense provide those services whenever they were reasonably necessary. A contract provision giving a designated official discretionary authority to make a determination requires that the designated official act in accordance with a reasonable standard in making his determination. *Albert C. Rondinelli,* ASBCA Nos. 9900 & 10197, 65-1 BCA 4674. The supervisor, in his zeal to avoid furnishing vendor engineers to assist the contractor in doing work for which the government was responsible, erred in the opposite direction by failing to provide such engineers. Since the government had failed to discharge its responsibility in a timely and proper manner, the contractor was justified in procuring the needed engineer services directly from the equipment manufacturers and was entitled to be compensated for such services.

On appeal, the Court of Claims held that the government's delay in reaching a decision was so long and so unjustified that the government must be held to have breached its implied covenant to render a timely and appropriate decision. Not only was the mere lapse of time inexcusable, but also this delay was compounded by the improper attempt to have the wrong officer decide the dispute, and then only in a summary fashion. Where the administrative remedy has proved to be unavailable or inadequate, the court's practice has long been to try the case judicially. Where the Contracting Officer fails to perform the duties imposed on him by the contract, it is the duty of the court to perform this service and pass on the legal rights of the plaintiff. *New York Shipbuilding Corp. v. United States,* 180 Ct. Cl. 446, 385 F.2d 427 (1967).

## DELEGATION OF AUTHORITY BY CONTRACTING OFFICER

By definition, the term "Contracting Officer" includes certain authorized representatives of that official acting within the limits of their authority as delegated by the Contracting Officer. FAR § 2.1. The scope of power of authorized representatives is generally severely restricted, and such representatives are rarely given the authority to legally commit the government by signing contracts or contract modifications or to direct that changes be made to contract specifications. *Chalker & Lund Co. v. United States,* 123 Ct. Cl. 381 (1952). Nevertheless, considerable litigation has arisen concerning the authority of such representatives when they interpret contract specifications or drawings, or direct a change in the scope of work of the contract by exceeding their power. In such cases, recovery by the contractor will generally be found, based on a finding that the representative was authorized to carry out such functions, or that the representative's course of conduct impliedly included such authority, or that such power is an integral part of the representative's official duties. And if the Contracting Officer knew, or should have known, that the representative was interpreting contract specifications, recovery can be had on the basis of an erroneous interpretation.

In *Fox Valley Engineering v. United States,* 151 Ct. Cl. 228 (1960), an official was sent to the contractor's facility by the Contracting Officer for the express purpose of giving guidance in connection with the contract. The contractor was justified in relying on that official's representations, especially where the Contracting Officer ratified field decisions made by his representative, in writing, with the proviso that such decisions were not to be applied retroactively. Three lots conforming to the revised specifications were nevertheless rejected. The Contracting Officer had authority to reject the sketches to be delivered under the contract for a number of specified reasons or for any deficiency that in the opinion of the Contracting Officer would adversely affect their reproduction quality. It is elementary, of course, that broad opinion clauses in contracts of this type must necessarily be given wide scope. It is equally elementary that the discretion involved must be exercised reasonably and fairly. Such a provision does not permit the Contracting Officer arbitrarily to accept work of a certain quality as meeting the specification standards, while simultaneously rejecting work of identical or even better quality as not meeting such standards. If work is to be accomplished at a higher standard, a change order is required. Failure to accept conforming work was a breach of contract, and an appropriate change order to compensate the contractor for the changed requirements it imposed with respect to such work, as well as the balance of the work submitted under the contract, should have been issued.

Under similar circumstances, it was held that a contractor was entitled to an equitable adjustment under its contract for the development of cable assemblies because it had to do extra work to comply with the government's demands concerning the format of documents required under the contract. The problem arose because a technical representative of the Contracting Officer directed that changes be made in drawings and in the final report to be submitted under the contract. The Board held that interpretation of contract data requirements was a normal part of the regular duties of the technical representative and that those duties included the power to make erroneous decisions. The Board also found that the Contracting Officers involved had reason to know that their technical representatives were interpreting contract data requirements and that their silence regarding such interpretations was conduct amounting to consent for the performance of such duties. *Triangle Mfg. Co.*, ASBCA No. 15995, 74-2 BCA 10,783. Liability for the actions of a government agent, who carried out exactly what he was ordered to do, cannot be avoided by pointing to labels. *Centre Mfg. Co. v. United States*, 183 Ct. Cl. 115, 392 F.2d 229 (1968).

In *Tasker Industries*, DOTCAB No. 71-22, 75-2 BCA 11, 372, the Board held that the authority denied by the government was authority expressly granted by the Contracting Officer under the contract. And insofar as this authority was concerned, it was delineated in specific detail, telling the designee that he was licensed to "make engineering determinations" to ascertain that the product met the engineering requirements of the contract and that he could also make "engineering interpretations concerning broad specification requirements." In a number of cases, the Court of Claims has indicated that when a Contracting Officer licenses technical personnel, such as engineers or inspectors, to give guidance about specification problems to contractors, the government is liable for the guidance given. *Max Drill v. United States*, 192 Ct. Cl. 608 (1970); *Centre Mfg. Co. v. United States*, 183 Ct. Cl. 115 (1968); *General Casualty Co. v. United States*, 130 Ct. Cl. 520, 533 (1955). And, as in all the cases cited, liability attaches where the actual exercise of authority is in error and hence induces the contractor to perform work that is beyond the scope of the contract.

Generally, an inspector is authorized to determine compliance with plans and specifications, but he is not authorized to direct changes in the work, *Tellico Lumber Co.*, AGBCA No. 80-149-31, 80-2 BCA 14, 787, and, absent a clause granting him the power, a government inspector does not have the authority to change specifications, *National Concrete & Foundation Co.*, ASBCA No. 6711, 61-2 BCA 3231.

Whenever the government orders work done that the contractor thinks is in violation of the contract, or in addition to its requirements, the contractor is required to lodge a protest against doing it. It is basic to all contracts that the contractor cannot do work that he is not required to do by the contract without registering a protest against being required to do it, or securing an order for the extra work, and then later making a claim against the government for additional compensation. *J. A. Ross & Co. v. United States*, 126 Ct. Cl. 323 (1953); *Barton & Sons Co.*, ASBCA Nos. 9477 & 9764, 65-2 BCA 4874.

Where a contractor voluntarily performs services outside the scope of the contract and the government refuses to make payment for the services, there is no legal remedy available to the contractor under the contract. *Iowa Engineering Co.*, GSBCA No. 4622, 79-2 BCA 12, 156. It is well established that a contractor who voluntarily incurs extra expense when such services have not been ordered by an authorized representative of the government, at least orally or by an act that would amount to an order, does so at his own risk and cannot require the government to assume the cost of such volunteered work. *Plumley v. United States,* 226 U.S. 545 (1913).

# 4

# Acquisition by Sealed Bidding

## INTRODUCTION

It is the policy of the United States to obtain the goods and services required by its agencies and departments from the private sector. Acquisition of these materials and services is accomplished by one of two methods authorized by the procurement statutes: sealed bidding and negotiation. In accomplishing their acquisitions, the procuring agencies are required to promote and provide for full and open competition. 10 U.S.C. § 2304; 41 U.S.C. § 253. Sealed bidding, as a method of acquisition in its more rigid procedural aspects, is almost entirely a creation of Congress and the executive branch. Acting through its agents, as it must of necessity, the government may for the purpose of keeping its own house in order lay down guideposts by which its agents are to proceed in the acquisition of supplies and services, and which create duties to the government alone. It has done so in the Armed Services Procurement Act and the Federal Property and Administrative Services Act, as amended by the Competition in Contracting Act. *Perkins v. Lukens Steel Co.,* 310 U.S. 113 (1940). The rigid procedural requirements of sealed bidding, as the system exists today, derive from these procurement statutes, the FAR, and the decisions of the courts, the Boards of Contract Appeals, and the Comptroller General.

## ACQUISITION PLANNING

Acquisition planning is the first, and most important, step in the lengthy acquisition process. Effective advance planning is required to ensure that contracts are entered into as a consequence of full and open competition, and it is through the planning process that these policy objectives of Congress are fulfilled. Acquisition planning is a joint undertaking of both program offices and procurement departments, in coordination with the agency competition advocate and Small Business Administration representative. The entire process is overseen by the agency head, or his designee, who is ultimately responsible for the agency acquisition program.

The degree of formality employed in agency planning processes is dependent on the complexity and the cost of the acquisition itself. The more costly and complex the goods or services being acquired, the more detailed the written plan. While detail may be dispensed with as to smaller acquisitions, there is nevertheless a requirement for at least informal planning with regard to such acquisitions. FAR § 7.103. The overriding objective of acquisition planning is that of specifying needs, developing specifications, and soliciting bids or offers in such a manner as to promote and provide for full and open competition with due regard to the nature of the supplies and services to be acquired. 10 U.S.C. § 2305(a)(1)(A); 41 U.S.C. § 253A(1)(a).

Because of the variances involved, it is essential that both the contract type to be awarded and the method of acquisition to be employed be resolved in the early stages of the planning process. Prospective sources of supply or services should be identified, together with source selection procedures for the specific acquisition.

### Specifications

The specification is a description of the technical requirement for material, products, or services that includes the criteria for determining whether these requirements have been met. Specifications form the cornerstone of government contracts and establish a base line for performance on which initial pricing and schedule are predicated. They likewise establish criteria for measuring performance, inspection, and acceptance. In order to be used effectively, specifications must be complete (to include drawings and plans), clear and unambiguous, and concise.

The process of creating new, or using previously prepared, specifications should be undertaken with the view of developing nonrestrictive specifications that reflect a statement of the government's minimum needs. Restrictive specifications will prevent the government from obtaining its needs at the most reasonable price, as well as bringing an element of partiality into the acquisition process. On the other hand, prescribing requirements in excess of the government's minimum needs is merely a waste of public monies.

In soliciting bids or proposals, procuring agencies are required to develop specifications in such a manner as to obtain full and open competition with due regard for the nature of the property or services to be acquired. The type of specification to be developed depends on the needs of the agency and the market available to satisfy such needs. Specifications may be stated in terms of *function*, in order that a variety of products may qualify; *performance*, including statements of the range of acceptable characteristics or of the minimum acceptable standards; or *design requirements*. 10 U.S.C. § 2305(c); 41 U.S.C. § 303(a)(3). Though Congress has expressed a preference for *functional* specifications, it has left it to the procuring agencies to use whatever type of specification will ensure timely performance and promote full and open competition. U.S. Code & Admin. News, 98th Cong. 2d Sess. (1984) Vol. 5, p. 2116.

Functional and performance specifications express requirements in the form of output, function, or operation of a product. The details of design or fabrication are left to the discretion of the contractor. Hence, these types of specifications must indicate requirements in terms of minimum acceptable, rather than optimum achievable, performance characteristics. The contractor accepts full responsibility for design, engineering, and achievement of the stated functional-performance characteristics and may use any commercial product that might meet these requirements. While the use of these forms of specifications enhances the government's "buy commercial" policy, it must be recognized that the drafting of specifications for a new item can be a difficult undertaking. Care must be exercised to assure that the specification does not reflect the product of a specific supplier since such practice would give that producer a distinct competitive advantage. However, the government may model the specification on one product if the features enumerated for that product are justifiably necessary to meet the government's minimum needs. *American Electrical Contracting Co. v. United States*, 217 Ct. Cl. 388, 579 F.2d 602 (1978).

Design specifications set forth all the data necessary to produce the end item, to include such details as material to be used, composition, physical and chemical requirements, weight, size, dimensions, and plans and drawings. The government accepts full responsibility for any errors in the design specification, though its use does ensure that the government will receive precisely what is required to satisfy mission requirements, while simultaneously enhancing standardization. The design specification may limit competition and restrict buying commercially.

### Contract Type

The contract selected for award by the Contracting Officer determines the ultimate risk of performance borne by each party. Under the sealed bidding method of acquisition, only a firm-fixed-price contract, or a fixed-price contract with escalation features, is authorized for use. Fixed-price contracts provide for a firm price or, in appropriate cases, an adjustable price. Those fixed-price contracts providing for an adjustable price may include a ceiling price, a target price, or both. Unless otherwise specified in the contract, the ceiling or target price is subject to adjustment only by operation of contract clauses providing for equitable adjustment or other revision of the contract price under stated circumstances. FAR § 16.201.

The firm-fixed-price contract provides for a price that is not subject to any price revision on the basis of the contractor's cost experience during contract performance. This type of contract establishes the relationship between cost and profit at the time of contract award and places on the contractor maximum risk and full responsibility for all costs and resulting profit or loss. It provides maximum incentive for the contractor to control costs and perform effectively, while imposing a minimum administrative burden on the government. The firm-fixed-price contract is suitable for use with either the sealed bidding or the negotiated method of acquisition, but should be used only for acquiring commercial or commercial-type products or for acquiring other supplies or services on the basis of reasonably definite functional-performance or design specifications when the Contracting Officer can establish fair and reasonable prices at the outset. *See* FAR § 16.202.

The fixed-price contract with economic adjustment features provides for upward and downward revision of the stated contract price upon the occurrence of specific contingencies set forth in the contract. Economic price adjustments may be based on increases or decreases in established prices from an agreed-on level in published or otherwise established prices of specific items or the contract end items. Adjustments may also be made for increases or decreases based on specified costs of labor or material that the contractor actually experiences during contract performance or for increases or decreases based on cost standards or indexes that are specifically identified in the contract. FAR § 16.203.

## ELEMENTS OF SEALED BIDDING

Sealed bidding is a method of acquisition that involves (1) the preparation of the Invitation for Bids (IFB), (2) the publicizing and issuing of the IFB, (3) the submission of sealed bids by qualified prospective contractors, (4) a formal bid opening, and (5) the contract award to responsible contractors based on price and price-related factors. Acquisition by the sealed bid method results in the award of firm-fixed-price contracts or of fixed-price contracts with economic price adjustment features when some flexibility is necessary, feasible, and authorized.

Contracting Officers are required to use the sealed bidding method of acquisition if time permits the solicitation, submission, and evaluation of bids, and if the award will be made on the basis of price and price-related factors. In using this method of acquisition, discussions are not permitted with respondees concerning their bids, but there should be a reasonable expectation of receiving more than one bid.

To be effective, the IFB must describe the requirements clearly, accurately, and completely. Unnecessarily restrictive specifications or contract terms and conditions, which may unduly restrict competition, are prohibited. FAR § 14.101. The IFB must also include all documents, whether attached or incorporated by reference, necessary to enable prospective bidders to prepare and submit bids.

In preparing IFBs, acquiring agencies are statutorily required to include a statement of all significant factors, to include price-related factors, which the Contracting Officer reasonably expects to consider in the evaluation of bids, and the relative importance assigned to each such factor. 10 U.S.C. § 2305(a)(2); 41 U.S.C. § 303A(b)(1). The following price-related factors may be applicable to the evaluation of sealed bids and are to be included in the IFB when appropriate:

- Foreseeable costs or delays resulting to the government from such factors as differences in inspection, location of supplies, and transportation. If bids are on an F.O.B. origin basis, transportation to the designated destination should be considered to determine the lowest cost to the government.
- Changes made, or requested by the bidder, in any of the provisions of the IFB, if such change does not constitute a ground for rejecting the bid.
- Advantages or disadvantages to the government that might result from making more than one award. Individual awards are to be made for the items or combination of items that results in the lowest aggregate cost to the government.
- Federal, state, and local taxes.
- Origin of supplies. *See* FAR § 14.201-8.

Invitations are publicized through distribution of IFBs to prospective bidders, posting in public places, and such other means as may be appropriate—to include publication in the *Commerce Business Daily.* The IFB must be publicized sufficiently in advance of the public opening of bids to enable prospective bidders adequate time to prepare and submit their bids.

To be considered for award, a bid must comply in all material respects with the requirements of the IFB. This policy enables all bidders to stand on an equal footing and maintains the integrity of the sealed-bidding method of acquisition. Once bids are received by the acquiring agency, they are publicly opened at the specified time and place by the Bid Opening Officer and read aloud. All bids received and opened are recorded on an abstract, which includes the IFB number, the bid opening time and date, a general description of the acquisition, the names of bidders submitting timely bids, the prices bid, and any other pertinent information required for bid evaluation. When completed, the abstract is available for public inspection.

After bids are opened and recorded, they are evaluated without discussion with bidders, except where necessary to determine if a mistake in bidding has occurred. 10 U.S.C. § 2305(a)(2)(B); 41 U.S.C. § 303A(b)(2)(A). An award will be made with reasonable promptness to that responsible bidder whose bid, conforming to the requirements of the IFB, is most advantageous to the government, considering only the price and the price-related factors set forth in the IFB. FAR § 14.101.

## BIDDING TIME

In order that the sealed-bidding method of procurement can function effectively, prospective bidders must be given a reasonable period of time in which to prepare and submit bids. Section 14.202-1 of the FAR provides that the time between the issuance of the solicitation and the opening of the bids shall be at least 30 calendar days, unless the Contracting Officer determines that a shorter period is reasonable or is both reasonable and necessary to satisfy an urgent requirement. The situation must be urgent to justify compressing bidding time because competition may be restricted and bidders responding to the IFB may be forced to include contingencies in their bids that, with additional time, could have been eliminated.

Since first becoming involved in rendering opinions as to bid protests, the Comptroller General has consistently ruled that adequate bidding time is the cornerstone to full and open competition. As early as 1936, the Comptroller General ruled that section 3709 of the Revised Statutes contemplated that, in purchasing the government's needs, the widest possible competition be had and that all qualified bidders be given an opportunity to compete. To confine invitations to a comparative few of those in a position to supply the needs of the government is not in compliance with the statute. The procurement regulations specifically provide that purchases and contracts for supplies or services shall be made after advertising a sufficient time previously, when the public exigencies do not require immediate delivery. Those qualified to bid should be given a reasonable time to consider the specifications and submit their bids. A telegraphic invitation for bids affording prospective bidders not more than 48 hours to prepare and transmit their bids is not in compliance with statutory provisions, in the absence of a public exigency. Such practice deprives the government of whatever benefit it might derive from the competition of the market. The widest publicity should be given to invitations for bid. All qualified persons should be afforded an opportunity to compete and given a reasonable time within which to prepare and submit their bids. What is a reasonable time is in some measure dependent on the circumstances of a particular case.

## AMENDMENTS TO IFB

An IFB may be amended prior to the time set for bid opening if it becomes necessary to make changes in quantities, specifications, delivery dates, and contract terms or to correct an ambiguous or defective invitation. Prior to issuing the amendment, the Contracting Officer is required to consider whether a reasonable extension of time is necessary. When only a short time remains before the time set for bid opening, consideration should be given to extending the bid preparation time. *See* FAR § 14.208. What is reasonable must be determined on a case-by-case basis. In one case, the Contracting Officer was found to have acted reasonably when bidders were given one day to consider an amendment that was simple in nature and when no bidder objected to the time allowed. *Pacific Contractors,* 78 CPD 297. In another, the award was set aside where the amendment was issued two days before the bid opening date and no additional time for bidding was granted even though six bidders did receive and were able to acknowledge receipt of the amendment. The Federal Procurement Regulations then in effect were specific that all prospective bidders receive amendments in sufficient time to consider their impact. Comp. Gen. B-158766 (1966). *See* FAR § 14.208(c).

Bidders are required to acknowledge receipt of amendments, and failure to do so could result in the rejection of their bids as being nonresponsive to the requirements of the IFB. Thus, a low bidder's failure to acknowledge receipt of an amendment to an IFB for containerized seedlings could not be waived as a minor informality because the amendment significantly reduced the specified quantity of trees and had more than a trivial effect on price. The government reasonably determined that the amendment's 62 percent reduction in quantity could affect unit costs, and that the low bidder, by not bidding in response to the amendment, could have an advantage over other bidders. Since there was no evidence that competition and reasonable prices had not been obtained, there was no reason to waive the low bidder's failure or to cancel and resolicit the requirement. Comp. Gen. B-195481 (1980). Minor informalities can be treated as such only if the government can waive the provision. *Grade-Way Constr. v. United States,* 7 Cl. Ct. 263 (1985). A bidder who received a garbled telegraphic amendment could not change his erroneous bid after bid opening since the bidder had a duty to seek verification of the telegram from either the telegraph company or the Contracting Officer. Comp. Gen. B-153248 (1964).

A bidder's failure to expressly acknowledge receipt can be waived under the constructive acknowledgment theory if the bid received clearly indicates that the bidder received the amendment. Such would be the case where the amendment added another item to the solicitation and the bidder submitted a bid on that item. The government may also waive formal acknowledgment where the amendment involves only a matter of form or has either no effect or merely a negligible effect on price, quantity, quality, or delivery of the item bid on. *See* FAR § 14.405.

Cancellation of a contract to purchase government property was proper where the high bid was improperly determined to have been nonresponsive because of a failure to acknowledge receipt of an amendment to the IFB.

Award had been made to the protestor, the low bidder, solely because of an administrative error that occurred when the high bid was rejected for failure to file a formal acknowledgment of the IFB amendment. The failure to acknowledge receipt should have been waived or cured as a minor informality since the bid itself indicated that the bidder had received the amendment. In the case of the rejected high bid, an end-use certificate submitted with the bid was dated on the same date as the amended bid opening date. Moreover, the fact that the protestor received a written notice of award did not prevent cancellation because statutory authority permitted award only to the highest bidder, the property was still in the possession of the government, and title did not pass until its removal. Comp. Gen. B-195017 (1979).

## TIMELINESS OF BID SUBMISSION

A bid is timely only if it is received in the office designated in the IFB no later than the precise time set for the opening of bids. A bid received after the time set for bid opening is a late bid and will be considered for award only if received before contract award and (1) the lateness is due solely to a delay in the mails when the bid was sent by registered or certified mail and was mailed not later than five calendar days before the bid receipt date specified in the IFB; (2) the bid was sent by mail, telegram, or facsimile, if authorized by the solicitation, and was received at the government installation in sufficient time to be delivered to the office designated for the opening and would have been received in such office but for delay due to mishandling at the government installation; or (3) the bid was sent by U.S. Postal Service Express Mail not later than 5:00 P.M. at the place of mailing two working days prior to the date set for the receipt of bids.

The only acceptable evidence to establish the date of mailing of a late bid, modification, or withdrawal sent by either registered or certified mail is a U.S. or Canadian Postal Service postmark on the wrapper or on the original receipt from either of these postal services. If neither postmark shows a legible date, the bid, modification, or withdrawal will be deemed to have been mailed late. For purposes of establishing government mishandling, the only acceptable evidence to establish the time of receipt at the agency is the time-date stamp on the bid wrapper or other documentary evidence of receipt maintained by the agency. *See* FAR § 14.304-1. There are no provisions for considering a late bid sent by regular mail, and late hand-carried bids are not eligible for award under any circumstance.

A protest against the government's refusal to consider a bid hand-carried by the contractor was denied, even though the bid was delivered less than a minute late, because the IFB provided that late bids would be considered only if submitted by certified or registered mail or by telegram. In addition, the procurement regulations provided that any late bid not submitted by mail or telegram would not be considered for award. Comp. Gen. B-150516 (1963).

On the other hand, even though a bid was date-time stamped as being received 45 minutes after the scheduled bid opening, it was not late because there was acceptable evidence to show that it had in fact been received at the designated place prior to bid opening. The sworn affidavit of the bid opening clerk demonstrated that all registered and certified mail received in the bid opening room had been delivered at 11:00 A.M. and that at 11:15 A.M., when she had to stop stamping the mail in order to proceed with the bid opening, she had not stamped all of the mail received. After the bid opening, the remaining mail, including the bid in question, was stamped as received at 11:56 A.M. Furthermore, a log prepared by the installation mail clerk and signed by the bid opening clerk showed the certified number of the bid in question and therefore proved that the bid was received along with other mail delivered to the bid opening room on the bid opening date. Comp. Gen. B-195589 (1980).

## MODIFICATION OR WITHDRAWAL OF BIDS

Bids may be modified or withdrawn by written or telegraphic notice, by facsimile if the solicitation authorizes the submission of facsimile bids, or in person by the bidder, provided notice thereof is received at the office designated in the IFB prior to the specific time prescribed for the opening of bids. Modifications or withdrawals received after the time set for bid opening are treated in the same manner as late bids, except that the late modification of the otherwise acceptable bid is to be opened by the Contracting Officer whenever it is received, and if the terms of the modification make the bid more acceptable to the government, it will be considered and may be accepted. *See* FAR §§ 14.303, 14.304-1(e).

Telegraphic bid modifications, when authorized, can be considered only if received before bid opening in order to put all bidders on an equal basis and to prevent any bidder from obtaining an advantage over others by permitting him to modify his bid after securing information as to other bids received. *Scherr Constr. Co. v. United States,* 5 Cl. Ct. 249 (1984).

Where a telegraphic price modification to the low bid was received 30 minutes after bid opening, the Contracting Officer was not only authorized, but also required to consider the late modification. The procurement regulations were issued under statutory authority and have the force and effect of law; thus, they were controlling, for the Contracting Officer is an agent of the United States only in accordance with the authority granted by statute or regulation. Consideration of an already low bidder's late reduction of his bid price is in the financial interest of the United States and does not prejudice the rights of other bidders since the low bidder would be entitled to award in any event. *Condec Corp. v. United States,* 177 Ct. Cl. 958, 369 F.2d 753 (1966).

A bidder's attempt to make a late modification was unsuccessful because the Late Bid clause permitted late modifications only of an "otherwise successful" bid and his bid had not been the low bid at the time of bid opening. The protestor claimed that he had submitted the low bid. He had offered a unit price with a 10-day prompt payment discount, while the awardee had offered his price with a 20-day prompt payment discount. The IFB provided that prompt payment discounts shorter than 20 days would not be considered in evaluating bids. Although the protestor's bid evaluated on the basis of a 20-day discount would have been the low bid at bid opening time, the late attempt to make the discount available for bid evaluation could not be considered under the Late Bid clause. Comp. Gen. B-197016 (1980).

The "firm bid rule" is one of the most rigid features of the sealed-bidding method of acquisition. Its purpose is to prohibit modification or withdrawal of bids for a reasonable period of time after bid opening. It is against public policy to permit the revocation of a bid after the public opening and during the acceptance period. Government agents should be allowed a reasonable time after the opening to ascertain whether collusion or fraud has been perpetrated against the United States by the bidders. To allow withdrawals after the results of the bidding are known would open the way to fraud against the government. *Scott v. United States,* 44 Ct. Cl. 524 (1909). The rationale for this rule is the preservation of the integrity of the sealed-bidding system. A bidder will not be permitted to attend a public bid opening, determine the prices offered by his competitors, and then either submit a modified bid undercutting the other bidders' prices or withdraw his bid.

## RESPONSIVENESS OF BIDS

To be eligible for award, a bid must conform to the requirements of the IFB. Compliance with every aspect of the IFB is essential to assure that all bidders are treated equally as to timeliness and method of submission and as to the substance of any resulting contract. Bids submitted under the following circumstances are considered nonresponsive:

- A bid that fails to meet the essential requirements of the IFB shall be rejected.
- A bid that does not conform to the specifications shall be rejected, unless the IFB authorizes an alternate bid and the alternate meets the requirements specified.
- A bid that fails to conform to the delivery schedule or the permissible alternatives set forth in the IFB shall be rejected.
- A bid received from any person or concern that is suspended, debarred, or ineligible for contract award shall be rejected if the period of suspension, debarment, or ineligibility has not expired as of the bid opening date.

- A bid requiring the submission of a bid bond shall be rejected if none was furnished in conformance with the IFB.
- A bid seeking to qualify the terms and conditions of the IFB, or otherwise seeking to limit contractor liability or to limit the government's rights, shall be rejected.
- A low bid from a concern determined to be nonresponsible shall be rejected. *See* FAR § 14.404-2.

While a bid may not be in conformance with the terms and conditions of the IFB, it may not necessarily be nonresponsive. The issue becomes one of determining whether the nonconformance is a major or minor informality. A minor informality or irregularity is one that is merely a matter of form and not of substance. It also pertains to some immaterial defect in a bid or variation of a bid from the exact requirements of the invitation that can be corrected or waived without being prejudicial to other bidders. Examples of such nonconformances would include failure to return the required number of copies of the bid; failure to execute a required certificate; failure to acknowledge receipt of an amendment, but only if the bid reflects the requirements of the amendment; and failure to sign the bid document, but only if the bid is accompanied by other material indicating the bidder's intent to be bound by the bid. *See* FAR § 14.405.

## MISTAKES IN BIDS

One of the most troublesome areas in sealed bidding is that of mistakes in bids. Whereas a bidder for a commercial contract may be able to withdraw or submit a corrected bid at any time prior to the acceptance of his offer, bidders for government contracts are generally not permitted to withdraw or modify their bids after the public bid opening. In sealed bidding, the type of mistake most often made is generally reflected in, or confined to, bid prices. This is attributable to the fact that IFBs are normally quite explicit as to what is required of the bidder, to include specific terms and conditions of the contemplated contract. Other types of mistakes (i.e., failure to sign the bid, failure to acknowledge receipt of amendments) relate to bid responsiveness.

The rules applicable to correction of mistakes in bid prices apply only to bids that are otherwise responsive to the requirements of the IFB. Accordingly, the Contracting Officer is required, after bid opening, but prior to contract award, to examine each bid received to determine if it contains a mistake. If the Contracting Officer has actual knowledge, or should have known, that a mistake has been made, he cannot in good faith bind the bidder to his erroneous bid price by awarding the contract.

Clerical mistakes, apparent on the face of the bid, may be corrected by the Contracting Officer upon verification of the bid actually intended by the bidder. Examples of apparent clerical mistakes include obvious errors in the placement of a decimal point, obvious figure transposition, obvious discount errors, and mathematical errors in the computation of unit and total prices. Other types of mistakes could involve failure to include a vendor or subcontractor quotation or failure to price out some critical aspect of the work to be performed. *See* FAR § 14.406.

Once a mistake is suspected, the Contracting Officer is required to request verification of the bid. This is accomplished by notifying the bidder that a mistake is suspected, calling the bidder's attention to the mistake or to the reason a mistake is suspected, and requesting that the bidder verify the correctness and accuracy of the bid. As to suspected clerical errors, the Contracting Officer may permit correction of the mistake by verification of the bid intended. Correction of all other mistakes may be made upon a determination by the agency head that clear and convincing evidence establishes the existence of a mistake and of the bid actually intended, unless the correction would result in displacing one or more bids.

In most cases, a bidder's unequivocal confirmation of his bid price is sufficient to enable the government to award a contract to him. There are instances, however, where a bidder's confirmation of his bid may be inadequate to dispel doubts as to its accuracy, requiring the agency to reach a determination as to its acceptability. On the other hand, an award may be improper where the bidder is not adequately informed as to the reasons for suspecting that a bid mistake has occurred.

A protestor's claim that an award was improperly made was sustained because the Contracting Officer revised the awardee's bid downward after bid opening, thereby displacing a lower acceptable bid. The awardee's bid, which was increased by a timely telegraphic modification, was decreased after bid opening on the showing that the upward modification was erroneous. Contracting Officers may correct clerical mistakes apparent on the face of the bid after obtaining verification of the mistake from the bidder, but all mistakes that cannot be processed by the Contracting Officer must be referred to the appropriate office in the acquiring agency for a legal determination. Bids may be corrected where there is clear and convincing evidence of a mistake, but if correction would displace a lower acceptable bid, the correction may not be made, unless the mistake and the bid actually intended are ascertainable from the bid and the invitation. Thus, where the Contracting Officer permitted correction without first submitting it for a legal determination, such action was unauthorized because the error was due to a "phone misunderstanding," and an error of this type is not a clerical error that may be corrected unilaterally by the Contracting Officer. Comp. Gen. B-162740 (1968).

A contract was properly terminated where the awardee's low bid, having been improperly corrected upon verification of a suspected mistake, was brought to within 0.5 percent of the next lowest bid, thereby putting the bidding system's integrity in jeopardy. The awardee had quoted $0 for certain of his labor charges under an IFB for a requirements-type contract for furniture moving. The government evaluated the bid by applying $7.10 where each $0 was entered and made award to him as the lowest bidder. When the displaced next low bidder protested the award, the Comptroller General found the original bid responsive and held that the $0 was intended to mean at no cost. It was therefore recommended that the contract be terminated, which was accomplished by the agency. The court, finding the actions of the Comptroller General and the government to be rational and in accordance with law, upheld the decision and the subsequent termination of the contract. *Keahy's Moving & Storage Co. v. United States,* 25 Govt. Cont. Rep. (CCH) 214 (1980).

The request of a low bidder for an upward correction of his bid due to a mistake in the arithmetical computation of the bid was granted because the bidder provided clear and convincing evidence of the intended bid. The bidder inadvertently used a multiplier of 26 months rather than 112 weeks, the multiplier he should have used to arrive at his indirect cost estimate. It was clear from the bidder's worksheet that a mistake had been made. The manner in which it had occurred and the intended bid price were also clear. Although the percentage of costs computation may have seemed excessive, there was no evidence that the awardee did not intend to use it. And, once the intended bid price was proven, the slight disparity between the low bid and the second low bid became irrelevant. Comp. Gen. B-198711 (1980).

But it was improper for a contracting agency to accept a low bid with an obvious error in it, despite the fact that the Contracting Officer sought and received verification of the bid, because by allowing the bidder to verify an obvious error in his bid, he displaced the apparent low bidder. One item of the bid required the insertion of a unit price and the statement of an intended price. The unit price in the protestor's bid was $14.00, but the intended price was based on a unit price of $1,400. All other bidders on this item bid at least $1,000 per unit, and it was obvious that the extended price was correct and that the unit price was in error. Allowing the bidder to verify the unit price as the correct price was detrimental to the basic precept of competitive bidding since it provided the bidder with an opportunity to decide, after bid opening, whether the erroneous unit price or the correct extended price was most advantageous. By using the unit price, the bid was reduced by approximately $29,000, making it the low bid. Comp. Gen. B-191708 (1979).

Contracting agencies have authority to allow the withdrawal of a bid containing an alleged mistake upon the request of a bidder if there is clear and convincing evidence of the mistake, and if legal counsel representing the agency concurs in the determination. However, if the evidence is clear and convincing, both as to the existence of a mistake and as to the bid actually intended, and if the bid in both its corrected and uncorrected states is the lowest bid received, a determination may be made to correct the bid and consider it for award on a corrected basis. *See* FAR § 14.406-3.

## CONTRACT AWARD

Unless all bids are rejected by the acquiring agency, the Contracting Officer is required to make an award to the responsible bidder whose bid, conforming to the requirements of the IFB, is most advantageous to the government. In arriving at the award decision, the Contracting Officer must make certain judgments, to include (1) an examination of all bids to determine whether they are responsive to the IFB, (2) a determination of the relative order of preference based on bid prices by applying the price-related factors incident to the acquisition, and (3) a finding as to whether the most desirable bid was submitted by a responsible bidder. The award decision must be supported by preparing a statement and certificate of award and by indicating that award was made to the bidder submitting the lowest price; or, alternatively, the rationale for rejecting all lower bids received must be provided. In reaching this decision, the Contracting Officer may not apply any factor other than price or price-related factors expressly set forth in the IFB.

Contract awards may be made by mailing or otherwise furnishing the successful bidder with a properly executed award document on an appropriate form prescribed by the procuring agency. The Contracting Officer must notify the successful bidder of award within the time specified in the IFB, or in an extension thereto, in order to create a valid contract. It is not necessary to deliver a formal, fully executed contract document to the awardee at once, but such documents must be delivered to the contractor as soon as is practicable after notice of award.

A bidder's acceptance of an award after expiration of the acceptance period prescribed by the IFB does not necessarily invalidate the award. The only right that is conferred by the expiration of the acceptance period goes to the bidder, and he may waive the right if he is still willing to accept the award based on his original bid. Comp. Gen. B-193548 (1979).

In order to establish a valid acceptance, the offer and acceptance must conform strictly to the terms and conditions of the IFB. Government acceptance of a bidder's highest alternate price for the purchase of stockpile ore did not operate as a valid acceptance. The IFB required bidders to specify items desired, including alternates, and to specify the price bid for each unit. The bidder submitted a principal bid and alternate bids in descending order of preference. The bids were all within the market price range and were considered reasonable to the government. The government awarded the contract at the highest alternate of his last preference, contrary to the terms and conditions of the IFB, which specified that items were to be bid in descending order of preference and expressly limited the power of acceptance to the order of preference. Consequently, the government was not entitled to obtain payment from the bidder in excess of the amount to which it would have been entitled under a valid award. Comp. Gen. B-193828 (1977).

Although a contract may have been improperly awarded to other than the low bidder, it was not invalid because the mistake in award resulted from an error on the part of the government in applying improper freight rates in the evaluation of bids. The General Services Administration acknowledged that the protestor was the low bidder and should have been awarded a contract to supply briquettes. The agency also acknowledged that it mistakenly applied the higher transportation rates for charcoal briquettes, rather than the lower rates for petroleum briquettes, in evaluating the protestor's bid. Since the error occurred without the awardee's knowledge and was not otherwise due to any action by him, the Comptroller General recommended (1) that the government terminate the contract for the convenience of the government as to the undelivered quantity and (2) that it award a contract to the protestor for the remaining quantity due to be delivered. Comp. Gen. B-194144 (1979).

## CONTRACT REFORMATION BASED ON MISTAKES IN BIDS

A request for correction of alleged bid mistakes after contract award amounts to a request for reformation, rescission, or amendment of the contract. If correction of the mistake would make the contract more favorable to the government, without changing the essential requirements of the specifications, the Contracting Officer may correct the mistake by supplemental agreement. Where the correction is not in favor of the government, the Contracting Officer's authority to rescind or reform a contract based on mistake after award is severely limited. Correction can only be accomplished on the basis of clear and convincing evidence that the mistake was mutual or that it was so obvious that the Contracting Officer should have known a mistake had occurred. The government is generally reluctant to rescind or reform a contract based on the contractor's unilateral mistake. The FAR does permit agencies to rescind a contract or to reform it in order to delete the items involved in the mistake or to increase the bid price if the corrected price does not exceed that of the next lowest acceptable bid under the original IFB. *See* FAR § 14.406-4.

Where the government makes an adequate request for verification and the awardee has verified his bid, a request for reformation will generally be denied. For example, the awardee alleged that his bid was approximately $25,000 too low because he had failed to multiply an hourly rate for the projected 137 days of performance by eight hours per day. The evidence disclosed that, during bid evaluation, the government had determined that the awardee's bid was approximately $40,000 less than the other bid received. The Contracting Officer therefore requested the awardee to verify his bid and advised him of the pricing discrepancy between the two bids. Proper verification requires that, in addition to requesting confirmation of a bid price, the government must apprise the bidder of the mistake that is suspected and the basis for such suspicion. Since the only basis to suspect an error was the pricing differential between the two bids and this information was conveyed to the bidder, the request for verification was adequate. Acceptance of the verified bid resulted in a valid contract. The alleged mistake was unilateral, not mutual, and provided no basis to reform the contract. Comp. Gen. B-196711 (1979).

The equitable remedy of reformation to correct a unilateral mistake in a contractor's bid is available only if the government knew, or should have known, of a mistake in a bid costly to the bidder and is designed to avoid governmental overreaching. If the Contracting Officer has knowledge, whether actual or imputed as something he should know, that the bid is based on or embodies a disastrous mistake, and if he accepts the bid in the face of that knowledge, there is overreaching. There is no overreaching by the government and the contract will not be reformed in cases where the government requests and receives verification of the bid price from the bidder prior to contract award. Verification, to be legally adequate, must include the reasons the Contracting Officer suspects that the bid may contain a mistake. It is settled that a contract will not be reformed because of a unilateral mistake in a bid, unless the contractor establishes that the error resulted from a clear-cut clerical or arithmetical error or from a misreading of the specifications. *Carrier Corp. v. United States,* 6 Cl. Ct. 169 (1984). Where it was impossible to identify the error specifically because the work was bid on a lump sum basis, the Contracting Officer was not placed on constructive notice of the nature of the error beyond the significant differences between the bid prices. Comp. Gen. B-194056 (1979).

A request for adjustment, based on a bidding error, alleged five months after completion of the contract work, was denied because the verification request prior to contract award was legally adequate. The contractor claimed that in verifying his bid, he had relied on its closeness to an erroneously low government estimate and had discounted the significance of two other considerably higher bids. The government did not know that its estimate was erroneous when it requested verification and therefore could not know that it was "getting something for nothing." Since the bidder has the responsibility for undertaking an examination of the bid to assure its accuracy after being advised as to the possibility of error, the Comptroller General could not find the contract to be unconscionable even though the second low bid was 130 percent higher than the awardee's bid. Comp. Gen. B-194610 (1980).

The test in these cases is whether, considering all the facts and circumstances of the case, there were any factors that reasonably should have raised the presumption of error in the mind of the Contracting Officer. *Connelly Containers v. United States,* 7 Cl. Ct. 423 (1985). But the adequacy of a bid verification request is irrelevant where a Contracting Officer is not on notice of possible error in a bid. In a case in point, the protestor argued that the verification request was inadequate because he had been pressured into making an on-the-spot verification and had been allowed only three hours to do so. Since the Contracting Officer was deceased and there were no records to establish his reason for having requested confirmation since the bid price was significantly higher than the government's estimate, the presumption of error would not have been raised in the Contracting Officer's mind. Comp. Gen. B-196543 (1980).

# 5

# Acquisition by Negotiation

## INTRODUCTION

Acquisition by negotiation is defined as contracting through the use of either competitive or other-than-competitive proposals and written or oral discussion with offers in the competitive range. The negotiated method of acquisition employed by the government closely resembles commercial contracting practices. The method provides the government with significant flexibility, and acquisition officials have a great deal of discretion in arriving at an award decision. Negotiation procedures properly permit the Contracting Officer to take actions in awarding a contract that would be considered a radical violation of the law if the procurement were being accomplished by sealed bidding. 47 Comp. Gen. 279, 284 (1967). In negotiation, discussions are generally conducted between the government and the contractor, whereas discussions concerning the technical merits and pricing of a bid are strictly prohibited in sealed bidding. As a general rule, the concept of responsiveness is not applicable to negotiation where the Contracting Officer is normally expected to conduct oral or written discussions with offerors whose proposals may vary the requirements of the solicitation itself. In negotiated acquisitions, "non-responsiveness" is generally considered to be a subject of negotiations. 59 Comp. Gen. 298 (B-195935); (1979) 51 Comp. Gen. 247, 250 (1971). With respect to the extent of discussions, unless initially unacceptable proposals are found not subject to being made acceptable, except through major revisions, prospective contractors should be afforded the opportunity to satisfy the government's requirements. 51 Comp. Gen. 431 (1972). Finally, in contrast with sealed bidding, offers may be modified or withdrawn at any time prior to contract. The firm bid rule has no application in negotiation.

## CHARACTERISTICS OF NEGOTIATION

The negotiated method of acquisition is characterized by the issuance of a solicitation instrument; in response, proposals, which may subsequently be modified or changed entirely, are submitted to the acquiring agency. Negotiation is a flexible procedure, which includes the receipt of proposals, permits bargaining, and affords offerors an opportunity to revise their offers in response to discussions with the government prior to contract award. Bargaining—in the sense of discussion, persuasion, alteration of initial assumptions and provisions, and give-and-take—may apply to price, schedule, technical requirements, type of contract, or other terms and conditions of a proposed contract. Negotiation is a method of acquisition designed to stimulate competition even though definitive specifications are not available. Hence, a broader range of contract types is available for use in this method of acquisition than is authorized for use in sealed bidding.

Acquisition planning, discussed in Chapter 4, *supra,* is equally as important in negotiation as it is in sealed bidding. The more comprehensive and complete the planning process, the better the ultimate position of the government when discussions are opened with respect to a given acquisition.

Agency heads have authority to convert an acquisition initiated under the sealed-bidding method to negotiation under certain circumstances. In such event, the agency head must determine in writing that inadequate or ambiguous specifications were included in the IFB; that all otherwise acceptable bids were unreasonable as to price; that only one bid was received, and that its price was unreasonable; that no responsive bid had been received; or that other reasons in the public interest require such a change. *See* FAR §§ 14.404-1, 15.103. There have been frequent protests involving a low responsive bidder who later loses out in the competition when award is made by the government to an offeror quoting a higher price in negotiation. As a general rule, the Comptroller General has upheld the government's position in this type of protest.

## TYPES OF CONTRACTS AUTHORIZED

The Contracting Officer has authority to award any type, or combination of types, of contract that will promote the government's interest in negotiation except the cost-plus-percentage-of-cost contract, which is prohibited by law. 10 U.S.C. § 2306(a); 41 U.S.C. § 254(a). The contract type ultimately selected for award by the Contracting Officer determines the performance risk to be borne by the parties. The fixed-price group of contracts places cost and performance risk on the contractor, whereas the cost reimbursement group places cost risk on the government.

Selecting the type of contract to be awarded is a matter of negotiation between the parties and requires the exercise of sound judgment on the part of the Contracting Officer. The objective is to negotiate a contract type that will result in reasonable contractor risk and provide the greatest incentive for efficient and economical performance.

A firm-fixed-price contract, which best utilizes the profit motive of business enterprise, is required for use when the risk involved is minimal or can be predicted with an acceptable degree of certainty. When a reasonable basis for firm pricing does not exist, other contract types should be considered, and negotiations should be directed toward selecting a contract type, or combination of types, that ties profit to contractor risk and performance.

### Fixed-Price Contracts

In addition to the contract types discussed in Chapter 4, the Contracting Officer may use any of the contracts discussed here in the negotiated method of procurement. The firm-fixed-price incentive contract provides for adjusting profit and establishing the final negotiated total cost to total target cost. Under this form of contract, both cost and performance characteristics can be incentivized. It is appropriate for use when the nature of the acquisition is such that the contractor's assumption of a degree of cost responsibility will provide a profit incentive for effective cost control or performance.

The fixed-price prospective-price-redeterminable contract is suitable for use for long-range quantity production or service contracts, when it is impossible to negotiate prices for the entire period of performance. A fair and reasonable price is negotiated for the initial period of the contract and redetermined upward or downward at a specific point in time established during negotiations.

The fixed-ceiling-price contract with retroactive price redetermination features is generally appropriate for research and development contracts of $100,000, or less, when it is established at the time of contract award that a fair and reasonable contract cannot be negotiated for the entire period of performance. A ceiling price is negotiated at levels that reflect a reasonable sharing of risk by the contractor.

The firm-fixed-price term type of contract requires that the contractor deliver for a fixed price a specified level of effort over a stated period on work that can be stated in general terms. While it is suitable for investigations or research and development efforts, and the contractor may furnish a report at the end of contract performance, payment is based on actual hours delivered. Under this form of contract, the contractor assumes negligible risk.

### Cost Reimbursement Contracts

Cost reimbursement contracts provide that the government will reimburse the contractor for all incurred costs, given that they are reasonable, allowable, and allocable to the contract. A ceiling is established at the outset for the purpose of fixing a ceiling on the contract and obligating funds; such ceiling cannot be exceeded by the contractor except at his own risk. Limitation of Cost or Limitation of Funds articles apply to these contracts, requiring that the contractor place the government on notice if the contract ceiling is to be either exceeded or underrun. A cost reimbursement contract may be used only when the contractor has an adequate accounting system, appropriate government surveillance is available to assure that effective cost controls and efficient performance methods are employed by the contractor, and a determination and findings have been prepared by the Contracting Officer. The contractor assumes little, if any, risk under these types of contracts, and there is little incentive to control costs.

The cost contract is suitable for research and development efforts with nonprofit organizations. Under this form of contract, the contractor receives no fee, but all incurred costs are reimbursed by the government.

The cost-sharing contract is suitable for use where the contractor agrees to absorb some portion of the costs in return for some compensating benefit, such as the right to commercially market the item. The contractor receives no fee and absorbs some mutually agreed-on portion of costs incurred under this contract arrangement.

Under the cost-plus-incentive fee contract, a target cost, target fee, minimum and maximum fees, and a fee adjustment formula are negotiated at the time of contract award. This form of contract is suitable for development and test programs, under which a cost reimbursement contract is necessary and a target cost and a fee adjustment formula can be negotiated that are likely to incentivize the contractor to manage effectively. While cost control will always be incentivized under this contract, it is also possible to incentivize performance characteristics. The amount of fee payable is determined at the completion of contract performance, based on the formula agreed to at contract award.

The cost-plus-award fee contract provides for a base fee, which may be zero, fixed at contract award, and an award amount judged by the government to be sufficient to motivate excellence in contract performance. Cost controls and performance characteristics may be incentivized. This form of contract requires the development of evaluation criteria at the outset of performance, against which the contractor's performance will be measured in accordance with agency regulations. The single most important disadvantage to this form of contract lies in the administrative burden placed on the acquiring agency in administering the contract.

The cost-plus-fixed-fee contract is a cost reimbursement contract that provides for payment of a fixed fee that is negotiated at the time of contract award and that does not vary with actual costs incurred. The fixed fee may be adjusted as a result of changes in the work to be performed. This form of contract presents the contractor with little incentive to control costs.

All cost reimbursement contracts are subject to statutory limitations as to the amount of fee that may be awarded. Research and development contracts shall not exceed 15 percent of the contractor's estimated cost, whereas all other cost reimbursement contracts are subject to a ceiling of 10 percent. A deviation to the maximum-fee limitation on cost-plus-award fee and cost-plus-incentive fee contracts may be obtainable in accordance with subpart 1.4 of the FAR. The ceiling on architect and engineering contracts has been fixed at 6 percent of the estimated cost and engineering of construction of the public work. *See* 10 U.S.C. § 2306(d); 41 U.S.C. § 254(d).

### Other Contract Types

Indefinite delivery contracts permit the government to maintain stocks at minimum levels and direct shipment to users when appropriate. The definite quantity contract provides for delivery of specific supplies or services within a fixed period, with deliveries to be scheduled at designated locations upon order. The requirements contract provides for filling all actual purchase requirements for specific supplies or services within a fixed period, with deliveries being scheduled by placing orders under the contract. This form of contract contains a total estimated quantity, whereas the indefinite quantity contract provides for stated minimum and maximum levels of supplies and services.

The time-and-materials contract provides for the contractor to supply direct labor hours at fixed hourly rates, which include overhead, general and administrative expenses, and profit. Materials are furnished to the government at cost and may include a materials-handling charge. The labor hour contract is a variation, which differs only in that the government furnishes materials.

The letter contract is a written preliminary instrument that permits the contractor to commence performance immediately, pending definitization of the agreed-to contract. It should be as complete as possible, to include a price ceiling where appropriate. The letter contract should be definitized within 180 days or before completion of 40 percent of the work.

The basic ordering agreement is not a contract as such. Rather, it is a written instrument of understanding that sets forth appropriate terms and conditions, a description of the supplies and services that may be furnished thereunder, and the methods of pricing, issuing delivery orders, and making deliveries under the agreement.

## SOLICITATION OF PROPOSALS

Requests for Proposals (RFPs) and Requests for Quotations (RFQs) are used by the government to communicate its needs to prospective contractors, but each has a separate and distinct function. The RFP contemplates the ultimate award of a contract and is therefore not used to obtain informational or planning data. The RFQ, on the other hand, is used only when the government does not intend to award a contract, but does want to obtain pricing or information for planning purposes.

Except as indicated below, procuring agencies are required to issue written solicitations that contain information necessary to enable prospective contractors to properly prepare proposals or quotations. It is essential to the integrity of the process that all prospective offerors be furnished identical information and that government personnel refrain from releasing information concerning the acquisition to any offeror that would give him an advantage over others.

Oral solicitations are authorized when the purchase of perishable subsistence is involved or when the processing of a written solicitation would delay the acquisition of the supplies or services to the detriment of the government. If this method of soliciting requirements is used, the Contracting Officer is required to furnish identical information concerning a proposed acquisition to all prospective offerors, as well as to follow the same procedures as would be used if a written solicitation were issued.

Presolicitation notices are available for use by the Contracting Officer, and a synopsis of the acquisition must appear in the *Commerce Business Daily* as a means of fostering full and open competition. The presolicitation conference, when its use is approved at a level above the Contracting Officer, provides the government with an opportunity to assure that competing offerors fully understand the requirements of the RFP.

## AMENDMENTS TO RFPs

If the government finds it necessary to make changes in specifications, quantity, quality, delivery schedules, or closing dates or to correct a defect or ambiguity in the RFP, prior to the date set for the receipt of proposals, such changes must be accomplished by issuing a written amendment to the RFP. Where only a short period of time remains before the date set for the receipt of proposals, the Contracting Officer may extend the closing date orally or by telegram, either of which must be followed by a written amendment to the RFP; any extension of time granted to one offeror must be granted to all offerors. Similarly, any other information given to any one prospective offeror must be furnished to all other offerors if the information is necessary for the preparation and submission of proposals, or if the lack of such information would be prejudicial to uninformed offerors.

As was the case with sealed bidding, failure to acknowledge receipt of an amendment to an RFP could be fatal. Thus, a proposal from an offeror who failed to acknowledge receipt of RFP amendments was properly rejected even though in negotiation such failure may properly be the subject of discussions, provided other offerors are not prejudiced thereby. In this case, other offerors could have been prejudiced by such discussions. The amendments were considered material because they revised performance requirements. Inasmuch as the RFP indicated that award could be made on the basis of initial offers, it would have created a competitive advantage if negotiations were conducted with the offeror, whose proposal did not meet the government's amended requirements.

Where the RFP specified that amendments had to be acknowledged and that the government reserved the right to make an award based on initial offers without discussion, a low offer was properly rejected for failure to acknowledge receipt of an amendment. The amendment itself warned that failure to acknowledge receipt could result in rejection of the offer. Despite the low offeror's contention, the Comptroller General accepted the government's argument that the price was significantly affected by the amendment. Although negotiated procurement procedures are designed to be flexible and to permit actions that would violate the law if done in sealed-bid acquisitions, each case involving negotiated procurement is dependent on the circumstances. In view of the urgency of this "public exigency" acquisition, there was no legal basis on which to question the rejection of the protestor's offer as being nonresponsive because no opportunity existed for curing the defect through negotiation. Depending on the circumstances, however, failure to acknowledge receipt of an amendment is ordinarily curable through discussions.

## LATE PROPOSALS AND MODIFICATIONS

Late proposals and modifications thereto are generally processed in the same manner as was prescribed for use in the sealed-bidding method of acquisition, with but two principal exceptions. First, a late proposal or modification may be considered for award at any time if it is the only proposal received. *See* FAR § 52.215-10. Second, the rules apply to the receipt of both initial proposals and "best and final" offers submitted after the closing of discussions.

## SELECTION OF OFFERORS FOR DISCUSSIONS

Written or oral discussions must be held with all responsible offerors who submit proposals within the competitive range. These requirements are not applicable to acquisitions (1) in which prices are fixed by law or regulation, (2) of the set-aside portion of a partial set-aside procurement, or (3) in which full and open competition or accurate prior cost experience with the product or service demonstrates that acceptance of the most favorable initial proposal without discussion would result in the lowest overall cost to the government at a fair and reasonable price, provided that the agency reserved the right to make an award without opening discussions and that the award was in fact made without oral or written discussions with any offeror. *See* FAR § 15.610.

Proposals in response to an RFP are normally submitted in two parts and are subsequently evaluated in two distinct phases: technical and management. The offeror's technical proposal describes the manner in which the prospective contractor proposes to accomplish the work required by the government. The management proposal includes the offeror's cost or pricing data and any other pertinent business information required by the agency to determine whether the prospective contractor has the necessary prerequisites to accomplish the proposed effort.

## Evaluation Factors

It is a fundamental policy of the government that competitive proposals shall be evaluated solely on the factors specified in the solicitation. *See* FAR § 15.608. These factors are included in the evaluation criteria, which consist of evaluation factors specifically tailored to meet the agency's requirement for a given procurement, standards for applying such factors, and the relative importance of the factors. Price or cost to the government is required as an evaluation factor in every solicitation, as are quality considerations. Quality, as an evaluation factor, may be expressed in terms of technical excellence, management capabilities, personnel qualifications, prior experience, past performance, and ability to comply with schedule requirements. Any other relevant factors, such as cost realism, may also be included. *See* FAR § 15.605.

Though the agency has broad discretion in determining evaluation factors to be applied to a given procurement, and the relative importance of such factors, the solicitation is defective unless such criteria are clearly set forth in the RFP. This is especially true with respect to the importance of cost or price in relationship to technical considerations.

Failure to show the relative importance of price is contrary to the longstanding view of the Comptroller General that intelligent competition requires, as a matter of sound procurement policy, that offerors be advised of the evaluation factors to be used and the relative importance of those factors. Each offeror has a right to know whether the procurement is intended to achieve a minimum standard at the lowest cost or whether cost is secondary to quality. Competition is hardly served if offerors are not given any idea of the relative value of technical excellence and price. A complaint is justified if in such circumstances a materially superior offer is rejected in favor of one offering a lower price. *University Research Corp.,* Comp. Gen. B-196246 (1981). If the RFP states that technical considerations are more important than cost in evaluating proposals, a clearly superior technical proposal could be accepted even at a higher cost. Price is secondary under such circumstances. *Tymeshare,* Comp. Gen. B-198020 (1980). On the other hand, if the solicitation does not indicate the relative value of cost or price, there is clearly a deficiency in the RFP's evaluation provision. *A.R. & S. Enterprises,* Comp. Gen. B-196518 (1980).

## Implied Warranty of Fair and Honest Evaluation

It is an implied condition of every RFP issued by the government that each proposal submitted in response thereto will be fairly and honestly evaluated in accordance with statutory requirements, procurement regulations, agency procedures, and the stated criteria set forth in the RFP. Neither the Comptroller General nor the courts and Boards of Contract Appeals will interfere with an agency's evaluation process, unless there is a showing of abuse of discretion on the part of the agency. Though reluctant to intervene in the evaluation process, they may examine the record to determine whether the judgment of the Contract Officer has a rational basis. Accordingly, it is imperative that the record reflect the basis for the judgment.

Procurement officials enjoy significant discretion in the evaluation of the relative merits of technical proposals, and their determinations will not be disturbed unless shown to be arbitrary or without a rational basis. *Space Age Engineering v. United States,* 4 Cl. Ct. 739 (1984). Judicial review of an agency's pre-award procurement decision is and should be extremely limited in scope. Thus, where an agency's decisions are highly technical in nature, judicial restraint is appropriate and proper. *Electro-Methods v. United States,* 7 Cl. Ct. 755 (1985).

## Establishing the Competitive Range

The Contracting Officer determines which proposals are to be included in the competitive range for the purpose of conducting written or oral discussions. This determination is based on price and other factors, as set forth in the RFP. Normally, the competitive range will include all proposals that have a reasonable chance of being selected for award. When there is doubt as to whether a proposal is in the competitive range, that doubt should be resolved by including it. FAR § 15.609. A proposal must be considered to be within the competitive range so as to require discussions unless it is so technically inferior or out of line with regard to price that meaningful discussions are precluded. 48 Comp. Gen. 314 (1968). Thus, an agency may properly exclude a technically unacceptable proposal from the competitive range after an initial evaluation, without considering cost. *Marketing Information Service,* 79-2 CPD 428 (1979), *Macro Systems,* Comp. Gen. B-195990, (1980).

Procuring agencies use a variety of systems to score proposals during evaluation, which is acceptable so long as the record shows that there is a rational basis for the award decision. *Tracor-Jitco,* 54 Comp. Gen. 896

(1975). Technical point ratings are useful as guides for intelligent decision making in the procurement process, but whether a given point spread between two competing proposals indicates the significant superiority of one proposal over another depends on the facts and circumstances of each procurement and is primarily a matter within the discretion of the procuring agency. The question of whether a difference in point scores is significant is for determination on the basis of what that difference means in terms of performance and what it would cost the government to take advantage of it. *The University Foundation, California State University, Chico,* Comp. Gen. B-200608 (1981); *Grey Advertising,* 55 Comp. Gen. 1111 (1976). The determinative element is not the difference in technical scores per se, but rather the considered judgment of the procuring agency concerning the significance of that difference. 52 Comp. Gen. 358 (1972). Thus, even where cost is assigned evaluation points, a higher combined score (cost plus technical) does not in itself necessarily justify an award without considering price. 51 Comp. Gen. 153 (1971).

A determination of competitive range based on a comparison of an offeror's score with a predetermined score for acceptability is improper. *Moxon, Inc.,* Comp. Gen. B-179160 (1974); 50 Comp. Gen. 59 (1970). The competitive range should be determined by examining the array of scores for all proposals submitted, 52 Comp. Gen. 382 (1972), and borderline proposals should not automatically be excluded from consideration if reasonably susceptible of being made acceptable, Comp. Gen. B-176761(2) (1973).

It is not the function of the Comptroller General to evaluate the technical merits of proposals, to resolve disputes over the scoring of technical proposals, or to substitute his judgment for that of the procuring agency as to which offeror should have received the award. *Sogitec,* Comp. Gen. B-196158 (1980); *Decision Sciences Corp.,* Comp. Gen. B-182558 (1975). Nor is it the function of that office to make determinations as to the acceptability or relative merits of proposals. *New York University,* Comp. Gen. B-195792 (1980); *Joanell Laboratories,* 56 Comp. Gen. 291 (1977). Technical evaluations and award determinations by procuring agencies will be questioned only on a showing that they were arbitrary or unreasonable or inconsistent with the specified evaluation. *Decision Sciences Corp.,* Comp. Gen. B-196100 (1980); *Group Operations,* 55 Comp. Gen. 1315 (1976).

The government properly excluded a proposal containing informational deficiencies that could not have been corrected without a major revision of the entire proposal. The RFP required an offeror to show his proposed methods of solving technical problems in sufficient detail to permit a comprehensive engineering evaluation by the government. The protestor did not specifically define his proposed methods, nor did he include sufficient information regarding tooling and fabrication methods, his quality assurance program, and other essentials, in spite of the fact that the RFP emphasized that the offeror's technical and management proposal would be the most important factor in selection for award and that it should be specific and complete. Comp. Gen. B-194157 (1980).

Where a protesting contractor alleged that the awardee had not submitted a responsive proposal since the system he offered was not based on existing, proven, and previously developed technology as required by the RFP, the Comptroller General ruled that questions of responsiveness are inappropriate in a negotiated procurement. The agency had based its determination on its experience with the system under a previous contract and on extensive research by the awardee. Moreover, extensive reviews by agency engineers in the field established that the awardee satisfied the RFP's technical requirements. The agency's determination that the system was acceptable had a rational basis. Comp. Gen. B-191756 (1979).

## WRITTEN AND ORAL DISCUSSIONS

Meaningful discussions, whether oral or written, are normally required in negotiated federal acquisitions. The agency must usually furnish information to offerors concerning the areas of deficiencies in their proposals so that they are given the opportunity to satisfy the solicitation requirements. *WASSEA Technical Systems & Research Co.,* Comp. Gen. B-189573 (1979); *Okaw Industries,* Comp. Gen. B-191730 (1978). Though negotiations should be conducted to the extent practical and meaningful in order to stimulate competition, *American Nucleonics Corp.,* Comp. Gen. B-193546 (1979), the content and extent of discussions needed to satisfy the requirement for meaningful discussions are a matter primarily for determination by the contracting agency; its judgment will not be disturbed unless clearly without a reasonable basis, *Arthur Young & Co.,* Comp. Gen. B-196220 (1980). A request for best and final offers will satisfy the discussions requirement where a proposal contains no technical uncertainties. *Information Management,* 84-1 CPD 76 (1984). Moreover, there is no requirement that the same matter be discussed with each offeror, *see Okaw Industries, supra;* and an agency's decision not to engage in technical discussions is unobjectionable where a proposal contains no technical uncertainties, *Weinschel Engineering Co.,* Comp. Gen. B-217202 (1985).

During the conduct of oral or written discussion, the Contracting Officer is required to attempt to resolve any uncertainties regarding the offeror's technical proposal, as well as any other terms and conditions imposed by the offeror. *See* FAR § 15.610(b). An attempt must also be made to seek the resolution of any suspected mistakes as specifically as possible under the circumstances, but without revealing any information concerning other offerors' proposals or the results of the evaluation process itself. The disclosure of the strengths or weaknesses of competing offers or the disclosure of any information from one offeror's proposal that would enable another offeror to improve his proposal is likewise prohibited. Similarly, government disclosure of technical information that would result in any improvement of a competing proposal is not permitted. Moreover, the Contracting Officer, and all other government personnel associated with the acquisition, is prohibited from assisting an offeror to bring his proposal up to the level of other proposals through a series of discussions designed to improve the offeror's lack of diligence, competence, or initiative in preparing his proposal. Auction techniques are also strictly forbidden. Examples of such methods include indicating a price that has to be met by an offeror in order for his proposal to receive further consideration and informing an offeror of his price standing relative to another offeror. It is permissible, however, to inform an offeror that his cost or price is considered to be too high. *See* FAR § 15.610.

Offerors selected to participate in written or oral discussions are advised by the Contracting Officer of any deficiencies in their proposals and are given a reasonable opportunity to correct or resolve such deficiencies. This process provides an opportunity for the offeror to submit such price, cost, technical, or other revisions to his proposal that he deems appropriate, based on his discussions with the government. For the purposes of discussions, a deficiency has been defined as that part of the offeror's proposal that fails to satisfy the government's requirements. Informational deficiencies in a proposal in the competitive range should be remedied by discussions with the offeror, particularly where a slight improvement in the technical score could change the relative ranking of all offerors in the competitive range. The fact that deficiencies are described as being "weaknesses" in a proposal does not change the conclusion, nor is the obligation to conduct meaningful discussions fulfilled by the Contracting Officer if he merely requests cost information relative to the deficient areas, without discussing the deficiencies themselves. *Logistics Systems,* Comp. Gen. B-196254 (1980). An agency cannot limit its duty to conduct meaningful discussions by labeling some areas "weaknesses." *Harbridge House,* Comp. Gen. B-195320 (1980).

"Discussion" is defined as any oral or written communication between the government and an offeror, whether or not initiated by the government, that involves information essential for determining the acceptability of a proposal or that provides an offeror with an opportunity to revise or modify its proposal. "Clarification," on the other hand, means communication with an offeror for the sole purpose of eliminating minor irregularities or apparent clerical mistakes in a proposal. It is achieved by explanation or substantiation, either in response to a government inquiry or as initiated by the offeror. Unlike discussion, clarification does not give the offeror an opportunity to revise or modify its proposal, except to the extent that correction of an apparent clerical mistake results in a revision. *See* FAR § 15.601.

This distinction is exceedingly important to negotiations, and, unless care is exercised, clarification could be legally construed as having been discussion. For example, two offerors were awarded close technical scores during evaluation of a cost-plus-fixed-fee solicitation. Following discussions, best and final offers were requested and submitted. One offeror significantly reduced the number of labor hours proposed, as well as its proposed costs, without explaining how the reduction was to be achieved. When the Contracting Officer requested clarification of the significant reductions, such clarification was held to be discussion. *ABT Assoc.*, Comp. Gen. B-196365 (1980).

Inquiries to an offeror for the sole purpose of eliminating minor uncertainties or irregularities in a proposal constitute "clarifications," not "discussions." *John Fluke Mfg. Co.*, Comp. Gen. 79-2 CPD 367 (1979). On the other hand, discussions occur if an offeror is afforded the opportunity to revise or modify his proposal, 51 Comp. Gen. 479 (1972), or if the information requested and provided is essential for determining the acceptability of proposals, *Human Resources Co.*, 76-2 CPD 459 (1976). It is also the actions of the parties that determine whether discussions have been held, and not merely the characterization thereof by the Contracting Officer. *New Hampshire–Vermont Health Service*, 57 Comp. Gen. 347 (1978). If discussions are reopened with one offeror after receipt of best and final offers, they must be reopened with all offerors in the competitive range to give these offerors an opportunity to submit revised proposals. *University of New Orleans*, 56 Comp. Gen. 958 (1977).

## Best and Final Offers

Upon concluding discussions, the Contracting Officer is required to establish a final, common cutoff date for the submission of best and final offers. The date selected must be one that allows a reasonable time for the preparation and submission of revised offers, and all offerors remaining in the competitive range must be so notified. If oral notification is given, written confirmation is required. The notification must indicate that

1. Discussions are concluded.
2. Offerors are being given an opportunity to submit a best and final offer.
3. If any modification is submitted, it must be received by the date and time specified, or it will be processed in accordance with the late modification of proposals provision of the solicitation. *See* FAR § 15.611.

The initial number of proposals considered as being within the competitive range may be reduced when, as a result of oral or written discussions, it has been determined that a proposal no longer has a reasonable chance of being selected for award. FAR § 15.609. Thus, the Contracting Officer is not required to give a firm an opportunity to submit a best and final offer if it is no longer in the competitive range. Comp. Gen. B-195624 (1980).

After receipt of best and final offers, discussions may be reopened if it is clearly in the government's best interest. Hence, a government request for a second round of best and final offers under an RFP for diesel generator sets was proper because the Contracting Officer exercised reasonable discretion in acting on the advice of his technical experts and in deciding to request technical clarification from all offerors concerning their proposals. The government was concerned about the low offeror's ability to meet the engine specifications for minimum horsepower levels. Although it would have been preferable to ascertain whether the engines conformed to the specifications before the receipt of initial best and final offers, the decision to reopen the negotiations was not arbitrary or lacking a reasonable basis. Comp. Gen. B-194570 (1980).

Receipt of a late modification to an otherwise timely proposal should raise questions in the mind of the Contracting Officer as to whether to open, or reopen, discussions. The FAR does not, and was never intended to, preclude opening discussions with all offerors in the competitive range upon the receipt of a late modification that fairly indicates that such discussions would prove highly advantageous to the government. 47 Comp. Gen. 279 (1967); Comp. Gen. B-161782 (1968).

### Award Without Discussions

The requirement for written or oral discussions need not be applied in acquisitions in which it can clearly be demonstrated from the existence of full and open competition or from accurate prior cost experience with the product or service that acceptance of the most favorable initial proposal without discussion would result in the lowest overall cost to the government at a fair and reasonable price. However, (1) the solicitation must have notified all offerors of the possibility that award might be made without discussions, and (2) the award must in fact have been made without any written or oral discussions with any offeror. FAR § 15.610(a).

The regulatory stipulation that award on the basis of initial proposals result in the lowest overall cost to the government reflects an express statutory requirement of the Competition in Contracting Act, Pub. L. No. 98-369. *Sperry Corp.*, Comp. Gen. B-220521 (1986). The previous statutory language did not require that the award result in the lowest overall cost to the government. Rather, it merely required that the award result in a fair and reasonable price to the government. *See* 10 U.S.C. § 2304(g) (1982).

## COST AS A BASIS FOR CONTRACT AWARD

In awarding cost-reimbursement contracts, the cost proposal should not be controlling since advance estimates of costs may not be valid indicators of final actual costs. There is no requirement that cost reimbursement contracts be awarded on the the basis of lowest proposed cost, lowest proposed fee, or lowest total proposed cost plus fee. If award decisions are based solely on estimated costs, such practices may encourage the submission of unrealistically low estimates and increase the likelihood of cost overruns. The primary considerations should be which offeror can perform the contract in a manner most advantageous to the government, as determined by evaluation of proposals according to the evaluation criteria established in the solicitation.

When the government contemplates the award of a cost reimbursement contract, the issues of buy-in and cost realism become proper issues for review by the Comptroller General. As a general rule, buying in on fixed-price contracts (e.g., submitting a below-cost proposal) provides no basis for protest so long as the offeror is responsible since it is the offeror's loss and not the government's if the cost of providing the required service or item exceeds the contract price. *Fresh Flavor Meals*, Comp. Gen. B-208965 (1983). But when the contract to be awarded is of the cost reimbursement type, the risk of loss as a result of a cost overrun shifts to the government. It is necessary in cost reimbursement contracting to be aware of the possibility of a buy-in and guard against its occurrence by analyzing costs in terms of their realism since, regardless of the costs proposed by the offeror, the government is bound to pay the contractor actual and allowable costs. *Bell Aerospace Co., Computer Sciences Corp.*, 54 Comp. Gen. 352 (1974).

It is therefore improper to award a cost reimbursement contract on the basis that the proposed costs are reasonable per se merely because they are low when compared to other offers, without an appropriate analysis that adequately measures the realism of such low costs. Where the award of the contract is based ultimately on the estimated cost for performance of the contract, a determination of cost realism requires more than the acceptance of proposed costs as submitted. See *Joule Technical Corp.* Comp. Gen. B-192125 (1979). For these reasons, the evaluation of competing cost proposals requires the exercise of informed judgment, which must be left to the administrative discretion of the contracting agencies involved. They are in the best position to assess "realism" of cost and must bear the major criticism for any difficulty or expenses resulting from a defective cost analysis. 50 Comp. Gen. 390 (1970). Since the cost analysis is a function of the contracting agency, its determination will not be disturbed unless it lacks a reasonable basis. *Moshman Assoc.*, Comp. Gen. B-192008 (1979).

Where the cost factor is clearly secondary or low in the list of evaluation factors in cost reimbursement acquisitions, it cannot be elevated to the ultimate decision-making factor, unless there is a very close clustering of proposals based on the more important technical and management approach factors. If cost is not a major factor in the evaluation scheme, and if the difference between the best evaluated technical proposal and the evaluated technical proposal of the low offeror is substantial, cost should not be the determinant of which offeror will receive the contract award. If a greater weight is assigned to technical considerations than to cost, it is improper and an abuse of agency discretion to reject a technically superior proposal on the basis that an inferior proposal offered a lower price.

The government also recognizes that profit or fee prenegotiation objectives do not necessarily represent net income to contractors. Rather, they represent that element of the total remuneration that contractors may receive for contract performance over and above allowable costs. It is in the government's interest to offer contractors opportunities for financial rewards sufficient to stimulate efficient contract performance, attract the best capabilities of qualified large and small business concerns to government contracts, and maintain a viable industrial base. Both the government and its contractors should be concerned with profit as a motivator of efficient and effective contract performance. Negotiations aimed merely at reducing prices by reducing profit or fee, without proper recognition of their function, are counterproductive and not in the government's best interests. Negotiations of extremely low profits or fees, use of historical averages, or automatic application of predetermined percentages does not provide proper motivation for optimum contract performance. *See* FAR § 15.901.

For each contract in which profit or fee is negotiated as a separate element of the contract price, the aim of negotiations should be to employ the profit or fee motive so as to impel effective contract performance and efficient control of costs. To this end, the profit or fee objective should be fitted to the circumstances of the particular acquisition, giving due weight to the effort required of the contractor; risks to be borne by the contractor and the government, respectively, during contract performance; the facilities investment required of the contractor; and other pertinent performance factors. In establishing profit or fee objectives, agencies are not permitted to establish administrative ceilings or to create administrative procedures that could be represented to contractors as de facto ceilings.

## UNSOLICITED PROPOSALS

It is the policy of the government to encourage the submission of unsolicited proposals, as well as to avoid either agency or regulatory constraints that could inhibit prospective contractors from developing and submitting ideas to its departments and agencies for its consideration. Unsolicited proposals are an extremely valuable means for government agencies to obtain innovative or unique methods or approaches to accomplish their missions from sources outside the government. Accordingly, acquiring agencies are required to assist potential offerors where possible, to include encouraging preliminary contacts with the agency and making available certain information that would assist in the preparation of a proposal acceptable for evaluation.

The government will not consider an unsolicited proposal unless it (1) is innovative or unique, (2) is independently originated and developed, (3) is prepared without government supervision, (4) includes sufficient cost and technical detail to permit a determination by the Contracting Officer that government support could be worthwhile and that the proposed work could benefit the agency's research and development and other responsibilities, and (5) is not an advance proposal for a specific documented agency requirement that can be acquired by competitive methods. FAR § 15.503(b). The government does not consider advertisements, commercial product offers, or technical correspondence to be unsolicited proposals. Moreover, because of the government's continuing search for unique or innovative ideas, agencies receiving unsolicited proposals that are not related to their mission or functional requirements may identify those agencies having missions bearing a relationship to the subject matter of the proposal.

Potential offerors are encouraged by the government to make preliminary contact with appropriate agency contracting and technical officials prior to expending significant time and effort in the development of an unsolicited proposal. Such contacts should include discussion of (1) the agency's need for the contemplated effort, (2) the content of an unsolicited proposal, (3) information to further an understanding of the agency's missions and responsibilities relative to the contemplated effort, (4) the content of the specific unsolicited proposal, and (5) the agency's evaluation procedures with respect to such proposals.

The question frequently arises as to whether the government can freely use the ideas and contents of an unsolicited proposal as the basis for a competitive acquisition. Under the provisions of section 15.508 of the FAR, government contracting and technical personnel are prohibited from using any data, concepts, ideas, or other parts of an unsolicited proposal, or any part of the basis, for a solicitation or in negotiations with any other person or firm, unless the offeror is notified and agrees to such intended use. Government personnel are prohibited from disclosing restrictively marked information included in an unsolicited proposal. The disclosure of any information concerning a party's trade secrets, processes, operations, style or method of work, apparatus, and other matters, except as authorized by law, could result in criminal sanctions under 18 U.S.C. § 1905. To protect original concepts and ideas, the offeror should include the nondisclosure statements referred to in section 15.509 of the FAR.

# 6

# Express Changes

## INTRODUCTION

Constant changes in the government's requirements or funding, significant advances in technology, errors in plans or specifications, unanticipated subsurface or latent site conditions, and delays are but a sampling of contract performance problems that mandate flexibility in the government contract. Such flexibility is contained in the standard Changes articles, which trace their origin to the period immediately following the American Civil War when the Navy Bureau of Yards and Docks included a provision in its contracts that permitted the government to make unilateral changes during contract performance. Following World War I, the Bureau of the Budget promulgated Standard Form 23 for use with construction contracts and Standard Form 32 for use with supply contracts, both of which included a standard Changes article. These clauses gave the government the unilateral right to order changes during contract performance and introduced the concepts of equitable adjustment and the contractor's duty to proceed, which have been carried forward in the current versions of the Changes articles.

## CONTRACT MODIFICATIONS

A contract modification is any written alteration to the terms, conditions, or performance requirements of an existing contract, whether accomplished unilaterally or bilaterally.

The unilateral modification is signed only by the Contracting Officer. A unilateral modification may be used to make administrative changes in contract provisions, issue change orders when time or circumstances do not permit the negotiation of a full agreement as to the consequences of the change itself, make changes authorized by articles other than the Changes clause (i.e., Property clause, Suspension of Work clause, etc.), issue termination notices, or increase funding levels under the contract, in the form of a unilateral determination, when agreement cannot be reached as to a fair and reasonable price for the changed work.

The bilateral contract modification, frequently referred to as a supplemental agreement, is executed by both parties to the contract. It is essentially a wholly new agreement negotiated by the parties, which does not necessarily modify all parts of the original agreement. Bilateral agreements are used to make negotiated equitable adjustments resulting from the issuance of a change order, definitize letter contracts, and reflect other agreements of the parties modifying the terms of the contract. *See* FAR § 43.103. To be legally effective, however, the bilateral modification must demonstrate mutuality of consideration. Otherwise, it is a nullity.

## SUPPLY CONTRACT CHANGES ARTICLES

Although the same principles apply to all forms of contracts authorized by the FAR, and although the rights and obligations of the parties are similar under the various Changes articles, the standard fixed-price supply contract clause in section 52.243-1 of the FAR will be relied on in the discussion that follows.

The clause provides that the Contracting Officer may at any time, by written order and without notice to sureties, if any, make changes within the general scope of the contract in any one or more of the following: (1) drawings, designs, or specifications, when the supplies to be furnished are to be specifically manufactured for the government in accordance with the drawings, designs, or specifications; (2) method of shipment or packing; or (3) place of delivery.

The clause also provides that if the change causes an increase or decrease in the cost of, or the time required for, performance of any part of the work under the contract, whether or not changed by the order, the Contracting Officer shall make an equitable adjustment in the price, the delivery schedule, or both, and modify the contract. The contractor is required to submit any proposal for adjustment within 30 days from the date of receipt of the order, unless the Contracting Officer determines that the circumstances justify a longer period in which to prepare the proposal. Though failure to reach agreement on any adjustment could result in a dispute, the contractor is not excused from proceeding with performance as changed by the order.

## WRITTEN OR ORAL CHANGE ORDERS

The standard Changes articles provide that the Contracting Officer, *by a written order,* may make changes within the general scope of the contract. A literal interpretation of this provision leads to the conclusion that if the change is to be effective, a formal change order must be issued by the Contracting Officer, in the form of either a letter to the contractor followed by a formal modification to the contract or a formal modification to the contract at the outset. This conclusion is in keeping with the decision of the Supreme Court in *Plumley v. United States,* 226 U.S. 545 (1913). In *Plumley,* the contract provided that changes increasing or diminishing the cost must be agreed on in writing by the contractor and the architect, with a statement of the price of the substituted work and material. The Court ruled that there was a total failure to comply with these provisions of the contract, and though it might have been a hard case since it was found that the work was in fact extra, the contractor could not recover for that which, though extra, was not ordered by the Contracting Officer and in the manner prescribed by the contract.

For some years, judges interpreted the Changes articles with strict literalism, refusing to grant relief for work not expressly changed by the order. One result was to accord relief only for consensual modifications in plans, specifications, or design. Since the early 1940s, the courts have been less rigid and have recognized the validity of oral change orders. The legality of oral orders was sanctioned by the Court of Claims in *W.H. Armstrong & Co. v. United States,* 98 Ct. Cl. 519 (1943), when it said:

> When one party writes a contract in its own language, and inserts in it two separate provisions, either of which might apply to a given set of facts, but different legal consequences would result if one, rather than the other, of the two provisions was applied, the other party to the contract is, in the absence of a contrary intent, entitled to have applied the provision which is least burdensome to him. What should be done in a case in which the responsible representative of the Government has not done nor has the contractor insisted upon his doing what the contract enjoined him to do at the time; a case in which, moreover, the contractor, has pursuant to an oral rather than a written order, performed just what the Government wanted to be done, and the Government has taken the product of that performance but refuses to pay for it. When the Contracting Officer orally directed plaintiff to use . . . [substitute material], and promised it that an adjustment would be made when the work was completed and the fair amount determined, and when that direction was performed by plaintiff by doing the work and using the required material, a contract to pay plaintiff the reasonable cost of the work resulted. We recognize that the decision of the Supreme Court in *Plumley v. United States,* 226 U.S. 545 (1913), is contrary to what we have said. We see no distinction, in principle, between that case and the cases of *United States v. Andrews,* 207 U.S. 229 (1907) and *St. Louis Hay and Grain Co. v. United States,* 191 U.S. 159 (1903). All the authorities in comparable legal situations are in accord with the latter cases, and we think fit our duty to fol-

low this general trend of authority, which leads to what we regard as just decisions, rather than the *Plumley* case, which seems to stand alone.

*Accord Whitman v. United States,* 124 Ct. Cl. 464 (1953), which held that although a contract may require a written change order, an oral order may be enforced.

The Court of Claims in *Len Co. & Associates v. United States,* 181 Ct. C1. 89, 385 F.2d 438 (1967), stressed the need to carefully review the requirements of individual clauses to determine whether an oral change order could form the basis for an equitable adjustment. In interpreting the standard Changes clause, the courts have not insisted on strict literalism. Where such a clause (or a comparable one) is included in a contract, the Claims Court, as well as the Armed Services Board of Contract Appeals, has held that if a Contracting Officer compels the contractor to perform work not required under the contract, his order to perform, albeit oral, constitutes an authorized but unilateral change in the work called for by the contract and entitles the contractor to an equitable adjustment in accordance with the Changes provision.

The court has considered it to be idle for the contractor to demand a written order from the Contracting Officer for an extra when the Contracting Officer was insisting that the work required was not extra and therefore has often dispensed on these occasions with the formality of issuing a written change under the standard clause. *Fox Valley Engineering v. United States,* 151 Ct. Cl. 228 (1960); *Fleischer Engineering & Constr. Co. v. United States,* 98 Ct. Cl. 139 (1942). But each of the other elements of the standard Changes or Extras clause has been present—the Contracting Officer has the contractual authority unilaterally to alter the contractor's duties under the agreement, the contractor's performance requirements are enlarged, and the additional work is not volunteered, but results from a direction of the government's Contracting Officer. *Len Co., supra.*

## CHANGES WITHIN THE GENERAL SCOPE OF THE CONTRACT

The standard Changes clause permits the government to make changes only within the "general scope" of the contract. Because of this phrase in particular, and the structure of the article in general, the courts have consistently ruled that such a change provision does not authorize a drastic modification beyond the scope of the contract. Rather, a fundamental alteration of this nature is a contract breach, or cardinal change as it is sometimes referred to, entitling the contractor to breach damages. *Air-A-Plane Corp. v. United States,* 187 Ct. C1. 269, 408 F.2d 1030 (1969). Because such a change fundamentally alters the contractual undertaking of the contractor, it is not comprehended by the normal Changes article. *Mann Constr. Co.,* AGBCA No. 76-111-4, 81-1 BCA 15,087.

The basic test to determine whether a change was within the general scope of the contract has been defined by the Supreme Court in the following language:

It is, of course, wise and necessary that Government agents in binding their principal in contracts for construction, [supplies,] or services should make provisions for alterations in the plans, or changes in the services, within the four corners of the contract, and thus avoid the presentation of unreasonable claims for extras. This Court has recognized that necessity and enforced various provisions to which it has given rise. But sometimes such contract provisions have been interpreted and enforced by executive officials as if they enabled those officers to remold the contract at will. The temptation of the . . . [agency] to adopt such clauses arise out of the fact that they avoid the necessity of labor, foresight and care in definitely drafting the contract. This does not make for justice; it promotes the possibility of official favoritism as between contractors, and results in enlarged expenditures, because it increases the prices which contractors, in view of their added risk, incorporate in their bids for Government contracts. These considerations, especially the first, have made this Court properly attentive to any language or phrase of these enlarging provisions which may be properly held to limit their application as having been fairly and reasonably within the contemplation of the parties when the contract was entered into.

*Freund v. United States,* 260 U.S. 60 (1922).

Under established case law, a change outside the scope of the contract is a breach. It occurs when the government affects an alteration in the work so drastic that it effectively requires the contractor to perform duties materially different from those originally bargained for. *Allied Materials & Equipment Co. v. United States,* 215 Ct. Cl. 406, 569 F.2d 562 (1978); *Edward R. Marden Corp. v. United States,* 194 Ct. Cl. 799, 442 F.2d 364 (1971).

The Comptroller General will review an allegation that a modification went beyond the contract's scope and should have been the subject of a new proposal only on the basis that such a modification could be viewed as an attempt to circumvent the competitive procurement statutes. *Aero-Dri Corp.,* Comp. Gen. B-192274 (1978). Thus, the basic standard as to whether there has been a cardinal change has been defined as whether the original purpose or nature of the contract has been so substantially changed by the modification that the contract for which competition was held and the contract to be performed are essentially different. *American Air Filter Co.,* 57 Comp. Gen. 285 (1978).

It is exceedingly difficult to establish a concise definition of a change outside the scope of the contract that will withstand all tests. The reported decisions do not establish clear lines of demarcation between changes that may be said to come properly within the Changes article and cardinal changes that constitute breaches of contract. *Keco Industries v. United States,* 176 Ct. Cl. 983, 364 F.2d 838 (1966). A determination of the permissive degree of change can be reached only by considering the totality of the change, and this requires recourse to its magnitude, as well as its quality. The point at which a change must be considered to be beyond the scope of the contract and inconsistent with the Changes article is a matter of degree, varying from one contract to another. *Saddler v. United States,* 152 Ct. Cl. 557, 287 F.2d 411 (1961). The existence of a change beyond the scope of the contract is principally a question of fact, requiring that each case be analyzed in light of the totality of the circumstances. *Wunderlich Contracting Co. v. United States,* 173 Ct. Cl. 180, 351 F.2d 956 (1965).

While there is no exact formula for determining when a change is not authorized by the contract, the fact that a large number of changes may have been ordered during contract performance is hardly determinative. *Saddler v. United States, supra; Magoba Constr. Co. v. United States,* 99 Ct. Cl. 662 (1943). Neither the number of changes nor the characteristics of the work to be performed are of themselves the determinative factors. *Aragona Constr. Co. v. United States,* 165 Ct. Cl. 382 (1962). A single change of sufficient magnitude or quality suffices. *Coley Properties Corp.,* PODBCA No. 291, 75-2 BCA 11,514. A series of changes, even if taken cumulatively, does not result in a fundamental alteration of the contract, or the physical results in the perspective of the overall project, if the finished project was substantially the same as originally contracted for. *Aragona Constr. Co., supra.*

Cases that have held that changes ordered by the Contracting Officer are cardinal changes and hence not permitted under the contract have involved changes that altered the nature of the thing to be constructed. Thus, where an illegal change order eliminated an entire building from the hospital complex the contractor had contracted to build, a breach of contract was found. *General Contracting Co. v. United States,* 84 Ct. Cl. 570, (1937). And in *Saddler v. United States, supra,* the change orders purported to obligate the contractor to construct a larger embankment, having almost twice the quantity of material the parties had agreed was required.

Time expended to perform changes in relation to their actual cost has never been used as a criterion in determining whether the changes ordered are beyond the permissible limits of the Changes article. Similarly, arguments that changes were issued at the end of the project, therefore making them unreasonable, are not well founded. There is no contract requirement or any obligation imposed by law that restricts the government's power to order changes within a specified period. The only restrictive language found in the Changes article is the phrase "within the general scope thereof." This means that the Contracting Officer can order changes so long as the finished project was the same as originally contracted for. *J.D. Hedin Constr. Co. v. United States,* 171 Ct. Cl. 70, 347 F.2d 235 (1965). The government cannot be held liable for the exercise of this contractual privilege unless it exceeded the permissible limits of its discretion under the Changes article and ordered changes that were cardinal in nature. *Wunderlich Contracting Co. v. United States, supra.* When confronted with a cardinal change, the contractor has the option of abandoning performance under the contract and suing for any damages that had been sustained as of the time of the breach or of proceeding with the work and then, after contract completion, instituting an action for damages sustained as a result of breach of contract. *H.R. Henderson & Co. v. United States,* 169 Ct. Cl. 228 (1965).

## IMPACT OF CHANGE ORDERS ON UNCHANGED WORK

In *United States v. Rice,* 317 U.S. 61 (1942), the Supreme Court held that the contract provided that payment was to be made for the reasonable cost and expenses of the changes made, but that no provision was made for any increase in the cost of work not changed. According to the court, it was never contemplated that delays incident to changes would subject the government to damages beyond those involved in the changes themselves. It seemed wholly reasonable to the court that an "increase or decrease in the amount due" should be met with an alteration in price. Increase or decrease of cost plainly applied to the changes in cost due to the structural changes required by the altered specifications and not the consequential damages that might flow from delay taken care of in the Difference in Time provision. "An increase or decrease in the time required" should be met with an alteration of the time allowed. If there were rights to recover damages where the government exercised its reserved powers to delay, they must be found in the particular provisions fixing the rights of the parties.

Under the *Rice* doctrine, a contractor was only entitled, in conformance with the Changes clause, to the increased costs of the changed work and a time extension equal to the delay period. The doctrine prohibited recovery of the increased cost of unchanged work even though this category of cost, now commonly referred to as impact costs, could frequently be more expensive to the contractor than those costs attributable to the structural change itself. The doctrine ignored the fact that when a change order is issued, it all too frequently disrupts the scheduled sequence of the work and delays completion of work in progress that was not affected by the change order.

### Delay Costs

The Court of Claims developed an exception to the general rule enunciated by *Rice* by holding that when the government unreasonably delays a contractor's performance because of its failure to provide properly drawn specifications or is otherwise at fault, it has committed a breach of contract and is answerable in damages. The grant of an extension of time by the Contracting Officer carries with it the administrative determination or admission that the delays resulted through no fault of the contractor. *J.D. Hedin Constr. Co. v. United States,* 171 Ct. Cl. 70, 347 F.2d 235 (1965); *Laburnum Constr. Corp. v. United States,* 163 Ct. Cl. 339, 325 F.2d 451 (1963).

This theory enabled the courts, but not the Boards of Contract Appeals, to grant relief since, by definition, the fact situations of these cases were not covered by contract clauses and therefore did not arise under the contract. The settled construction of the Disputes clauses excluded breach of contract claims from their coverage, whether for purposes of granting relief or for purposes of making binding findings of fact that would be reviewable under Wunderlich Act standards. *See United States v. Utah Constr. & Mining Co.,* 384 U.S. 394 (1966).

Eventually, and in order to give the Boards of Contract Appeals jurisdiction over delay cases, the Suspension of Work clause was adopted by the government. The purpose of this article is to provide a mechanism for an equitable adjustment in those cases where the procuring agency suspends, delays, or interrupts contract performance by an express order or for an unreasonable period of time.

### Impact Costs

The problem of impact costs was not so easily resolved. The problem arises when the direct, foreseeable, reasonable, and inevitable result of the altered specifications is to increase the cost of the unchanged work and subject the contractor to various kinds of delay expenses. See Shedd, *The Rice Doctrine and the Ripple Effect of Changes,* 32 Geo. Wash. L. Rev. (1963). Shedd took the position that the *Rice* decision was a misinterpretation of the contract provisions and of earlier cases cited in support of the decision. He advocated a more realistic treatment of impact costs as being simply another category of costs incident to a contract change, with recognition that a series of changes might have ripple effects that extended far beyond the individual change orders themselves, affecting work quite removed for a given change order.

The Engineer Board of Contract Appeals broke away from the "consequential damages" restriction of *Rice* by applying the term in its more common legal understanding, rather than as a label for all costs of unchanged work. In *Ivey Brothers Construction Co.,* ENG BCA No. 1762 (1960), the Board granted an equitable adjustment that included the increased costs of unchanged work on the ground that they "flowed directly and not consequentially from the change."

In 1968, the construction contract Changes article was amended for the specific purpose of circumventing the applicability of *Rice* to the cost of unchanged work by inserting the words "whether or not changed by any order." Applying the revised clause, the Court of Claims followed *Ivey*

*Brothers, supra,* in *Merritt-Chapman & Scott Corp. v. United States,* 192 Ct. Cl. 848, 429 F.2d 431 (1970), in holding that:

Wholly apart from the Suspension of Work clause, it is established that under the Changes and Changed Conditions articles the equitable adjustment can include costs which were the direct and necessary result of the change or changed condition, where that condition or change directly leads to disruption, extra work, or new procedures.

*Accord Savoy Constr. Co. v. United States,* 2 Cl. Ct. 338 (1983); *Law v. United States,* 195 Ct. Cl. 370 (1971).

The issuance of change orders will, of course, have varying effects in different situations depending on the scope and location of the work required by the orders and the timing and manner of the issuance of such orders. The issuance of a large volume of change orders could adversely affect the contractor's ability to efficiently perform the basic contract. Since such dislocation is a normal and natural consequence of the circumstances, a contractor would be entitled to recover a fair and reasonable amount for the additional costs it sustained. *See Freuhauff Corp.,* PODBCA No. 477, 74-1 BCA 10,596. The cumulation of changes requiring the contractor to perform a great portion of the work out of sequence and in a manner that reduces normal efficiency flows from the changes made by the government and entitles the contractor to recover for the increased costs incurred in completing the unchanged work. *Coley Properties,* PODBCA No. 291, 75-1 BCA 11,514.

The basis for recovery of an impact claim is that the effect of changes can and does create costs beyond those attributable to the changes themselves. Recognition of the reality of this effect is what led to the abrogation of the *Rice* doctrine by the 1968 revisions to the Changes and Suspension clauses. *Ingall's Shipbuilding Division, Litton Systems,* ASBCA No. 17579, 78-1 BCA 13,038.45.

## DUTY TO PERFORM CHANGES

The standard Changes articles provide that "nothing in this clause shall excuse the contractor from proceeding with the work as changed." *See* FAR § 52.243-1, -2, & -3. The Disputes article mandates that the "contractor shall proceed diligently with performance of this contract, pending final resolution of any request for relief, or action under this contract, and comply with any decision of the Contracting Officer." See FAR § 52.233-1. Since the government has reserved the right to make changes in the work within the general scope of the contract, and since the contract itself provides a remedy to protect the contractor through the Disputes article, the contractor has a clear obligation to continue with the work as directed. If the contractor fails, or refuses, to perform the work as changed, he is in breach of contract and subject to termination for default proceedings, as well as to breach damages.

This rule was clearly enunciated in *Max M. Stoeckert d/b/a University Brick & Tile Co. v. United States,* 183 Ct. Cl. 152, 391 F.2d 639 (1968), where the court said:

> At the outset, it must be observed that the termination of plaintiff's contract for default was proper if for no other reason than that he refused to follow the Contracting Officer's directive. . . . Instead he elected to abandon the work and refused to proceed except at Government expense and by a method specified by the Government. However, such an election is simply not open to a Government contractor under the standard disputes clause. . . . Thus, plaintiff could not justifiably abandon the work simply because of his disagreement with the Contracting Officer.

*H&H Mfg. Co. v. United States,* 168 Ct. Cl. 873 (1964). But see *Wingate Construction Co. v. United States,* 164 Ct. Cl. 131 (1964), where, after protesting a direction by the Contracting Officer, the contractor nevertheless continued with the work under the contract and was compensated therefore. In its legal effect, a contractor's failure to proceed as directed pending resolution of his dispute with the government has been equated with anticipatory breach of contract by repudiation. *James G. Henderson,* ASBCA No. 15353, 72-2 BCA 9567; *Kirk Casavan,* AGBCA No. 76-192, 78-2 BCA 13,459.

The duty to comply with the directions of the Contracting Officer was explained in *Appeal of Wiggins,* ASBCA No. 4022, 58-1 BCA 1644, where the Board said:

> Having received the list of deficiencies with instructions to correct them, the contractor under the Inspection and Changes articles of the contract was required to comply. To the extent that such list of deficiencies constituted a change in specifications or performance of work not required by the contract, the contractor would have been entitled to an equitable adjustment in the amount due and/or in the time required for performance provided he had complied with procedural requirements of the contract. The contractor, however, elected not to follow this course. The contractor clearly abandoned further work on this contract. Upon proper notice and because of the abandonment and failure to make satisfactory progress, the Contracting Officer terminated the contract for default. Under the circumstances, he could do no less.

Similarly, the Board upheld a termination for default when the contractor withdrew his men and equipment from the job site and indicated that he would not return unless the government met his demands for an increase in the contract price and time extension on the basis of a change order. Under such circumstances, it is well established that the government has a right to terminate the contract for default. *Dimastinis Tsambaurakis,* ASBCA No. 18142, 75-1 BCA 11,313. Under the contract—absent impossibility or other causes beyond its control and without its fault or negligence—the contractor is not privileged to stop work pending the decision on disputes that have arisen under the contract. *D.H. Dave & Gerber Contracting Co.,* ASBCA No. 6257, 1962 BCA 3493. Even if the Contracting Officer has erroneously interpreted the requirements of the contract, the contractor is obligated to continue performance. *Brenner Metal Products Corp.,* ASBCA No. 25294, 82-1 BCA 15,462.

The Disputes article has been construed to mean that if there is a dispute as to the meaning, rights, or obligations arising under a contract provision, and even if the contractor's interpretations of certain contract requirements may be correct, the contractor is still obligated to perform in accordance with the directions of the Contracting Officer and to seek relief in additional compensation under the appropriate contract provision. *Max M. Stoeckert, supra; H&H Manufacturing Co., supra.*

Neither the Boards of Contract Appeals nor the courts are prepared to conclude that the Contracting Officer must issue a directive to do specific work only by way of a final decision. Nor are these forums prepared to conclude that only a final decision affords a contractor protection if he elects not to proceed. The Contracting Officer is authorized by the Changes clause to direct a contractor to take certain actions without issuing a final decision. The Contracting Officer is authorized by the Inspection clause to direct the contractor to take corrective action without issuing a final decision. The Disputes article requires the contractor to continue performing in accordance with the Contracting Officer's directions. The Changes clause provides for an equitable adjustment, should the Contracting Officer's directive entail work in excess of contract requirements and cause an increase in the contractor's costs. *See Tester Corp.,* ASBCA No. 21312, 78-2 BCA 13,725, *aff'd, Tester Corp. v. United States,* 227 Ct. Cl. 648 (1981).

## GOVERNMENT BREACH OF CONTRACT

Under certain circumstances a contractor could justifiably refuse to continue performance even though directed to do so by the Contracting Officer. This would be the case where such direction constituted a material breach of contract. *Seven Sciences,* ASBCA No. 21079, 77-2 BCA 12,730. It is axiomatic that the government has the right to obtain precisely what is specified in the contract, *Arnold M. Diamond, Inc.,* ASBCA No. 12335, 68-1 BCA 6872; regardless of the technical soundness of the government's requirements, a contractor must comply with them and cannot substitute his own views for those of the government, *Maxwell Dynamotor Co. v. United States,* 181 Ct. Cl. 607, 386 F.2d 855 (1967). On the other hand, an experienced contractor cannot rely on government-furnished production documents where, on the basis of such documents, he either knows, or should have known, that the documents could not produce the desired result, for he has no right to produce a useless thing and charge his customer for it. *J.D. Hedin Constr. Co. v. United States,* 171 Ct. Cl. 70, 347 F.2d 235 (1965); *S.W. Electronics & Mfg. Corp.,* ASBCA Nos. 20698 & 20860, 77-2 BCA 12,631.

It is equally well established that one side cannot continue, after a material breach by the other, to act as if the contract remains fully in force, although stopping performance would be fair and convenient, and to run up damages and then go to court. *Ling-Temco Vought v. United States,* 201 Ct. Cl. 135, 475 F.2d 630 (1973). A contractor could properly refuse to perform upon a material breach by the government. As a result of a material breach, the contractor has a legal right of avoidance, thereby discharging his duty to perform and relieving him of a default termination and the consequences that flow therefrom. *G.W. Galloway,* ASBCA No. 17436, 77-2 BCA 12,640. Whether the contractor has the right to refuse performance depends on the seriousness of the government's breach and the impact on the contractor's ability to perform. See the cases cited in *National Linen Co.,* ASBCA No. 18379, 75-2 BCA 11,400. Short of commercial impossibility, a contractor is not entitled to refuse performance on the ground that performance would entail substantial expenses not taken into account in its bid price. Absent clear government direction to proceed with the manufacture of useless articles, the contractor is not obliged to do so. But the consequences of the government's breach must be so severe as to provide the contractor with the right of avoidance. *See Seven Sciences, supra.*

Failure or unreasonable delay in making payment has also been held to constitute a material breach of contract, justifying abandonment by the contractor. In a contract that provides for periodic installment payments, a failure to make a payment at the time specified is a breach that justifies abandonment of work; whenever one party to a contract is guilty of such a breach, the other party may treat the contract as broken and may abandon it. *Ernest C. Whitbeck v. United States,* 77 Ct. Cl. 309 (1933). A contractor has a right to assume from the inception of the contract that he would be paid according to the requirement of the contract, and the failure of the government to pay justified his refusing to proceed. Whatever might have been his faults up to the time payment was refused, the government, having permitted him to proceed, having accepted the performance of the contract, and having received the benefit of his labor, was not within its rights to withhold the pay in order that it might be secured against the consequences of a probable or possible failure. *Brooklyn & Queens Screen Mfg. Co. v. United States,* 97 Ct. Cl. 532 (1942).

Thus, avoidance or rescission by the contractor has been upheld where the government refused to pay any of its invoices, *Contract Maintenance,* ASBCA Nos. 19409 & 19509, 75-1 BCA 11,207; where the government's untimely invoice payments were the ultimate cause of the contractor's failure to perform, *Q.S.V., Inc.*, ASBCA No. 3722, 58-2 BCA 2007; and where wrongful withholding of progress payments was the basis for avoidance by the contractor, *Robert O. Redding*, AGBCA No. 272, 69-2 BCA 7888.

It has also been held that a service contractor is not required to continue performance when payments due under the contract are not being made. Though the government is authorized to deduct amounts reasonably reflecting the reduced value of the services it receives, the contractor should be paid at least the reduced amount when he submits his invoices. If the government unreasonably refuses to pay the contractor even those amounts known to be due under the contract, such refusal relieves him of any obligation to continue performance. *Valley Contractor*, ASBCA No. 9397, 1964 BCA 4071.

Under current Progress Payments clauses, a number of situations constitute appropriate justification of suspension or curtailment of payments by the Contracting Officer. But, as set forth in the regulation governing his actions, there is a warning that these drastic measures can only be invoked after (1) providing the contractor with an opportunity for discussions; (2) evaluating the effect of the action on the contractor's operations, based on his financial condition, projected cash requirements, and existing or available credit arrangements; and (3) giving consideration to the general equities of the particular situation. *See* FAR § 32.503-6. The Contracting Officer is expected to act fairly and reasonably and must prepare written findings, based on substantial evidence that the conditions for invoking the terms of the contract clause do exist. *See generally National Radio Co.*, ASBCA No. 14707, 72-2 BCA 9486; *Connecticut Cartridge Corp.*, ASBCA Nos. 12656 & 12662, 70-2 BCA 8559.

Where the government's failure to make progress payments impairs the contractor's financial ability to continue performance, such failure excuses the contractor from continuing. The contractor does not have the burden of proving that he would have been able to perform but for the government's breach. In spite of an inability, in a particular case, to ascertain the ultimate facts of causation between the failure to make such payments and the contractor's own default, such inquiry is not relevant where the evidence indicates that the contractor is dependent on such financing and that the suspension of payments deprived the contractor of a means of financing other progress. *R.H.J. Corp.*, ASBCA No. 9922, 66-1 BCA 5361.

The presence of the Progress Payments clause and the manipulation intended to increase the amounts payable to a contractor must be deemed a recognition of the importance attached to the clause as a financing device. The careful safeguards established to protect contractors against any arbitrary cutoff of such financing reflects the concern that the government's policy assure the availability of financial support for contract performance. Even though the suspension and curtailment of financing may not result in outright failure to complete, arbitrary financial restrictions must be considered as a factor that, together with those causes attributable to a contractor, could result in delayed performance. Where the causes for delay are concurrent, and at least one is attributable to the government, while the others were either inexcusable or otherwise chargeable to the contractor, neither party may use the occasion for an affirmative recovery against the other; and where liquidated damages are involved, a contractor will not be subjected to assessments during such periods. *Acme Missile & Constr. Corp.*, ASBCA No. 11786, 69-2 BCA 8057.

## EQUITABLE ADJUSTMENTS

The phrase "equitable adjustment" is a term of art used to describe the compensation to which a party may be entitled for a change within the general scope of the contract. Inasmuch as the Changes articles do not prescribe any criteria or standards for determining the equitable adjustment, the term has of necessity been defined by the courts and Boards of Contract Appeals. The Supreme Court has stated that an equitable adjustment involved merely the ascertainment of the cost to perform the change and the addition to that cost of a reasonable and customary allowance for profit. *United States v. Callahan-Walker Constr. Co.*, 317 U.S. 56 (1942). Equitable adjustments in this context are simply corrective measures utilized to keep a contractor whole when the government modifies a contract. Since the purpose underlying such adjustments is to safeguard the contractor against increased costs engendered by the modification, it appears patent that the measure of damages cannot be the value received by the government, but must be more closely related to and contingent on the altered position in which the contractor finds himself by reason of the modification. *Bruce Constr. Corp. v. United States*, 163 Ct. Cl. 97, 324 F.2d 516 (1963).

The making of an equitable adjustment cannot be reduced to the application of a mathematical formula. If the intended meaning was reasonable costs plus a fair profit, it would have been easy for the clause to have been so written. What constitutes an equitable adjustment depends in substantial part on the facts of the particular case. It cannot be said that as a matter of law an equitable adjustment must include a profit allowance in all cases. *Paccon, Inc.*, ASBCA No. 7890, 65-2 BCA 5227. An equitable adjustment normally includes an allowance for overhead and profit, and this is true whether the equitable adjustment is upward or downward. The key is always to put the contractor in as good a position as he would have been in, but for the government's action. *E.V. Lane Corp.*, ASBCA No. 9741, 65-2 BCA 5076.

When the government makes a change, it should not alter the contractor's position from making a profit to suffering a loss, but should merely compensate for the change made, leaving the contractor in the same relative position as before the change. *S.N. Nielson Co. v. United States,* 141 Ct. Cl. 793 (1958). However, in order to effectuate a downward adjustment, the government must draft the revised specifications so as to change the amount of work the contractor is required to do. Otherwise, there is no substantive change in the work. *Continental Service Co.,* DOTCAB No. 73-27, 74-1 BCA 10,538.

## ACCORD AND SATISFACTION

Accord and satisfaction has been defined as the discharge of a contract, or of a disputed claim arising under or related to a contract, by the substitution and execution of a new agreement between the parties in satisfaction of such contract or disputed claim. Accord generally refers to the execution of a bilateral agreement requiring additional performance or payment, whereas satisfaction occurs when the additional performance or payment is accomplished.

In the course of doing business with the government, contractors frequently sign contract modifications containing language to the effect that the amount stated shall constitute full compensation for said delays or that the amount stated shall constitute full compensation for said changes incorporated herein. The government later may assert that these signed modifications serve to bar future claims under the contract. However, such language has been narrowly construed by the courts and Boards of Contract Appeals, particularly if there is any indication that the claimed costs were not considered when the price adjustment was negotiated.

As a general rule, the execution by a contractor of a release that is complete on its face reflects the contractor's unqualified acceptance and agreement with its terms and is binding on both parties. It is well established that where a contractor has the right to reserve claims from the operation of a release, but fails to exercise that right, it is neither improper nor unfair, absent some vitiating or aggravated circumstance, to preclude the contractor from maintaining a suit based on events that occurred prior to the execution of the release. *Clark Mechanical Contractors v. United States,* 5 Cl. Ct. 84 (1984).

Thus, a modification to a contract that compensated a contractor for excusable delays encountered during contract performance and that contained the words "which amount shall constitute full compensation for said delays" has been held to bar further recovery. *Cannon Constr. Co. v. United States,* 168 Ct. Cl. 94 (1963). However, an amendment to compensate the contractor for changed work has been held to cover the costs resulting from the change, but not the cost of work based on the defective specifications prior to the issuance of the change. *Crane Carrier Corp.,* ASBCA No. 9822, 65-2 BCA 4945. Similarly, a prime contractor's claim for costs of settling with its subcontractors following a partial termination for the convenience of the government is not barred by accord and satisfaction, unless there was an actual mutual intent to settle the partial termination for an amount that included no such allowance. When the supplemental agreement is interpreted in accordance with the rules applied in interpreting releases, it cannot be found to manifest a mutual intent to do so, unless specifically addressed. *Stewart Avionics,* ASBCA No. 10226, 65-2 BCA 5111.

Modifications to a contract after performance has been completed, which include general language releasing the government from further liability and which adjust the contract price, are generally held to be an accord and satisfaction. If the modification was executed as a bilateral agreement by the parties and, by its terms, increased the price of the contract to reimburse the contractor for additional costs incurred due to discrepancies and errors in drawings and changes in contract requirements, but contained no limitations, exceptions, qualifications, or reservations, it will be considered to be an unconditional settlement of the additional costs incurred in performing the contract. It has been consistently held that in the absence of any showing of fraud, collusion, or mutual mistake, an agreement is binding on both parties. Such an agreement should not thereafter be unilaterally disturbed. *Columbus Jack Corp.,* ASBCA No. 7249, 1962 BCA 3288. See FAR § 43.204 for an example of such release.

The granting of a time extension, "with no increase in funds," to perform government-requested work does not preclude recovery of additional compensation for that work because the limiting clause does not constitute an accord and satisfaction releasing all claims or surrendering the contractor's rights under the contract. In interpreting a change order as a release or an accord and satisfaction as to any claim not clearly included in the agreement, the intent of the parties as to the effect of the agreement and the matters included or excluded is a primary factor that must be resolved on the basis not only of the language of the agreement, but also of the circumstances surrounding the agreement, including negotiations between the parties and their actions and conduct with respect to the agreement. *Technology Incorporated,* VACAB No. 1168, 76-1 BCA 11,752.

Unless there is some documentation in the record to indicate that an accord and satisfaction was expressed in the final payment, one cannot be implied from the bare fact of final payment, particularly in the absence of any release given by the contractor. *Leader Mfg. Co.,* ASBCA No 3532, 57-1 BCA 1169. Final delivery, final acceptance, and final payment do not operate to divest the Contracting Officer of his authority to act under the contract. It follows as a corollary that the finality of a delivery, acceptance, and payment does not necessarily bar the consideration of a claim. *Korshoj Constr. Co.,* IBCA No. 321, 1963 BCA 3848.

## NOTICE REQUIREMENTS

The standard Changes article requires that any claim for an equitable adjustment be asserted within 30 days after receipt of a change order, unless the Contracting Officer determines that the facts justify a time extension. In any event, under the Changes clause, the claim must be asserted prior to final payment. The Contracting Officer lacks authority under the clause to accept a claim submitted after final payment has been made under the contract. *Futuronics*, DOTCAB No. 67-15, 68-2 BCA 7079. Final payment occurs when a payment is made in the normal course of events following delivery, acceptance, and submission of an invoice requesting payment, and such final payment generally extinguishes all rights between the parties to a contract.

The invocation of the final payment provisions of the Changes clause is an affirmative defense, and the government has the burden of proving those facts on which the affirmative defense is based. If the government fails to present sufficient probative evidence as to the occurrence of "final payment" beyond the mere assertion that a final payment had in fact been made prior to the date that a claim is filed, it fails to carry the burden of proving that a final payment had been made. *Human Advancement*, HUDBCA No. 77-215, 81-2 BCA 15,317. Where a contractor has verbally informed the Contracting Officer on numerous occasions that he was concerned about equipment deletions and the consequent loss of revenue, this constitutes timely notice for purposes of the Changes clause. Thus, where the contractor informally puts the government on notice of his position or where the government is aware, or should be aware, of the facts giving rise to a claim, strict compliance with the notice requirement is not mandatory. *Raytheon Service Co.*, GSBCA No. 5264, 82-1 BCA 15,546.

# 7

# Excusable Delays

## INTRODUCTION

Delays in contract performance can be caused by a wide variety of factors, both excusable and unexcusable, resulting in either late completion or increased costs, or both. The Excusable Delays clause provides relief for the contractor for a performance failure if the failure arose from well-defined causes beyond the control and without the fault or negligence of the contractor. Similar provisions are contained in the Default articles. The Default clause for fixed-price construction contracts contains the additional proviso that the contractor's right to proceed shall not be terminated, nor shall the contractor be charged with damages if the delay in completing the work arises from *unforeseeable causes* beyond the control and without the fault or negligence of the contractor.

## THE EXCUSABLE DELAYS CLAUSE

The Excusable Delays clause provides that, except for defaults of subcontractors at any tier, the contractor shall not be in default for any failure to perform the contract if the failure arises from causes beyond the control and without the fault or negligence of the contractor. Examples of such causes include acts of God or of the public enemy, acts of the government in either its sovereign or its contractual capacity, fires, floods, epidemics, quarantine restrictions, strikes, freight embargoes, and unusually severe weather. *See* FAR § 52.249-14.

As to performance failures of subcontractors at any tier, the contractor shall not be in default if the cause of the failure was beyond the control and without the fault or negligence of either the prime contractor or the subcontractors. The delay is not excusable as to the prime contractor if the contracted supplies or services were obtainable from another source, or if the Contracting Officer ordered the contractor to obtain the supplies or services from another source and the contractor failed to comply reasonably with that order.

If the completion date was delayed by the inability of the contractor or his subcontractor to procure necessary materials, through a failure either to obtain timely commitments or to ascertain the availability of such materials prior to the submission of the bid, that is a matter for which relief cannot be granted even in equity. A prime contractor is excused from nonperformance or delays, to the extent that they render performance impossible, caused by defaults of subcontractors or suppliers if such defaults cannot be charged to the fault or negligence of the prime contractor, and it is immaterial whether or not the default of the subcontractor can be placed under one of the enumerated causes of excusability because such causes are illustrative and not exclusive. 39 Comp. Gen. 343 (1959).

In order to avail himself of the article, the contractor is required to request a time extension of the Contracting Officer, setting forth the facts and extent of the failure. If the Contracting Officer determines that the delay is in fact excusable, the delivery schedule is to be revised.

## PURPOSE OF THE ARTICLE

The purpose of the article is to remove uncertainty and needless litigation by defining with more particularity the otherwise hazy area of unforeseeable events that might excuse nonperformance within the contract period and to protect the contractor from the unforeseeable. Contractors thus know they are not to be penalized for unexpected impediments to prompt performance, and since their bids can be based on the foreseeable and probable, rather than possible, hindrances, the government secures the benefit of lower bids and an enlarged selection of bidders.

In its grammatical sense, the provision militates against holding that the listed events are always to be regarded as unforeseeable, no matter what the attendant circumstances are. Rather, the adjective "unforeseeable" must modify each event in the "including" phrase. *United States v. Brooks Callaway Co.*, 318 U.S. 120 (1943). Moreover, a contractor cannot benefit from delay, for it is unlikely that the government would accede to a contract provision providing for a price escalation for deliveries that were inexcusably late. *United States v. DeLoro Smelting & Refining Co.*, 161 Ct. Cl. 489, 317 F.2d 382 (1963).

## UNUSUALLY SEVERE WEATHER

A prudent contractor, in preparing bids for the commencement of work within a specified period and for the completion of the same within certain stipulated days thereafter, normally considers the weather conditions that ordinarily prevail during such season of the year at the site of the work. Inasmuch as weather conditions could adversely impact on the ability of a contractor, particularly a construction contractor, to perform, contractors are expected to include time in their bids or offers for foreseeable weather delays. *Carney General Contractor,* NASA BCA No. 375-4, 80-1 BCA 14,243; *Larsen-Meyer Constr. Co.,* IBCA No. 85, 58-2 BCA 1987. However, notice of lost time due to adverse weather conditions is not the same as notice of an excusable delay due to unusually severe weather because the Contracting Officer has no information as to what was foreseeable by the contractor. *Carney General Contractors, supra.*

The term "unusually severe weather" does not include any and all weather that prevents work under the contract, but only means weather surpassing in severity the weather usually encountered or reasonably to be expected in the particular locality and during the same time of year involved in the contract. 14 Comp. Gen. 431 (1934). It must be weather that could not have been reasonably anticipated and that impeded performance over and above the amount that work would been impeded in a normal year. *John E. Faucett,* AGBCA No. 396, 76-2 BCA 11,946. But the mere fact that the weather was cold enough to make performance of the work substantially more expensive than at other seasons of the year is not sufficient to substantiate an excusable delay, unless the contractor demonstrates that the weather was unusual. *T.C. Bateson Constr. Co.,* GSBCA No. 2656, 68-2 BCA 7263.

## ACTS OF GOD

Though rarely invoked as an excusable cause of delay, an act of God may occasion performance failures. Thus, a termination for default was held to be improper where the contractor was entitled to a time extension as a result of an act of God. The contract required tree planting within a certain period of time, but the eruption of Mt. St. Helens delayed performance, and it was determined to be an act of God sufficient to constitute an excusable delay even though the contractor was behind schedule before the eruption occurred. *Nogler Tree Farm,* AGBCA No. 81-104-1, 81-2 BCA 15,315.

## STRIKES

A contractor will not be automatically excused from performance merely because he establishes the existence of a strike. It must also be shown that the delay caused by the strike was beyond the control and without the fault or negligence of the contractor. *Sun Constr. Co.,* IBCA No. 208, 61-1 BCA 2926. He will not be excused where the strike resulted from his own unfair labor practices. *Transit Warehouse Corp.,* ASBCA No. 16761, 72-2 BCA 9696. Even if a contractor bears no initial fault for a particular cause of excusable delay, he must mitigate the effect of that delay. He cannot allow a possible cause of delay to develop, but must take such action as is reasonably available to him to prevent the delay. *Harris & Covington Hosiery Mills Co.,* 4 CCF 60,906 (1949). Therefore, if the strike involved a subcontractor or supplier, and if the contractor could have obtained the required supplies or materials from another source, but elected not to do so because of higher prices, he will normally not be excused. *Southern Steel Corp.,* ASBCA No. 6579, 61-1 BCA 2965. Similarly, the contractor will not be excused if he could not obtain the supplies delayed by the strike because he failed to place the order in a timely manner. *Bogue Electric Mfg. Co.,* ASBCA No. 16957, 73-1 BCA 9885.

## LACK OF ADEQUATE FINANCING

It is well settled that the contractor has the responsibility of either having adequate capital or having a reasonably established arrangement for obtaining the necessary capital required for contract performance at the time of contract execution. This is not intended to imply that the contractor must have on hand the cash reserves to finance the entire cost of performance. Rather, the contractor must have available reasonable financial resources in the light of business customs and practices to finance the expected cost of production or performance. *Security Signals,* ASBCA No. 4634, 58-2 BCA 2045.

Where the cause of the contractor's inability to perform lies solely in a conspicuous undercapitalization of the corporation with relation to the obligation it undertakes under the contract, rather than deriving from a contingency beyond its control, such undercapitalization is not a circumstance beyond the contractor's control as to be within the purview of any *force majeure* clause. *Williams Industries v. United States,* 155 Ct. Cl. 360 (1961).

If the contractor's financial condition was such that attempted performance of the contract would have rendered him hopelessly insolvent, or even an adjudicated bankrupt, he is not excused from the default in contract performance as a matter of law. Actual bankruptcy, a fortiori the mere possibility or threat of the same, is no excuse for nonperformance under the Default article and does not relieve the contractor from liability for excess costs of reprocurement. Bankruptcy, insolvency, or undercapitalization cannot be considered as a cause for nonperformance beyond the control and without the fault of the contractor. *Consolidated Airborne Systems v. United States,* 172 Ct. C1. 588, 348 F.2d 941 (1965).

Where a contractor's bank had disapproved a loan and was discontinuing further advances because of his accumulated losses from a prior undertaking, his demonstrated inability to control costs and to operate profitably under current contracts, and the increases in the amount of his delinquent payroll taxes, a clear case of breach and anticipatory repudiation was found by the Board. It is well established that a failure to obtain adequate financing, through no fault of the government, does not excuse a contractor's lack of performance. *Hughes & Brokers Corp.*, GSBCA No. 5765, 81-1 BCA 14,937.

Financial inability to perform a contract constitutes an excusable cause for delay under the Default articles only where it is "directly and inevitably caused by something beyond the contractor's control and without the fault or negligence of the contractor." *Southland Mfg. Corp.*, ASBCA No. 10519, 67-1 BCA 6128. It is well established that a contractor has the responsibility of providing the financing necessary for performance of a government contract. The problem rests squarely on the contractor, *Aircraftsmen Co.* ASBCA Nos. 3592 & 3695, 58-1 BCA 1667, and the lack of needed working capital does not constitute excuse for nonperformance, *Herf Industries*, ASBCA No. 20177, 75-2 BCA 11,461. But financial incapacity can be excusable when it was precipitated by causes beyond the control and without the fault or negligence of the contractor. This is *a fortiori* true when the precipitated causes are acts or omissions of the government. *National Eastern Corp. v. United States*, 201 Ct. Cl. 776, 477 F.2d 1347 (1973).

Thus, default has been found to be improper where various small contracts were terminated because the contractor's near bankrupt condition was the result of the government's inappropriate termination of a large Navy contract. The Navy contract was prematurely terminated for default when the Contracting Officer erroneously determined that a first delivery should have been made on a date earlier than that specified in the contract. As a consequence of the termination, the contractor lost credit sources, was unable to obtain a bank loan, and was sued by his supplier. The Board found no basis for concluding that the contractor may not have been able to complete its smaller contracts if it had not suffered these financial difficulties. Although completion of the smaller contracts was by no means secure, they were within reach, had the government not caused the contractor's financial difficulties by its improper action. *R&D Mounts*, ASBCA No. 14827, 71-1 BCA 8643.

The government's failure to compensate a contractor as required by the terms and conditions of the contract has also been held to excuse delayed performance. If the government, after due notice and without justification, fails to meet its obligations to make payment within the time required by the contract, such failure is a breach of a material condition. *Overstreet v. United States*, 55 Ct. Cl. 154 (1920). This being true, the contractor had a right to refuse to perform further under the contract and exercised this right by withdrawing equipment from the work site and declining to continue with the work. *Ernest E. Whitbeck v. United States,* 77 Ct. Cl. 309 (1933). It follows that the government cannot hold the contractor responsible for excess costs incurred on repurchase and that the contractor is entitled to payment in full for the amount earned prior to the date the contract was rescinded. *U.S. Service Corp.,* ASBCA Nos. 8291 & 8433, 1963 BCA 3703.

## ACTS OF THE GOVERNMENT

Acts of the government, in either its sovereign or its contractual capacity, may be excusable causes of delay under the Default article of the contract. If any government-ordered change in the work to be performed—whether formal or constructive—delays contract performance, the delay is excusable. *Jack Picoult,* GSBCA No. 752, 65-1 BCA 4519; *Mishara Constr. Co.,* ASBCA Nos. 8604 & 8688, 1964 BCA 4345. Where the government requires the contractor to perform work not called for by the contract or in any manner formally or constructively changes the specifications or other terms of the contract and performance is delayed thereby, the contractor is entitled to the benefits of an excusable delay. But if the contractor volunteered such changes, the delay is not excused. *Melrose Waterproofing Co.,* ASBCA No. 9058, 1964 BCA 4119; *Blanchard Constr. Co.,* ASBCA No. 7323, 1962 BCA 3489.

Where the government, without justification, refuses to permit a subcontractor to carry out his required effort under a prime contract and such refusal causes the prime contractor to fail to perform the work called for in the contract on time, a termination for default is not justified. Causes for delay that arose from unforeseeable causes and without the fault or negligence of the contractor include acts of the government in its contractual capacity. *Petroleum Engineering Service,* ASBCA No. 14111, 67-1 BCA 6126.

The government's failure to provide timely required approval of the contractor's efforts, plans, drawings, or reports may be a cause for excusable delay. The government, as a party to the contract, has rights and obligations similar to those of a private person under similar circumstances. *Percy v. United States,* 294 U.S. 330 (1935). Thus, when the government promises to approve or reject a contractor's preproduction samples, documentation, or report within a specified period after their submission, there is implicit in this promise an assurance to the contractor that the government is able to, and will, discharge its obligation in this respect. *Carnegie Steel Co. v. United States,* 240 U.S. 156 (1916). Even when the contract is silent regarding the amount of time available to the government for the review and approval of work in progress, the government is nevertheless obligated to either approve or disapprove the submission within a reasonable time. If it fails to do so, the contractor cannot be held liable for the assessment of any liquidated damages under the contract. *Wadena Sheet Metal & Heating,* GSBCA No.

2313, 67-1 BCA 6266. If the government encounters unforeseen difficulties in acting on preproduction samples that were due principally to the fact that the item to be procured under the contract was a new device and that the government could not be sure that existing test procedures were fully capable of measuring the performance characteristics of the item, these unforeseen difficulties do not excuse the government from discharging the plain obligation it had imposed on itself. *Specialty Assembling & Packing Co. v. United States,* 174 Ct. Cl. 153, 355 F.2d 554 (1966).

To establish that the failure to render approval caused the delay, it must be shown that an approval was required by a specific date and that it was delayed unreasonably, causing a delay in the contractor's performance. *Allied Paint Mfg. Co. v. United States* 200 Ct. Cl. 313, 470 F.2d 556 (1972); *Spectrum Leasing Corp.,* ASBCA Nos. 25724 & 26049, 85-1 BCA 17, 822. The contractor has the burden of establishing that the delay was unreasonable. *Kopper's Co.,* ENG BCA No. 2960, 71-2 BCA 8935; *C.C. Galbraith & Sons,* DOTCAB No. 67-45, 68-1 BCA 6895.

## GOVERNMENT INTERFERENCE

It is an implied warranty of every contract, whether it be between commercial parties or with the United States, that neither party to the contract will do anything that will prevent performance by the other party or that will hinder or delay him in completing the work. Willfully and wrongfully putting an end to a contract and preventing the other party from carrying it out constitute a breach of contract for which an action will lie for the recovery of all damages that the injured party has sustained. *United States v. Behan,* 110 U.S. 338 (1884).

It is a necessary corollary to this principle that one who, while not preventing the other party from carrying out the contract, nevertheless hinders or delays him in doing so, breaches the contract and is liable for the damages the injured party has sustained thereby. The law implies that the work should be done in a reasonable time and that the United States would not unnecessarily interfere to prevent this. Not only is the government liable for willful delay, but also it is liable for any delay except one caused by the exercise of a reserved right or one brought about by an act of God, of the law, or of the other party. *George A. Fuller Co. v. United States,* 108 Ct. Cl. 70, 69 F. Supp. 409 (1947).

In order to prevail, the contractor must establish that performance was in fact delayed by the government and that he took every reasonable precaution to avoid foreseeable causes for delay and to minimize their effect. He must establish the precise period of time during which such causes actually delayed performance. *Margold Electric Co.,* ASBCA Nos. 15894 & 15895, 77-2 BCA 9646. Once a breach of this type has been established, the contractor must still show, as in all contract cases, that damages ensued. *Com-*

*merce International Co. v. United States*, 167 Ct. Cl. 529, 338 F.2d 81 (1964). But when both parties contributed to the delay, settled law dictates that neither can recover damages, unless there is a clear apportionment of the delay and the expense attributable to each party. *Pittman Constr. Co. v. United States*, 2 Cl. Ct. 211 (1983).

Absent a warranty, the contractor's recourse for *mere delay* is to seek an extension of the time of his performance. But this general principle presupposes that the government has met the ever-present obligation to carry out its bargain reasonably and in good faith. *Walsh v. United States*, 121 Ct. Cl. 546, 102 F. Supp. 589 (1952). Unless expressly negatived, that duty is read into all bargains. It would be intolerable if the government could disregard that responsibility, or if it were free to stretch its tardiness for however long it fancied, without sterner control than the mere prolongation of the completion date of the contract. The rule is, rather, that when the government's delay in furnishing work or materials stems from its failure to do what it should under the particular contract, it will have to respond in damages for the resulting additional outlays that are proved to have been caused the contractor. But if the government exerts every effort to supply the contractor with the necessary materials on time, it cannot be held that it willfully or negligently interfered with performance. *Peter Kiewit's Sons Co. v. United States*, 138 Ct. Cl. 668, 151 F. Supp. 726 (1957). If a specific date is set for the completion of a contract and completion is dependent on the government's furnishing drawings to the contractor, for example, it is the duty of the government or its agents to furnish the necessary drawings in time for the contractor to complete his contract by that date. The government cannot escape its responsibility for having failed to furnish the drawings on time for completion of the work. *F.H. McGraw & Co. v. United States*, 113 Ct. Cl. 29 (1949).

The government frequently attempts to rebut allegations of excusable delay based on defective specifications on the ground that the Changes article permits it to delay a contractor's progress while the government makes the necessary changes to the specifications. The courts and Boards of Contract Appeals have not always reacted favorably to such defense, particularly where the government is the sole author of rigid specifications outlining in precise detail the work expected of the contractor.

In *Laburnum Constr. Corp. v. United States*, 163 Ct. Cl. 339, 325 F.2d 451 (1963), the contractor brought an action in breach of contract on the basis that defective government-furnished specifications delayed completion of the work. The contractor contended that the government's unreasonable delays, resulting from errors in its specifications and tardiness in correcting those errors, constituted a breach of contract. The government countered that the Changes article permitted it to delay the contractor while it made changes in the specifications. The Court of Claims did not share the government's viewpoint and held that the critical factor was that all of the delay to which the contractor was subjected came about because the specifications were deficient. Were this not the case, the contractor would have no right to complain if the government's exercise of its reserved right to make changes set his work schedule awry. *J.A. Ross & Co. v. United States,* 126 Ct. Cl. 323, 115 F. Supp. 187 (1953). At least this would be so if the government had acted with due alacrity. *Anthony P. Miller, Inc. v. United States,* 111 Ct. Cl. 252, 77 F. Supp. 209 (1948). In this case, however, the contractor had contracted to do the work in accordance with specifications the government had prepared, and he was therefore under a duty not to render the project more expensive than it would have been if he could have complied with its plans. In *United States v. Spearin,* 248 U.S. 132 (1918), the Supreme Court held that in a case where the specifications prescribe the character, dimensions, and location of the construction work, the government implicitly warrants that the contractor, if he complies with the specifications, will be able to complete the project within the contemplated period of time. This warranty is akin to the condition implied in every construction contract that neither party will do anything to hinder the performance of the other party. *J.A. Ross & Co. v. United States, supra; George A. Fuller Co. v. United States,* 108 Ct. Cl. 70, 69 F. Supp. 409 (1947). If faulty specifications prevent or delay completion of the contract, the contractor is entitled to recover damages for the government's breach of its implied warranty. *United States v. Spearin, supra; Warren Brothers Road Co. v. United States,* 123 Ct. Cl. 48, 105 F. Supp. 826 (1952). Those damages extend to the costs incurred by reason of the idleness resulting from mistakes in the plans. The government cannot, by errors in its specifications, cause delay in the contractor's completion of the work and then compensate him merely by extending the performance period and by payment of any added direct costs occasioned by changes to correct those errors.

Thus, there is no question that the government has the responsibility of furnishing correct specifications and that any delay caused by a failure to furnish correct specifications must be charged to the government. *D&E Constr. Co.,* VACAB No. 561, 67-2 BCA 6558. It is also clear that if the specifications are proven to be defective, the contractor need not prove that the delay due to defective government-furnished specifications is per se unreasonable and compensable. *Chaney & James Constr. Co. v. United States* 190 Ct. Cl. 669, 421 F.2d 728 (1970). If the contractor is delayed, he may recover extra costs resulting from delay due to mistakes in plans and drawings, and the recovery is not limited to an equitable adjustment for changes ordered to correct such mistakes. While the government is entitled to make necessary changes, where the change is necessitated by defective plans and specifications, it must pay the entire resulting damage without deductions for time to make the changes, as would be the case if the redesign were necessitated by a changed condition or the like. *Luria Brothers & Co. v. United States,* 177 Ct. Cl. 666, 369 F.2d 700 (1966).

In order to prevail, however, the contractor must establish that the specifications were defective and that it was in substantial compliance therewith. *United States v. Spearin,* 248 U.S. 132 (1918); *Laburnum Constr. Corp. v. United States,* 163 Ct. Cl. 339, 325 F.2d 451 (1963); *R.M. Hollingshead Corp. v. United States,* 124 Ct. Cl. 681, 111 F. Supp. 285 (1953); *Rosendin Electric,* ASBCA No. 22996, 81-1 BCA 14,827; *Davison Constr. Co.,* ASBCA No. 22237, 79-1 BCA 13,510.

## FAILURE OF DEFENSE

The courts and Boards of Contract Appeals have held on many occasions that the employment of qualified personnel is the contractor's responsibility and that the failure to employ or retain the services of qualified personnel necessary to perform a contract is not beyond the control and without the fault or negligence of the contractor. *Home Electronic,* ASBCA Nos. 8642 & 8707, 1963 BCA 3833. It is the contractor's responsibility to have available the means of performing the contract, and none of his labor difficulties can be charged to the government under most circumstances. The availability of labor is a market condition of which the contractor assumes the risk at the time of making the contract, and the assumption of that risk was in his control. *Ellis Constr. Co.,* GSBCA No. 2344, 68-1 BCA 6926; *Wisconsin Mfg. Co.,* ASBCA No. 9040, 1964 BCA 4391.

A contractor's inability to obtain an adequate work force will not generally be an excusable cause of delay or justify an extension of performance time. And this rule prevails even in circumstances requiring the services of highly skilled personnel in remote locations (e.g., lens grinders in Melbourne, Florida) on the basis that such scarcity was a prevailing market condition that was known, or should have been known, by the contractor at the time he entered into a contract. *Space Age Laboratories,* ASBCA No. 12162, 68-1 BCA 6859. It is also firmly established that the contractor has the responsibility to provide the machinery, equipment, or facilities to accomplish the contract work, *G. O'Connor,* AGBCA No. 75-154, 78-1 BCA 12,981, unless, of course, the government has assumed that obligation.

The Default articles provide that if a failure to perform is caused by a subcontractor at any tier, and if the cause of the default is beyond the control of both the contractor and the subcontractor and without the fault or negligence of either, the contractor shall not be liable for any excess costs for failure to perform, unless the subcontracted supplies were obtainable from other sources in sufficient time for the contractor to meet the required delivery schedule or other performance requirements. *See* FAR § 52.249-8, -9 & -10. The tenor of the clause suggests that the term "subcontractors," in the context in which it is used, means those whom the principal contractor could control or for whom it was contractually responsible, and not those concerning whose conduct and reliability a contractor could only hopefully and helplessly speculate. *Schweigert, Inc. v. United States,* 188 Ct. Cl. 1184, 388 F.2d 697 (1967).

The provisions of the clause limiting excusability for subcontractor delays that are beyond the control and without the fault of the subcontractor are applicable only in regard to those in privity with the prime contractor and do not apply to second-tier subcontractors or suppliers. The result is that if the delay is caused by the failure of a second-tier subcontractor to make delivery and this was beyond the control and without the fault of the prime contractor and first-tier supplier, the delay is excusable. In order for a late delivery by a second-tier supplier to be considered an excusable cause of delay, it must be shown that both the prime and the first-tier suppliers made reasonable efforts to assure that the necessary supplies would be delivered on time. *Blackhawk Heating & Plumbing Co.,* VACAB No. 809, 69-2 BCA 7773.

Where the contractor's default was occasioned by the default of a first-tier subcontractor and the record suggested that the latter's default was occasioned by the default of an unidentified second-tier supplier, the threshold question is whether the contractor is to be absolved on the basis of the rule laid down by the Court of Claims in *Schweigert, Inc. v. United States,* 188 Ct. Cl. 1184, 388 F.2d 697 (1967). According to that rule, a failure in delivery that is solely the fault of a second-tier subcontractor operates to excuse the default of the prime contractor. However, the evidence presented by the contractor did not fulfill the criteria of that rule. While it could be found that the contractor's evidence established that his own default was beyond his control and without his fault or negligence, the same finding could not be made with respect to the first-tier subcontractor. Insofar as the latter was concerned, the most that the record established was that the first-tier supplier did not deliver because an unnamed second-tier subcontractor failed to deliver. There was a failure of proof concerning the first-tier subcontractor's diligence in placing timely orders, in obtaining firm commitments, and in attempting to obtain supplies from alternate sources once the original second-tier supplier gave notice that he could not perform. *K Electronics,* ASBCA Nos. 14248 & 14452, 79-1 BCA 8097.

Though acts of the public enemy will excuse a delay in performance under the Default articles, contractors have not always been successful in the use of that defense. For example, it has been held that, in order to prevail, the contractor must do more than show that his costs were increased by the warlike atmosphere in Vietnam. It is well established that a contractor may not be relieved from the responsibility of performing a contract that was possible of performance because of unforeseen difficulties or unexpected expenses. *E.V. Lane Corp.,* ASBCA Nos. 9741, 9920 & 9933, 65-2 BCA 5076.

A contractor whose performance was in fact disrupted by an act of a public enemy in Vietnam was likewise unsuccessful. The contractor argued that the 1968 Tet offensive was an unknown condition that could not have been anticipated at the time of making the contract. The Board disagreed and held that the contract was made for rehabilitation of facilities in an active combat zone. Their very purpose was ancillary to the hostilities that were being conducted in that zone. There was no way to ensure that hostilities would not erupt in the construction area. *Keong Nam Enterprises,* ASBCA No. 13734, 69-1 BCA 7705.

## NOTICE REQUIREMENTS

As was the requirement with respect to the Changes article, the contractor must give the government timely notice if it is to prevail in an action for increased costs based on excusable delay. On numerous occasions, the courts and Boards have delineated the general criteria for assessing the existence of a claim against the United States. The principle set down is that oral and written communications between the parties will be liberally construed in determining whether a claim has been asserted before the Contracting Officer. But to demonstrate the existence of a claim, there must be some evidence of record (1) that the contractor, at the time the alleged claim was asserted, manifested a present, positive intention to seek an equitable monetary or other adjustment of the contract terms as a matter of legal right and (2) that the contractor placed before the Contracting Officer or one empowered to act for him an actual or constructive notice that a claim was being asserted. *Gulf & Western Industries v. United States,* 384 Ct. Cl. 77, 639 F.2d 732 (1980); *Jo-Bar Mfg. Corp. v. United States,* 210 Ct. Cl. 149 (1976).

# 8

# Constructive Changes

## INTRODUCTION

The constructive change is a concept that has been developed by the courts and Boards of Contract Appeals as a rule of law based on an inference that a change has occurred because of the government's action or fault vis-à-vis a formal change order under the Changes article. The doctrine serves as a mechanism by which the contractor may process a claim against the government under the Changes clause in those circumstances where there is no other apparent contractual authority that would permit government review. The constructive changes theory has served at least two purposes.

1. It prevents the unjust enrichment of the government when a contractor, at the direction of the government, performs work not specified in the contract. *C.A. Logeman Co.,* ASBCA No. 5692, 61-2 BCA 3232.
2. It permits the Boards of Contract Appeals to retain jurisdiction over actions that, prior to the passage of the Contract Disputes Act, would otherwise have been treated as breaches of contract triable only in courts of competent jurisdiction. *Midwest Spray & Painting v. United States,* 126 Ct. Cl. 1331, 389 F.2d 423 (1966). With passage of the Contract Disputes Act, this second purpose has become moot.

## THE CONSTRUCTIVE CHANGE THEORY

### Definition

By definition, a constructive change arises from either the conduct or the fault of the government. Conduct, circumstances that compel the contractor to accomplish work not called for by the contract, instructions (oral and written), and acts or omissions by the Contracting Officer or by other authorized government officials that are of such a nature that they are inferred as having the same effect as the issuance of a formal change order are construed as constructive changes. The doctrine is based on equitable tenets and recognizes that an informal requirement (i.e., one not formalized by the issuance of a change order) for the performance of additional work under a contract is substantially equivalent to a formal requirement and must therefore be governed by similar principles. Stated differently, any conduct by a Contracting Officer or any authorized government representative that is not a formal change order, but that has the effect of requiring performance different from that prescribed by the original terms of the contract is a constructive change.

When a Contracting Officer or other authorized government representative, by his conduct, causes a contractor to perform changed work, such conduct may form the basis for a claim by the contractor. If the Contracting Officer compels the contractor to perform work not required by the contract, his order to perform, even if oral, constitutes an authorized, but unilateral change in the work and entitles the contractor to an equitable adjustment in accordance with the Changes provision of the contract. *Len Co. & Assocs. v. United States,* 181 Ct. Cl. 29, 385 F.2d 438 (1967).

The drafters of the Federal Acquisition Regulation have recognized the validity and potential impact of the constructive changes doctrine as it pertains to contract performance. They have therefore mandated that government personnel refrain from acting in such a manner as to cause a contractor to believe that they have authority to bind the government, as well as refraining from directing or encouraging a contractor to perform work that should be the subject of a contract modification. *See* FAR § 43.102.

### Examples of Constructive Changes

Government conduct may be in the form of an affirmative act, *Fulfillment Corp. of America,* ASBCA No. 7094, 1963 BCA 3761; a failure to act, *F.H. McGraw & Co. v. United States,* 113 Ct. C1. 29 (1949); or a course of conduct, *J. Bell v. United States,* 186 Ct. Cl. 189, 404 F.2d 975 (1968). It may be in writing, *Gulf Coast Steel Building,* ASBCA No. 5552, 59-2 BCA 2348, or oral, *Len Co. & Assocs. v. United States, supra.* A constructive change may be couched in terms of a "request," *Tombigbee Constructors v. United States,* 190 Ct. Cl. 615, 420 F.2d 1037 (1970); result from "cumulative suggestions," *Skidmore Owings & Merrill,* ASBCA No. 8346, 1963 BCA 3727; or be expressed as "threats" to terminate the contract for default, *Holt Hauling & Warehouse Systems,* ASBCA Nos. 19136 & 20249, 76-2 BCA 12,185; *City Electric Anchorage,* ASBCA No. 6750, 1962 BCA 3605. A constructive change may be any act that, in practical effect, constitutes a requirement by an authorized representative of the government for a contractor to perform work not required by, or specified in, the contract. But "mere suggestions" by the government's representatives do not constitute a constructive change, *Scientific Equipment Mfg. Corp.*, ASBCA No. 10163, 65-1 BCA 4819; nor does the government's expression of its intent to assert its legal rights and remedies constitute duress sufficient to sustain a claim, *Pine River Assocs.*, CGBCA No. T-166, 66-1 BCA 5448.

Examples of government fault that have formed the basis for claims under the constructive changes theory include providing defective government specifications; requiring a contractor to adhere to a delivery schedule, when the contractor is in fact entitled to a time extension under the Excusable Delays clause, by failing either to grant the time extension or to accept the fact that a delay in the work was excusable; denying the contractor the opportunity to employ a permissible method or sequence of work; erroneously requiring a contractor to perform contrary to his correct interpretation of the requirements of the contract; or by interfering in the contractor's performance.

## ELEMENTS OF A CONSTRUCTIVE CHANGE

The constructive change doctrine is made up of two elements: the "change" element and the "order" element. To find the change element, actual performance must be examined to determine whether it went beyond the minimum standards demanded by the terms of the contract. *A.G. Bartlett Co.*, ASBCA No. 12692, 69-1 BCA 7547. The order element is also a necessary ingredient in the constructive change concept. To be compensable under the Changes clause, the change must be one that the government ordered the contractor to make. The government's representative, by his words or deeds, must require the contractor to perform work that is not a necessary part of his contract. This is something that differs from the advice, comments, suggestions, and opinions that government engineering and technical personnel frequently offer to a contractor's employees. And this is especially so where the contract standards are broad prescriptions of the performance specification type that give the contractor a wide measure of discretion in designing and manufacturing the end item. *Maverick Diversified*, NASA BCA No. 874-19, 75-1 BCA 11,081; *Industrial Research Assocs.*, DOTCAB No. WB-5, 68-1 BCA 7069.

In *A.G. Bartlett Co., supra*, a fuel services contract at an Air Force base required the contractor to provide on-call services 20.5 hours per day. In connection with a general overhaul program for certain aircraft, the Air Force worked around the clock for approximately one month and required similar response from the contractor. To comply with the demands of the Air Force, the contractor employed a midnight shift, which clearly went beyond the requirements of the contract. It was more than the casual or "emergency" call contemplated by the original contract. Quite clearly, the requirement was for extended services during some indefinite, but nevertheless continuous, period for the duration of the special emergency to support the base mission. The Contracting Officer's technical representative ordered the services as required, and, for all practical purposes, the contractor's manager had no real option as to the method of complying with the demand. Obviously, some fueling demand was to be expected during each night, but from the number of aircraft involved in the modification program, it is doubtful that any on-call servicing would have been adequate. Under the circumstances, the use of an on-duty crew for the midnight shift was reasonable, and the Government acquiesced therein. The midnight shift represented extra work, and even though a formal change order had not been initiated, the contractor was entitled to additional compensation on its account.

## DEFECTIVE SPECIFICATIONS

The cornerstone of the government contract is the specification, with its applicable descriptive material, on which the basic issues of pricing, performance, and contract terms and conditions are founded. The objective of the specification is to establish (1) a description, or specification, of the supplies or services being acquired; (2) criteria for inspection and acceptance of the work; and (3) a base line for performance on which initial pricing and schedule are predicated. Obviously, the adequacy and clarity of the specification are of paramount importance to both parties.

In *United States v. Spearin,* 248 U.S. 132 (1918), Justice Brandeis said that where one agrees to do for a fixed sum a thing possible to be performed, he will not be excused or become entitled to additional compensation because unforeseen difficulties are encountered. Thus, one who undertakes to erect a structure on a particular site assumes ordinarily the risks of subsidence in the soil. But if the contractor is bound to build according to plans and specifications prepared by the owner, the contractor will not be responsible for the consequences of defects in plans and specifications. Therefore, when the government specifies a method of performance or a design that calls for a usual and ordinary means of performance, there is an implied warranty that the results will be satisfactory.

A contractor is obligated to do what the plans and specifications direct him to do, and when he has done so in a good and workmanlike manner, he has discharged his responsibility under the contract. If the plans and specifications are deficient, or if they are inadequate or structurally wrong, it is the fault of the party preparing them and not of the contractor attempting to follow them. Where the government contracts for supplies or services in accordance with specifications it has prepared, there is an implied warranty that if the specifications are followed, a satisfactory product will result. Accordingly, a contractor attempting to perform to defective specifications may be entitled to costs incurred in attempting to meet the requirements of the original specifications, as well as to costs resulting from mistakes in the plans.

It is a basic tenet of contract law that a contract must be read as a whole and in its entirety. It is equally elementary that meaning must, if at all possible, be given to the language employed in the contract and that the proper interpretation of a provision is a question of law. Technical words and words of art are given their technical meaning, unless the context or a usage that is applicable indicates a different meaning. One primary purpose of interpreting a contract in this manner is to ensure that no word is rejected, treated as a redundancy, or assumed to be meaningless if any meaning that is reasonable and consistent with the other parts of the contract can possibly be given to it. Moreover, an interpretation that gives a reasonable meaning to all parts of an instrument will be preferred to one that leaves a portion of it useless, inexplicable, inoperative, void, insignificant, meaningless, or superfluous; nor should any provision be construed as being in conflict with another, unless no reasonable interpretation is possible. *Baltimore Contractors,* GSBCA No. 3066, 74-2 BCA 11,908.

If some substantial provision of a government-drawn agreement is fairly susceptible of a certain construction and the contractor actually and reasonably so construes it in the course of bidding or performance, that is the interpretation that will be adopted—unless the parties' intention is otherwise affirmatively revealed. This rule is fair to both the drafters and those who are required to accept or reject the contract so proffered without haggling. Although the potential contractor may have some duty to inquire about a major patent discrepancy, or an obvious omission, or a drastic conflict in provisions, he is not normally required (absent a clear warning in the contract) to seek clarification on any and all ambiguities, doubts, or possible differences in interpretation. The government, as the author, has to shoulder the major task of seeing that within the zone of reasonableness the words of the agreement communicate the proper notions—as well as the main risk of a failure to carry that responsibility. *WPC Enterprises v. United States,* 163 Ct. Cl. 1, 323 F.2d 874 (1963).

When both the contractor's and the government's interpretations lie within the zone of reasonableness, if some substantive provision of a government-drawn agreement is fairly susceptible of a certain construction and the contractor actually and reasonably so construes it, that is the interpretation that will be adopted. *BCM Corp. v. United States,* 2 Cl. Ct. 602 (1983). When the meaning of a provision is ambiguous and reasonable men could interpret the provision in different ways, the interpretation that will be given is the one that is more favorable to the party who did not draft the provision. *Tibshraeny Brothers Constr. v. United States,* 6 Cl. Ct. 463 (1984). It is also well established that where a contractor is relying on an interpretation of an alleged ambiguous contract, he must show that he relied on such interpretation. *Dale Ingram, Inc. v. United States,* 201 Ct. Cl. 50, 475 F.2d 1177 (1973).

If an ambiguous specification authored by the government is the subject of an exchange of views during negotiations that predated the contract and that resulted in an amendment to the specifications, the contractor may be precluded from obtaining relief. Thus, technical fact finding during negotiations, with an in-depth discussion and possible revisions to the specification, may result in a sharing of responsibility between the government and the contractor, precluding the applicability of the general rule of interpreting ambiguous language against the party who prepared such language. In effect, both parties may be deemed to have coauthored the specification, especially when the final product is the result of extensive negotiations at which the contractor was represented by counsel. *Olin Matheson Chemical Corp.,* ASBCA No. 7401, 1962 BCA 3596; *aff'd, Olin Matheson Chemical Corp. v. United States,* 179 Ct. Cl. 368 (1967).

In *Hol-Gar Manufacturing Corp. v. United States,* 175 Ct. Cl. 518, 360 F.2d 634 (1966), the contractor sought reimbursement for additional costs incurred in attempting to perform a contract with the Air Force under specifications that, prior to amendment, were so defective that the desired performance could not be attained by following them. The fixed-price supply contract called for the manufacture of generator sets. The specifications provided specific size and weight limitations for the generator unit and set out various environmental conditions under which the unit was to operate. They also called for an air-cooled, multicylinder, full stroke diesel engine and provided for the amount of cubic displacement, the direction of the rotation and the operating speed of the engine, the type of fuel to be used, and detailed specifics as to engine components. After limited testing, the parties became convinced that the specification would have to be amended to permit the substitution of a new engine. A supplemental agreement relaxed size and weight limitations to permit the use of an Onan engine. In accepting the change, Hol-Gar agreed that no claim would be made for any additional costs resulting from the substitution of the Onan engine, but reserved the right to submit a claim for costs incurred in attempting to meet the original specification requirements.

Hol-Gar completed the amended contract, was paid the contract price, and subsequently submitted a claim for costs incurred in attempting to perform to the original requirements. This claim was denied by both the Contracting Officer and the Board of Contract Appeals. However, the Court of Claims reversed both decisions, holding that the parties had agreed at the time of the execution of the contract that if, as a result of testing the preproduction samples, changes in specifications were required, such changes would be processed under the Changes article of the contract. That changes in the specifications were required was clear from the fact that after numerous negotiations, during which time the contractor was attempting unsuccessfully to comply with the specifications, they were changed by the execution of a supplemental agreement. The court was of the opinion that this change caused an increase in the cost of performance of the contract since the change in specifications made useless some of the expenditures the contractor had made up to that point. Because the contractor was out of pocket those costs, they had to be included in the cost of performance. Since the necessity for the change was not due to the contractor's fault, an equitable adjustment required that the contractor be paid for the increase in its costs over what they would have been had no change been required.

Where the change is necessitated by defective specifications or drawings, the equitable adjustment to which the contractor is entitled must, if it is to be equitable (i.e., fair and just), include the costs that he incurred in attempting to perform in accordance with the defective specifications and drawings. Under such circumstances, the equitable adjustment may not be limited to costs incurred subsequent to the issuance of the change order. *J. Bell v. United States,* 186 Ct. Cl. 189, 404 F.2d 975 (1986). They must include the costs that the contractor incurred in attempting to perform in accordance with such defective specifications and drawings. *Johnson & Sons Erectors,* ASBCA No. 24564, 81-2 BCA 15,082; *J.W. Hurst & Sons Awning,* ASBCA No. 4667, 59-1 BCA 2095.

When a defective product is manufactured as a result of inaccurate government specifications, the contractor is entitled to compensation for the subsequent repair of that product. When a contractor is delayed because of deficient government specifications, he can recover the additional costs incurred as a result of faulty plans. Once it is established that the government-furnished plans and specifications are defective, the government is liable. When, with the knowledge of government representatives, the contractor performs work to correct design deficiencies that should have been corrected by a change order, the courts and Boards treat as done what should have been done. *Joseph Penner,* GSBCA No. 4647, 80-2 BCA 14,604; *W. Southerland Jones,* ASBCA No. 6321, 61-2 BCA 3182.

The courts and Boards are sensitive to the need to protect the government from bearing the cost of extra work performed that is beyond the government's determined minimum needs (i.e., volunteered work). But when additional effort is required to correct defects in a device, the government has a need and a duty to correct the defects. So far as the government has notice of the added work before it was done, it had the opportunity to determine whether the particular cure was to its liking. In the absence of a specific warranty as to result, if a contractor follows the contract specifications, he may recover even though the item failed to function. *Dayton-Wright v. United States,* 64 Ct. Cl. 514 (1928). A claim based on work resulting from defective specifications is properly for consideration under the Changes clause of the contract since a change required by a defective design or specification is in effect a constructive change order for which the contractor is entitled to an equitable adjustment. *E. Arthur Higgins*, AGBCA No. 76-128, 79-2 BCA 14,050.

Equitable adjustments are legal corrective measures designed and utilized to safeguard a contractor against increased costs and delays when the government alters a contract. *Bruce Constr. Corp. v. United States*, 163 Ct. Cl. 97, 324 F.2d 516 (1963). Recovery can generally be had for all of the increase in costs that can be shown to result directly from the defective specifications or extra work required, including costs of delays, disruptions of work sequences, and loss of efficiency. The measure of adjustment must relate to the contractor's altered position. The contractor is entitled to be paid the amount the changed work reasonably cost him, and there is a presumption that his actual costs are reasonable. *Bruce Constr. Corp. v. United States, supra.* The proper measure of damages of an equitable adjustment, where the work has been performed, is the difference between the reasonable cost of the work required by the contract and the actual reasonable cost to the contractor for performing the changed work, plus a reasonable amount for overhead and profit. *General Builders Supply Co. v. United States*, 183 Ct. Cl. 477, 409 F.2d 246 (1949). But those expenses that would have had to be incurred had there been no change are not recoverable under the constructive change doctrine. *Dale Ingram, Inc. v. United States*, 201 Ct. Cl. 50, 475 F.2d 1177 (1973).

Nevertheless, an experienced contractor cannot rely on government-furnished production documents or specifications where, on the basis of such documents or specifications, he knows, or should have known, that the document or specifications could not produce the desired result, for he has no right to make a useless thing and charge his customer for it. *J. Hedin Constr. Co. v. United States*, 171 Ct. Cl. 70, 347 F.2d 235 (1965); *S.W. Electronics & Mfg. Corp.*, ASBCA Nos. 20968 & 20890, 77-2 BCA 12,631.

A different result will obtain where the contractor has no possible way of knowing that the specifications are defective until he commences performance. When a contractor encountered substantial quantities of large boulders during the excavation of a site, which constituted a differing site condition, he was entitled to an equitable adjustment for increased performance costs because the specifications did not indicate the presence of such large boulders and their presence was not ascertainable from a site inspection. Additionally, extra costs incurred in the construction of a lagoon were compensable to the contractor because the specifications, which set out the method of performance, were defective and forced the contractor to employ an alternate method of construction. *Southern Paving Corp.*, AGBCA No. 74-103, 77-2 BCA 12,813.

Under certain circumstances, such as extremely adverse weather conditions, a government failure to timely issue a stop work order, which in reality requires that the contractor continue performance by changing his planned method of accomplishing the work, may be construed as a constructive change order. In *J.R. Pope, Inc.,* DOTCAB No. 78-55, 80-2 BCA 14,562, the contractor was forced to continue the paving of a steep road even though the work area was the site of the heaviest rainfall experienced in a century. The Contracting Officer's actions of requiring the contractor to work under adverse road and weather conditions had the separate and distinct consequence of causing several constructive changes. *Hilltop Electric Constr.,* DOTCAB No. 78-6, 78-2 BCA 13,421. A constructive change results when (1) extra work was done beyond the minimum requirements of the contract, (2) an action by a government representative required the contractor to perform work not covered by the contract, and (3) the contractor gave sufficient notice of the change. *Environmental Consultants,* IBCA No. 1192-5-78, 79-2 BCA 13,937. Where the government has actual knowledge of facts pertaining to the constructive change claim, the claim is not precluded by the absence of specific notice itemizing the contractor's claim. *Smith & Pittman Constr. Co.,* AGBCA No. 76-131, 77-1 BCA 12,381. The Contracting Officer forced the contractor to pave on an excessively moist surface, which changed the contract specifications that required an asphalt thickness of two inches to be spread on a surface free of moisture. Since the contractor was required to perform more costly work than was called for in the contract, a constructive change occurred, and an equitable adjustment is warranted. *Hayes International Corp.,* ASBCA No. 21758, 79-1 BCA 13,596. By forcing the contractor to work when it was impossible to apply the minimum amount of asphalt because the air temperature was too low to allow it to be spread to the proper depth, the government constructively changed that minimum. *Hilltop Electric Constr., supra.* Moreover, the contract gave the contractor the option of spreading the asphalt with a mechanical spreader or with a blade and windrow. The contractor had decided to use the mechanical spreader, which heated the asphalt and spread it to a more uniform thickness, but was forced to use the less efficient and more costly blade and windrow method when the Contracting Officer forced him to perform under adverse weather conditions. Thus, a change in the specifications occurred, and the contractor was entitled to the reasonable cost of performing in a more costly manner. *Mann Constr. Co.,* AGBCA No. 444, 76-1 BCA 11,710. When the contractor elects to perform in a reasonable sequence and the government disrupts that plan for its own convenience, a constructive change results, and an equitable adjustment is in order. *Laburnum Constr. Corp. v. United States,* 163 Ct. Cl. 339, 325 F.2d 451 (1963).

## ACCELERATIONS

An acceleration in delivery or performance occurs when

1. The contractor is entitled to a time extension because of an excusable delay,
2. The Contracting Officer refuses or fails to grant the requested extension, or acts in such a manner as to require that the work be completed at the earliest possible date, and
3. The contractor incurred costs in an effort to comply.

While most of the cases have involved accelerated construction contracts, the necessary factual elements are no different under a supply contract. *Dynamics Consolidated Corp. of America, Fermont Division,* ASBCA No. 15086, 75-1 BCA 11,139. Recovery is not defeated if the completion date is not in fact improved, provided added costs are incurred in a reasonable effort to comply with the government's direction. Even absent a denial of the time extension, the government may be liable for acceleration if it delays inordinately in acting on a request for time extension, while directing the contractor to meet the unadjusted completion schedule. *Continental Consolidated Corp. v. United States,* 200 Ct. Cl. 737 (1972). A contractor who finishes the project within the contract time plus excusable delays is not disqualified as a matter of law from claiming acceleration costs. *Norair Engineering Corp. v. United States,* 229 Ct. Cl. 160, 666 F.2d 546 (1981).

The first element of a constructive acceleration is the contractor's entitlement to a time extension as a consequence of an excusable delay. As was seen in the preceding chapter, an excusable delay is one that is without the fault or negligence of the contractor. Thus, where the contractor claimed acceleration costs because of government insistence that he maintain the original delivery schedule in the face of strikes, the Board recognized the general rule that a contractor who has been excusably delayed, having given timely notice of the causes, may recover the cost of accelerating the work when the Contracting Officer refuses the request for a time extension and insists on adherence to the existing performance schedule. *National Radio Co.,* ASBCA No. 14707, 72-2 BCA 9486. The Boards have also found an implied acceleration in the government's refusal of a requested time extension based on excusable delay, coupled with the government's expression of urgency and its reading of the liquidated damages clause to the contractor in such a manner as to give him reason to believe that such damages would be assessed for completion any later than the originally scheduled date. *Pathman Constr. Co.,* ASBCA No. 14285, 71-1 BCA 8905.

It is, of course, possible that acceleration can be required, in effect, by a calculated withholding of a requested extension of time in conjunction with orders that force a contractor to take steps to overcome the excusable delay. *Electronic & Missile Facilities,* ASBCA No. 9031, 1964 BCA 4338. The government's failure to deliver government-furnished property in accordance with the contract schedule has also been found to have compressed the performance period, thereby accelerating performance. *Farnsworth & Chambers, Inc.*, ASBCA No. 5988, 60-2 BCA 2733.

Acceleration has been found where the contractor was entitled to a time extension for the amount of time that installation and testing of certain electrical equipment was delayed because of the Veterans Administration's failure to obtain a priority order under the government's priorities, allocation, and allotment system. The Contracting Officer had previously allowed a time extension for the same reason, and the government contended that that time extension was sufficient. However, there was evidence that the manufacturer failed to meet the delivery date on which the first time extension was based and that the failure was the result of the same priority system. *George E. Jensen, Contractor,* VACAB No. 606, 67-2 BCA 6506.

If the Contracting Officer refuses to consider a request for an extension even though it is evident that excusable delays have occurred, an acceleration will be found. In one such case, the government was adamant in its demands that the contractor adhere to its original progress schedule and forced the contractor to hire additional workmen and to work overtime hours in an attempt to do so. The orders of the Contracting Officer, requiring a speedup of the work at a time when the contractor was not behind schedule, constituted a constructive change for which the contractor was entitled to an equitable adjustment in the contract price. *J.W. Bateson Co.*, ASBCA No. 60691, 1962 BCA 3529.

It is well established that a mere denial of an extension of time or a mere failure of the Contracting Officer to grant an extension of time during the period that the work is being performed does not amount to an acceleration order. *Lewis Constr. Co.*, ASBCA No. 5509, 60-2 BCA 2732. Contracts with the government contemplate that disputes may arise during performance and therefore provide that the contractor proceed diligently with performance of the work pending settlement of the dispute. The fact that a Contracting Officer's denial of a time extension is later overruled by the courts or a Board, or the fact that the Contracting Officer may, after due consideration, allow an extension of time that he was either adverse to or uncertain of is not the equivalent of an acceleration order on the ground that the decision is too late to permit the contractor to use it in adjusting his completion schedule.

In order to justify a finding that the work has been accelerated, there must, in addition, be an express order or some actions that are the equivalent of an order to the contractor to adhere to the original completion date without regard to excusable delays. See, for example, *Mechanical Utilities*, ASBCA Nos. 7345 & 7467, 1962 BCA 3557, where the Contracting Officer was aware that the work had been excusably delayed, but informed the contractor that the contract would be terminated for default if the original completion date was not met. See also *Electronic & Missile Facilities*, ASBCA

No. 9031, 1964 BCA 4338, where the government withheld extensions of time for the calculated purpose of requiring the contractor to meet the original completion date and issued orders requiring the contractor to exert the effort necessary to meet that date. But a mere failure to make a timely award will not generally be viewed as an excusable delay for the purpose of prosecuting a claim for acceleration. *Freeman Electric Constr. Co.*, DOTCAB No. 74-23 A & B, 77-1 BCA 12,258.

Constructive acceleration requires that the government be afforded an opportunity to grant a time extension on account of the delay. Normally, that opportunity is afforded by the contractor's notice of the delay given to the government, together with sufficient supporting information to allow the Contracting Officer to make a reasonable determination as to entitlement to a time extension. The furnishing of supporting information may be dispensed with if the information is known to, or reasonably available to, the government. *Gruelich, Inc.*, ENG BCA No. 3832, 78-1 BCA 13,417. The Contracting Officer has an affirmative duty under the Default articles to conduct a prompt review of requests for time extension and to negotiate the matter within a reasonable time. *Fishback & Moore International Corp.*, ASBCA No. 18146, 77-1 BCA 12,300.

Failure to give timely notice may lead to the conclusion that the contractor was a volunteer or had otherwise acquiesced to the government's directive to maintain the original performance schedule. This requirement is bottomed on the presumption that if a contractor does not request a time extension, the Contracting Officer could not actually or constructively order an acceleration of the work. *Humphrey Constr. Corp.*, IBCA Nos. 555-4-66 & 479-7-66, 68-1 BCA 6820.

Strict adherence to this rule has been somewhat relaxed in recent years, to the extent that if the contractor puts the Contracting Officer on notice of problems that might result in excusable delays, and if the government unequivocally indicates that a delay in performance will not be accepted, the failure to specifically request a time extension may be excused.

*Gibbs Shipyard*, ASBCA No. 9809, 67-2 BCA 6499, clearly illustrates this exception. In *Gibbs*, the contractor contended that the government's insistence on completion of a dry dock by the original completion date, without regard to excusable delays, disrupted the entire operation and substantially increased the costs. In a letter to the contractor, the government stated:

> This will acknowledge receipt of your letter in which you offer explanations for various problems that have been under discussion with my staff here and at our yard. I have also received reports from both Washington and the field that there is a continuing slippage of work. This project is top priority and absolutely no relaxation of the operational date can be permitted. This letter is to advise you that if the final completion date is not met, I will issue an unsatisfactory construction performance report on this project regardless of the circumstances which you feel caused such delay.

In view of the language in the government's letter, any request for an extension of time would have been pointless except insofar as such request related to the number of days of delay the contractor was being called on to overcome. The order to complete the work by the originally scheduled date without regard to any excusable delays that had been or might be encountered in the future was an acceleration order. The need for notice was eliminated by unequivocal orders to complete by the scheduled date regardless of past or future delays. This decision is cited with approval in *Continental Consolidated Corp. v. United States,* 200 Ct. Cl. 737 (1972).

The central problem relating to constructive accelerations is that of determining what types of actions or statements constitute an order. Because the order is "constructive," it will generally be something less than a specific directive to accelerate the work. The underlying test is whether a prudent contractor could reasonably interpret the government's actions or statements (oral or written) as directives that the work be completed within the original schedule. At the very least, there must be government pressure in some form that requires the contractor to complete performance in accordance with that schedule.

In one case, at a meeting on March 28, 1958, the resident engineer "requested" that the prime contractor speed up work during the period June 1–July 5, 1958. Extra equipment was employed on the contract, and increased expenses were incurred for which the contractor sought reimbursement. The government contended that the speedup was not directed, but merely requested, and that the contractor voluntarily complied with the request because of the mutual interest of the parties in not extending the work into another winter. In contrast, a later directive was issued to accelerate the work, and increased expenses were paid for. It appears that the purpose of the speedup for which claim was made may have been to prepare taxiways for the anticipated arrival of some tanker aircraft. The Board was unable to distinguish between a request and an order under the circumstances. The initiative came from the government for its convenience. It made no difference whether the contractor complied willingly or unwillingly, or whether it also benefited from the compliance. The work was done in a manner different from that required by the contract, and the contractor was entitled to reimbursement for it. *Hyde Constr. Co.,* ASBCA No. 8393, 1963 BCA 3911; *cited with approval in Tombigbee Constructor v. United States,* 190 Ct. Cl. 615, 420 F.2d 1037 (1970).

The Board, in another case, held that a demand that excavation work be completed within seven days, given at a time when intended backfill was temporarily unsuitable because of climatic conditions, amounted to an acceleration order. This was so even though, under normal circumstances, the work could have been completed within this period and the government had already permitted the work to continue 30 days beyond the scheduled completion date. *Unicorn Management Corp.*, ASBCA No. 10195, 65-1 BCA 4774.

Moreover, a threat to terminate a contract for default may be viewed as an acceleration order under certain circumstances. *Olin-Matheson Chemical Corp.*, ASBCA No. 7605, 1963 BCA 3983. Thus, an order to accelerate, to be effective, need not be couched in terms of a specific directive. A request to accelerate, or even an expression of concern about lagging progress, may have the same effect as an order. The pressure applied, even if it is merely implicit, is particularly strong where liquidated damages hover in the background. *Norair Engineering Corp. v. United States,* 229 Ct. Cl. 160, 666 F.2d 546 (1981).

## GOVERNMENT MISREPRESENTATION

Absent a contract provision under which the government has agreed to pay for increases in the contractor's costs because he encountered unusually severe weather, the contractor cannot recover for delays in performance. *Keflavik Contractors,* ASBCA No. 6387, 61-2 BCA 3161. It is well established that while a contractor may be entitled to a time extension as a result of abnormal weather conditions, the government is not responsible, prior to acceptance of the work, for the damages that may occur at a construction site as a result of unusually severe weather. *B.D. Click Co.* ASBCA Nos. 17705 & 17757, 74-1 BCA 10,420. By the same reasoning, it is a general principle of law that neither party is responsible to the other for damages through a loss occasioned as an act of God, unless such an obligation is expressly assumed. *Arundel Corp. v. United States,* 103 Ct. Cl. 688 (1945).

However, a contractor has been allowed to recover extra costs incurred in constructing a navigation station on a remote atoll in the Pacific Ocean because the weather information furnished by the government was incorrect and the price of the successful bid was based on that incorrect information. The contractor's reliance on the government's representations that "Marcus Island is considered to be well outside the normal typhoon zone" was warranted, and the interpretations drawn therefrom were reasonable. The government's misrepresentations were misleading. *Chris Berg v. United States,* 189 Ct. Cl. 389, 404 F.2d 364 (1968).

## GOVERNMENT INTERFERENCE

Government interference with work in progress is another cause for concern in constructive changes. Although the government has the contractual right to inspect work in progress at any reasonable time, it may not do so in such a manner as to interfere with the contractor's performance. The major concern in cases dealing with the government's obligation not to hinder or interfere with the contractor's performance is in determining what conduct by the government constitutes a breach of that obligation. But it is clear that if the delay occurs despite the government's diligence and lack of fault, the contractor will not recover. *Peter Kiewit's Sons Co. v. United States,* 138 Ct. Cl. 668, 151 F. Supp. 726 (1957). On the other hand, if the delay is caused by the government's negligence or failure to exercise reasonable diligence, the government will be held liable. *Ben C. Gerwick, Inc. v. United States,* 152 Ct. Cl. 69, 285 F.2d 412 (1961).

Following this line of reasoning, improper or untimely inspection by the government's representative that causes a delay in contract performance may be compensable. Thus, it has been held that the government's failure to promptly inspect a contractor's erosion control and landscaping work and terminate his maintenance responsibility imposed an additional performance requirement on him over and above what was called for by the contract. In addition, the contractor's plant replacement obligation was concomitantly extended. Consequently, the contractor's entitlement to a change, and equitable adjustment thereto, was not limited solely to the expenditures incurred, but included compensation for the additional obligation and responsibility imposed on him by the government's unilateral extension of the maintenance period. *Paul G. Maddox,* ASBCA No. 11712, 67-2 BCA 6415.

The court, in *Adams Mfg. Co. v. United States,* 175 Ct. Cl. 288 (1966), found on equitable principles that the contractor was entitled to recover damages caused by overzealous and interfering acts of a government inspector. In essence, the inspector demanded a higher quality product than was called for by the contract. Hence, the court concluded that a substantial portion of the loss sustained by the contractor was directly traceable to delays in production brought about by the extremely rigid, unreasonable, and arbitrary conduct of the inspector.

Recovery of costs under the Suspension of Work clause may be granted only for delays that are unreasonable. "Reasonableness" is determined by considering all the relevant circumstances of the suspension, including whether the cause of the delay was due to the government's proper exercise of a contractual right. *Chaney & James Constr. Co. v. United States,* 190 Ct. Cl. 699, 421 F.2d 728 (1970).

In *Brand S. Roofing,* ASBCA No. 24588, 82-1 BCA 15,513, the parties were engaged in a good faith disagreement regarding a contractual requirement. The government quite properly suspended work in order to allow the Contracting Officer to fully evaluate the problem, to review it with his superiors, and to discuss some alternative solutions with the contractor. The "unreasonable" aspect of the suspension centered around the fact that the problem was not one that first came to the government's attention in mid-July. On the contrary, the record showed that the Contracting Officer had known of the contractor's procedures since late April. A suspension of over one month to formulate a position on a pre-existing contract problem was, at least to some extent, unreasonable. The contractor was therefore entitled to a contract adjustment under the Suspension of Work clause to the extent that the duration of the delay was unreasonable.

In *United Hoffman Machinery Corp.*, ASBCA No. 10906, 68-1 BCA 7027, the Board held that a rejection of gun projectiles was improper because of a misapplication of a projectile wall thickness standard by government inspectors. The inability of the contractor, over the period of one year, to obtain a definitive statement from the inspectors' superiors as to the proper method of applying the tests, while at the same time obtaining acceptance from those same officials of sample projectiles rejected by the inspectors, operated to permit an equitable adjustment in the contract price under the Changes article.

Economic duress has also been held to be a form of government interference under certain circumstances. The law of economic duress has been expanded somewhat in recent years, making it virtually impossible to arrive at any clear-cut definition. An examination of the cases makes it clear, however, that three elements are common to all situations where economic duress has been found to exist: (1) one side voluntarily accepted the terms of the other, (2) circumstances permitted no other alternative, and (3) said circumstances were the result of coercive acts of the opposite party.

In *Karnavas Painting Co.*, NASA BCA No. 28, 1963 BCA 3633, the government demanded that a contractor apply a third coat of paint to the stairs and hallway of a building he was renovating, which requirement was beyond the requirements of the contract, and threatened him with a termination for default if he did not comply. When the contractor at first refused to apply the paint as directed, the government in fact terminated the contract. It withdrew the termination only when the contractor acquiesced to its demands. The Board found that the test for proving economic duress had been met. The contractor was coerced into agreeing to apply the third coat of paint by the government's threat to terminate the contract for default, which threat was in actual practice carried out and withdrawn as the price for the contractor's agreement. The fact that termination was not only threatened, but also carried out and then only withdrawn as the price of the agreement was the *sine qua non* of economic duress.

## NOTICE REQUIREMENTS

When a contractor considers that the government has effected or may effect a change in the contract that has not been identified as such in writing, the contractor is required to notify the government as soon as possible. Notification will permit the government to evaluate the suspected change and (1) confirm that it is a change, direct the mode of further performance, and plan for its funding; (2) countermand the alleged change; or (3) notify the contractor that no change is considered to have occurred. *See* FAR §§ 43.104 & 52.243-7.

# 9

# Termination for Default

## INTRODUCTION

The discretionary rights of the government to terminate a contract for default following the contractor's breach and the obligations and liabilities of the parties following termination are set forth in standard FAR clauses. A default termination generally results from a contractor's failure, actual or anticipatory, to perform his obligations under the contract. The decision to terminate a contract for default is not one that Contracting Officers take lightly. Acquisition officials are required to exercise judgment in terminating an agreement for default, and they are not automatons. Moreover, the government's rights as expressed in the Default articles do not replace rights and remedies prescribed in other standard contract provisions. The Equal Opportunity article provides that the contract may be terminated, or suspended, in whole or in part if the contractor fails to comply with the clause or any rule, regulation, or order of the Secretary of Labor concerning the equal opportunity program. Labor laws contain similar provisions. The Service Contract Act of 1965 likewise provides that any failure to comply with the Act may be grounds for terminating the contract for default. In the discussion that follows, however, only the Default articles will be considered.

## DEFAULT ARTICLES

The termination of a contract for default is the exercise of the government's express right to completely or partially terminate a contract because of the contractor's actual or anticipatory failure to perform its contractual obligations. If the contractor can establish, or if it is otherwise determined, that the contractor was not in default, or if the failure to perform was excusable (i.e., the failure arose out of causes beyond the control and without the negligence of the contractor), the Default clauses set forth in section 52.249 of the FAR provide that the default termination will be considered to have been a termination for the convenience of the government. If so proven, the rights and obligations of the parties will be governed by the termination for convenience provisions of the contract.

The Default (fixed-price supply and service) clause provides that the government *may,* by written notice to the contractor, terminate the contract in whole or in part if the contractor fails to meet his obligations and duties under the contract. *See* FAR § 52.249-8. For the purpose of the discussion that follows, it is appropriate to analyze both the stated and the unstated bases for termination:

*Stated Grounds*

1. Failure to deliver within the time specified.
   a. Failure to deliver on time (i.e., the exact date specified in the delivery schedule).
   b. Failure of the item furnished to strictly comply with the specifications, even though the item is delivered on or before the date specified in the delivery schedule.
2. Failure to make progress.
   a. Failure to make such progress that it will be impossible for the contractor to deliver [or complete performance] on time.
   b. Abandonment, repudiation, demonstrated inability of the contractor to perform, or an act of bankruptcy.
3. Failure to perform other provisions of [the] contract.
   a. Buy American Act.
   b. Any of the labor provisions in the contract including equal opportunity employment provisions.
   c. Any other provision such as gratuities, covenant against contingency fees, et cetera.

*Unstated Grounds*

1. Submission of false claim[s] against the Government as defined in the False Claims Act.
2. Commission of fraud against the Government.
3. Being involved in a conflict of interest or kickback.[1]
4. Being convicted of a capital crime.

The Default articles do not *require* the government to terminate on finding a bare default, but merely give the acquiring agency the discretionary right to do so. The existence of discretion is undeniable. The clause says that the "Government *may* terminate," not "shall" or "must." It has been recognized that a decision to terminate for convenience is rooted in discretion, and though the factors the government will wish to consider may be different when a default is involved, there is no reason to read the Default article, contrary to its literal terms and accepted practice, as compelling termination. *Schlesinger v. United States,* 182 Ct. Cl. 571, 390 F.2d 702 (1968).

In general, the Default articles may be looked on as a limitation of remedies clause, which results in a forfeiture of rights by the contractor. The articles establish the rights of the government and the procedures it must follow in the event the contractor fails to perform his contractual obligation. In this light, it has been held that the Default articles are administrative substitutes for the common law breach of contract doctrine. *Gardner Constr. Co.,* DOTCAB No. 70-18, 73-2 BCA 10, 342.

When the Default articles are invoked, the government is not liable for the contractor's costs on undelivered work and is entitled to repayment of any advance or progress payments made to the contractor. The clause does not permit the Contracting Officer to use it as authority to acquire any completed supplies or manufacturing materials, unless it is ascertained that the government has acquired title under some other provision of the contract. If the government has acquired title, it is required to pay the contractor the contract price for such supplies or the amount agreed to by the parties for any manufacturing materials acquired by the government. Furthermore, the contractor is liable to the government for any excess costs incurred in acquiring supplies or services similar to those terminated for default and for any other damages, whether or not repurchase is effected. *See* FAR § 49.402-2.

## DESIGNATED OFFICIAL TO INVOKE DEFAULT

Settlement negotiations are often had with a Contracting Officer's superiors or with other authorized officials in the agency. Plainly, the superiors have at least normal authority to participate in settlements. The courts have often declared that a contractor is entitled to a finding by the contractually agreed-on officer and that a decision by someone else is a nullity. When the Contracting Officer fails to perform the duties imposed on him by the contract, the courts view it as their duty to perform this service and pass on the legal rights of the contractor. Moreover, the parties will not be required to exhaust the administrative procedures if it is shown by clear evidence that such procedure is inadequate or unavailable. *New York Shipbuilding Corp. v. United States,* 180 Ct. Cl. 446, 385 F.2d 427 (1967).

The extremely serious nature of a termination for default has long been recognized by the courts and Boards of Contract Appeals, and every reasonable presumption against the party invoking it will be drawn. It has been held that if the provisions of the contract are valid and binding on the parties thereto, the annulment of the contract must have been within the rights and authority of the officers of the government by whom it was annulled, and their actions in annulling the contract cannot be questioned or revised by the court, unless the officers are shown to have acted in bad faith. It has been conclusively settled by the courts that contract provisions of this character, vesting in the officer discretionary power over the prosecution of the work, are proper and valid and that the action of the officer in the exercise of such discretionary power cannot be revised or set aside by the courts unless it affirmatively appears that the officer acted in bad faith. *King v. United States*, 37 Ct. Cl. 428 (1902).

In *King, supra*, the contract provided that the "engineer in charge," with the prior approval of the chief of engineers, might annul the contract by giving written notice to the contractor. It called for the "judgment of the engineer in charge" and gave him alone "power" to annul the contract, assuming that he obtained the prior approval of his superior designated in the contract. The notice of termination was signed by an assistant engineer, and the termination was therefore found to be improper.

Where the Contracting Officer stated not only that he was directed to terminate a contract for default, but also that he did not feel that he had any choice after the receipt of the direction from a superior, the court held that the Navy used the termination article as a "device" and that it had never made a judgment as to the merits of the case. The courts have consistently refused to sanction such abdication of responsibility where there is administrative discretion under a contract. This protective rule should have special application for a default termination that has the drastic consequence of leaving the contractor without any further compensation. *Schlesinger v. United States*, 182 Ct. Cl. 571, 390 F.2d 702 (1968). A Contracting Officer's discretionary decision must reflect his reasoned judgment, based on the investigation and evaluation of the evidence reasonably available at the time the decision is made. *Apec International Management Services*, 60 Comp. Gen. 172.

## PROCEDURES FOR INVOKING DEFAULT

When a default termination is being considered, the procuring agency is required by the FAR to determine which type of termination action (i.e., default, convenience, or no-cost cancellation) is most appropriate under the circumstances. A default termination action may be initiated only after review by contractual and technical personnel and by counsel to ensure the propriety of the proposed action. In determining whether to terminate a contract for default, the Contracting Officer is required to consider such factors as

1. The terms of the contract and the applicable laws and regulations;
2. The specific failure of the contractor and the excuses for that failure;
3. The availability of the supplies or services from other sources;

4. The urgency of the need for the supplies or services and the period of time required to obtain them from other sources, as compared with the time delivery could be obtained from the delinquent contractor;
5. The degree of essentiality of the contractor in the government acquisition program and the effect of a termination for default on the contractor's capability as a supplier under other contracts;
6. The effect of a termination for default on the ability of the contractor to liquidate guaranteed loans, progress payments, or advance payments; and
7. Any other pertinent facts and circumstances. *See* FAR § 49.402-3.

## FAILURE TO MAKE TIMELY DELIVERY

It has long been held that time is of the essence in any government contract specifying fixed dates for delivery or performance. Accordingly, if the contractor fails to perform within the time specified, or an extension thereof, the Default article authorizes the government to terminate the contract, in whole or in part, by written notice to the contractor. As a practical matter, the government is habitually lenient in granting reasonable extensions of time for contract performance because it is more interested in production than litigation. Nevertheless, it may terminate the contract immediately after the close of business on the exact date specified in the schedule. *Texas Aerospace Services,* ASBCA No. 19278, 77-2 BCA 12,623; *motion for reconsideration denied,* 77-2 BCA 12,732.

The government need not issue a 10-day cure notice when it terminates for failure to make timely delivery. In a contract to provide lifeguard services, the contractor was found to have defaulted by stopping payment on the lifeguards' payroll checks, which caused the lifeguards to stop work for two hours. The general rule with respect to service contracts is that a failure to perform services that are required to be performed daily is not curable. It is equivalent to a failure to deliver supplies on time and will support a termination for default without prior notice. That rule is qualified by the condition that the failure must be substantial. The magnitude and severity of the failure must be considered, and if it is so minor or infrequent as to be insubstantial, then the contractor may not properly be defaulted under subsection (a)(i) of the Termination for Default clause. *Building Maintenance Specialists,* ASBCA No. 25552, 85-3 BCA 18,300. But, according to a decision handed down by the Claims Court in *Lewis B. Udis v. United States,* 7 Cl. Ct. 379, a contractor who fails to make timely delivery must nevertheless be given an opportunity to show the government why he is late. In this event, a show cause letter may suffice.

Similarly, a contract for lawn maintenance services required the contractor to mow lawns approximately once every two weeks and to edge properties and clip shrubbery once a month. The contractor stopped performance after a few cuttings in the early part of the season. His failure to mow the lawns in each biweekly period constituted a separate default under the contract, which did not require cure notices prior to termination. *Cleanway Janitorial Services,* HUD BCA Nos. 79-422-C41 & 79-423-C41, 80-2 BCA 14,792.

A contractor's contention that his failure to perform was excusable because the resignation of his key personnel caused a delay in the delivery of a first article test report was rejected because the evidence did not establish that the departure of those employees actually caused a delay. The record did not indicate the actual effect of the employees' departure on the performance of the contract. Consequently, the contractor was unable to prove that the delay was the result of causes beyond his control or without his fault or negligence, and, thus, he did not establish that the delay was excusable. *UOP Instruments Division,* ASBCA No. 14540, 70-2 BCA 8484.

In those instances where the contract requires delivery in increments, the entire contract can be terminated for default when the contractor fails to meet any incremental delivery schedule. Where the government is held to be estopped from terminating one or more increments for a delivery failure, it nonetheless retains the right to terminate subsequent increments for delivery failure since each delivery failure of later increments creates a new right in the government to terminate that increment or the entire remaining contract. *Prestex,* ASBCA No. 21284, 81-1 BCA 14,882.

A material breach does not automatically and ipso facto end a contract. It merely gives the injured party the right to end the agreement. The injured party can choose between canceling the contract and continuing it. If he decides to close the contract and so conducts himself, both parties are relieved of their further obligations, and the injured party is entitled to damages to the end of the contract term. If he elects instead to continue the contract, the obligations of both parties remain in force, and the injured party may retain only a claim for damages for partial breach. A contract—and the government's right to terminate—remains in effect, regardless of any prior breach by the government, where a contractor fails to put an end to the contract due to government breach before the government exercises its right to terminate. *National Helium Corp. v. United States,* 211 Ct. Cl. 222, 543 F.2d 1306 (1976). Moreover, the government may condone nondelivery without, at the same time, yielding its right to insist on a demonstration of progress toward contract goals. *A.B.G. Instrument & Engineering v. United States,* 219 Ct. Cl. 381, 593 F.2d 394 (1979).

## FAILURE TO MEET SPECIFICATION REQUIREMENTS

In the absence of unusual facts or circumstances, the government has the right to demand strict compliance with all contract provisions. Where performance fails to conform to the contract's specifications, this can be the basis for default termination, even if delivery is timely, since such failure constitutes nondelivery under the Default articles.

A contract for bearing shell assemblies was properly terminated for default because the contractor only offered bearings in which misdrilled holes were repaired and new holes drilled, rather than bearings drilled in exact compliance with the drawings and specifications of the contract. Since the government has the right to insist on performance in accordance with the specifications and other requirements of the contract, it was within its contractual rights in refusing to accept supplies not conforming to those requirements. The contractor had not at any time before the receipt of the termination notice offered to deliver bearings manufactured in conformity with the contract drawings and specifications. On the contrary, the contractor continued to offer bearings in which misdrilled holes were repaired and new holes drilled even though the government had stated unequivocally on several occasions that requested waivers or deviations would not be granted and that the repaired bearings would not be accepted. Under these circumstances, the contractor's failure to continue performance amounted to an abandonment of its contractual obligations, justifying an immediate termination for default. *Manistique Tool & Mfg. Co.*, ASBCA No. 19417, 74-2 BCA 10,832.

Under the doctrine of substantial compliance, the contractor may be entitled to relief even though the articles delivered did not conform precisely to the requirements of the specification. In order to obtain relief under the doctrine, the contractor must demonstrate in good faith that (1) the items shipped substantially compiled with the contract's specifications, (2) the items were timely delivered, and (3) the contractor had reasonable cause to believe that the items were acceptable and the defects minor and correctable within a reasonable time. Once these conditions have been met, the contractor must be given a reasonable time within which to cure the defects, thereby precluding the issuance of a default termination even if the time extends beyond the original delivery date. *Radiation Technology v. United States*, 177 Ct. Cl. 227 (1966); *Nanofast*, ASBCA No. 12545, 69-1 BCA 7566. And the doctrine applies to both supply and construction contracts. *HLC & Assocs. Constr. Co. v. United States*, 176 Ct. Cl. 285, 367 F.2d 586 (1966).

## GOVERNMENT WAIVER OF RIGHTS

If the government fails to exercise its right to terminate immediately upon a contractor's failure to make timely delivery, it may have waived that right. It has often been said that the term "waiver" is a troublesome term in the law. It is a flexible word with no definite and rigid meaning, and since it may be used in many senses, it is often of equivocal significance. While the term has various meanings depending on the context, it is nevertheless capable of taking a very definite meaning from the context in which it appears. Waiver is generally defined as an intentional relinquishment of a known right. As minimum requirements to constitute an implied waiver of substantial rights, the conduct relied on must be clear, decisive, and unequivocal, showing a purpose to waive the legal rights involved before such conduct constitutes a waiver. *United States v. Chichester,* 312 F.2d 275 (9th Cir. 1963).

If the government rejects items submitted for first article approval and does not terminate the contract as it could have, but instead notifies the contractor in writing of the defects it had found, its actions raise the presumption that the contractor was to rework and resubmit the items for approval. It was reasonable for the contractor to presume that if termination was elected, it would be forthcoming within the deadline for resubmission. Telling the contractor what the defects were, without more, and not accompanied by a termination, in effect was a notice of election that the government would not terminate and that the contractor was to make a second submission. The detailed listing of deficiencies would have been unnecessary if the government meant to terminate, but was vital to facilitate corrections if that option was elected. The courts have followed the principle that a default termination is a drastic sanction and have held the government to strict accountability for its actions in enforcing this sanction. By electing to permit a contractor to continue performance past a due date, the government surrenders its alternative under the Default clause to terminate, assuming that the contractor has not abandoned performance and that a reasonable time has expired for a termination notice to be given. This is popularly, if inaccurately, referred to as a "waiver" of the right to terminate. *H.N. Bailey & Assocs. v. United States,* 196 Ct. Cl. 156, 449 F.2d 387 (1971). In order to establish that the government intended to waive its right to terminate a contract for default, there must be evidence that the government manifested an intention not to terminate for failure to make timely delivery and that the contractor relied on that manifestation in continuing production. *Switlik Parachute Co. v. United States,* 216 Ct. Cl. 362, 573 F.2d 1228 (1973).

The determination as to what conduct constitutes an election or waiver is more conjectural than to prescribe the proper method of effecting a valid termination once the election has occurred. The necessary elements of an election by the nondefaulting party to waive default in delivery under a contract are (1) failure to terminate within a reasonable time after the default under circumstances indicating forbearance, and (2) reliance by the contractor on the failure to terminate and continued performance by him under the contract, with the government's knowledge and implied or express consent.

What is a reasonable time for the government to terminate a contract after default depends on the circumstances of each case. Notice of failure or of the possibility of termination for default is not required to be sent to the contractor before the actual notice of termination when the contractor has defaulted for failure to make delivery (*see* FAR § 49.402–3), implying that the Contracting Officer is required to issue a termination notice "at once." The period for default termination will naturally be greater where the contractor abandons performance, or where his situation is such as to render performance impossible or unlikely, than where he continues performance in reliance on the lack of termination and proceeds to incur obligations in an effort to perform.

Time is of the essence in any contract containing fixed dates for performance. When a due date has passed and the contract has not been terminated for default within a reasonable time, the inference is created that time is no longer of the essence so long as the constructive election not to terminate continues and the contractor proceeds with performance. The proper way thereafter for time to again become of the essence is for the government to issue notice under the Default clause, setting a reasonable, but specific, time for performance on pain of default. The election to waive performance remains in force until the time specified in the notice, and, thereupon, time is reinstated as being of the essence. The notice must set a new time for performance that is both reasonable and specific from the standpoint of the performance capabilities of the contractor at the time the notice is given. *D. Joseph DeVito v. United States,* 188 Ct. Cl. 979, 413 F.2d 1147 (1969); *see also* FAR § 49.402–3.

## FAILURE TO MAKE PROGRESS

The government may also terminate a contract for default before the specified delivery date if the contractor fails to make progress so as to endanger performance of the contract. This remedy is based on the policy that the government should not be required to stand idly by awaiting nondelivery by a contractor who obviously cannot meet a required delivery or performance date. Rather, the government should have the option to terminate inadequate performance in order to obtain needed supplies or services from a more capable source.

### Cure Notice Requirement

If termination for default appears appropriate after the Contracting Officer has considered the factors set forth in section 49.402-3(f) of the FAR, and if the contractor has failed to make progress, the government's right to terminate the contract for default may be exercised if the contractor does not cure such failure within 10 days after receipt of a notice from the Contracting Officer, specifying the failure. As a condition to a default termination for failure to make progress, the Contracting Officer is required to give the contractor written notice, specifying the performance failure and providing a period of 10 days (or longer, if necessary) in which to cure the failure. FAR § 49.402-3(d); *ElectroMagnetic Refinishers,* GSBCA No. 5035, 79-1 BCA 13,697; *Fairchild Scientific Corp.,* ASBCA No. 21151, 78-1 BCA 13,082; *Roberts International Corp.,* ASBCA No. 10954, 68-2 BCA 7074. Written notice, specifying such failure and providing a period of 10 days in which to cure the failure, is an established policy not to be ignored. *Dubrow Electronic Industries,* ASBCA No. 4864, 65-1 BCA 4859. If the government does not give the contractor written notice of his defects, the contractor will have no opportunity to correct them. *Bailey Specialized Buildings v. United States,* 181 Ct. Cl. 71, 404 F.2d 355 (1968). And if the contract calls for written notice, oral notice will not suffice. *United States v. Cunningham,* 125 F.2d 28 (D.C. Cir. 1941).

The cure notice must specify the progress failure in sufficient detail so as to enable the contractor to effectively utilize the opportunity to cure. Default terminations for failure to make progress have been frequently overturned on the basis that the notice to cure did not set forth performance defects with the particularity required of such a notice. *Valley Contractors,* ASBCA No. 9397, 1964 BCA 4071.

On the other hand, the termination will not be defective if the contractor was actually aware of the basis for default. If the contractor was not misled by the lack of particularity in the notice, the courts and Boards will generally find that the notice was sufficient. Hence, in a case involving a complex acquisition, the 10-day cure notice issued by the Contracting Officer merely stated that it "was apparent from the status of testing that you are failing to make progress as will permit delivery under the contract." In spite of the lack of specificity, the Board found the notice to be sufficient because (1) there had been constant communications between government representatives on the job site and the contractor concerning the contractor's performance difficulties, (2) those difficulties were well known to the contractor, and (3) the contractor was not misled or prejudiced by the Contracting Officer's failure to specify performance difficulties in greater detail. *Midwest Engineering & Constr. Co.,* ASBCA No. 5801, 1962 BCA 3289.

When deficiencies become the rule, necessitating corrections or deductions from the contract price virtually every day, overall performance of the contract can be deemed unsatisfactory even though individual problems are resolved. The repeated need for correction may itself serve as the default, making termination an appropriate remedy. It is entirely permissible for the government to make a tentative decision to terminate the contract before the expiration of the cure period, so long as the decision is subject to reconsideration if there are subsequent timely cure efforts. Similarly, there is no harm if a final decision to terminate is made before the expiration of the cure period if the contractor makes no further efforts to cure. But when an irrevocable decision to terminate is made before the end of the cure period and a contractor's timely efforts to cure are ignored, the termination is improper. *Cervetto Building Maintenance Co. v. United States,* 2 Cl. Ct. 299 (1983).

### Difficulties in Measuring Progress Failure

It is difficult at times to ascertain when a contractor's lack of progress sufficiently endangers progress so as to warrant a default termination. The Armed Services Board has held that the government properly terminated a contract for aircraft horizontal situation indicators, even though the termination came seven months after the contractor first failed to submit required test procedures, because the termination was based on lack of progress, rather than on a failure to meet the contract deadline for submitting the procedures. While the submission of the test procedures was an important indicator of the contractor's progress, it could not be considered a failure to deliver supplies or perform services under the contract, whereas the failure of submission did endanger contractor progress because the government required two or three months to finish the first article test results. The requirement for submitting the test procedures was a condition precedent, imposing a control on testing to assure the government that it could rely on the test results. *AAR Corp.,* ASBCA No. 16484, 74-1 BCA 10,653.

Where the contract required that, 10 days before the submission of preproduction samples, the contractor submit a statement to the effect that components had been manufactured, but failed to do so, it was held that the Contracting Officer properly issued a default termination prior to the earliest delivery specified in the contract because the contractor failed to make sufficient progress to assure compliance with the terms of the contract. It was found that the contractor did not at any time have a contract with his proposed supplier because he could not meet the supplier's financial guarantees. The contractor lost a great deal of time in negotiating with a supplier whose demands—not shown to be commercially unreasonable—it could not meet. The contractor also waited too long, and then failed, to find a reasonably reliable alternate source of supply. Such wasting away of time does not fulfill a contractor's obligation to make satisfactory progress toward performance of its contract. *Marmac Industries,* ASBCA No. 11861, 69-2 BCA 8067; *Mil-Craft Mfg.,* ASBCA No. 19205, 74-2 BCA 10,840.

## REPUDIATION

A separate basis for default termination is repudiation, or anticipatory breach of contract. Repudiation, as defined by section 2–610 of the Uniform Commercial Code, centers on an overt communication of intention or an action that either renders performance impossible or demonstrates a clear determination not to continue with performance. A repudiation occurs when (1) the contractor, by a positive and unequivocal statement made before performance is due, indicates that he will not perform the contract according to its terms and conditions; or (2) the contractor, although willing to continue performance, admits that he is totally unable to perform. The hallmark of anticipatory repudiation is that there must be a definite and unequivocal manifestation of intention on the part of the repudiator that he will not render the promised performance when the time fixed for it in the contract arrives. *Dingley v. Oler,* 117 U.S. 490 (1886). The government's remedy is based on breach of contract under the Default article, which provides that "the rights and remedies of the Government in this clause are in addition to any other rights provided by law or under this contract." *See* FAR § 52.249-8(h).

There could be a breach of contract before the time fixed for performance, and a positive and absolute refusal to carry out the contract prior to the date of actual default amounts to such a breach. *Roehm v. Horst,* 168 U.S. 1 (1900). Correspondence between the parties and other facts could warrant the conclusion that the contractor had abandoned the work and refused to complete the contract. Such abandonment would constitute an anticipatory breach by the contractor, which entitled the government to relet the uncompleted part of the work. *Midland Land & Improvement Co. v. United States,* 270 U.S. 251 (1926).

In those cases where anticipatory breach forms the basis for default termination, it is not necessary for the government to issue a 10-day cure notice. *Imperial Van & Storage,* ASBCA No. 11462, 67-2 BCA 6621. Termination prior to the contract performance date, without the issuance of a cure notice, on the ground of contract repudiation by the contractor requires that the government present clear and unmistakable evidence of an inability or refusal to perform. *Norfolk Air Conditioning Service & Equipment Corp.,* ASBCA No. 14000, 71-1 BCA 8617.

For example, a guard service contractor notified the Contracting Officer that it could not pay wages that were 45 cents an hour higher than the minimum wage specified in the Invitation for Bids. Because the Service Contract Act's successor contract provisions required the contractor to pay the higher wage notwithstanding the wage determination, the contractor's notice constituted an anticipatory breach of the contract. It justified the termination of the contract. *What Mac Contractors,* GSBCA No. 4766, 78-2 BCA 13, 279.

A repudiation will be found where it is evident that the contractor is totally unable to perform the contract. Accordingly, the Contracting Officer properly terminated a contract for default before the performance due date on the basis of letters from the contractor expressing an inability to perform, in which he requested that the contract be terminated for the convenience of the government. *Washington Scientific Industries,* ASBCA No. 9384, 65-2 BCA 4743. Similarly, the government was correct in terminating two requirements contracts for default because the contractor sent two letters to the Contracting Officer in which he clearly admitted an inability to continue performance due to his subcontractor's refusal to make further shipments under the contract. The letters constituted an anticipatory breach of the contract. *Charles J. Slicken Co.,* GSBCA No. 3666, 72-2 BCA 9666.

Repudiation will be found in those circumstances where a contractor makes an unequivocal statement that he will abandon the work. Hence, a termination for default was proper where the contractor, under a contract to deliver signal mixers, effectively manifested to the Contracting Officer (through correspondence and interrogatories) his abandonment of intent to perform, except under his own interpretation of the work required by the contract. The contractor persisted in his intent to abandon the contract notwithstanding the fact that the Contracting Officer, after the original delivery date had passed, but shortly before initiating termination action, had instructed the contractor to proceed with performance, thereby electing not to terminate for nonperformance and becoming obligated to afford the contractor a further reasonable time to complete performance. *Sterling Electronics,* ASBCA No. 8450, 1964 BCA 4092.

If the contractor fails to follow the instructions of the Contracting Officer to proceed with the work required by the contract, the courts and Boards, absent an adequate defense by the contractor, will view the government's default termination favorably. Hence, the Court of Claims upheld a Contracting Officer's decision to terminate a contract because the contractor refused to proceed with the removal and replacement of a tile floor, except at government expense and by a method of installation to be specified by the government. The court observed that the termination was proper if for no other reason than that the contractor refused to follow the Contracting Officer's directive. Instead, he elected to abandon the work, but such an election is simply not open to a government contractor under the standard Disputes clause, which specifically requires that "Pending final decision of a dispute hereunder, the contractor shall proceed diligently with the performance of the contract and in accordance with the Contracting Officer's decision." Therefore, the contractor could not justifiably abandon the work because of a disagreement with the Contracting Officer. *Max M. Stoeckert, d/b/a/ University Brick & Tile Co. v. United States,* 183 Ct. Cl. 152, 391 F.2d 639 (1968).

An improper omission of a cure notice and termination for default, based on acts that do not show that there has been an anticipatory repudiation of the contract, will not be upheld by the courts and Boards even though the contractor subsequently admits that he had abandoned all intention of performing the contract. The propriety of the default depends on what the government knew at the time of the termination. Although the government may reasonably infer that the contractor is not going to perform, inference is not enough. The issue of whether the contractor's alleged repudiation was unequivocally manifested to the government is not determined by reasonable inferences or educated guesses even if the inferences or guesses prove to be correct. The issue of anticipatory repudiation is determined by what was actually manifested to and perceived by the government and whether such manifestation was capable of being understood in only one way. In this connection, the settled principle that the government has the burden of proving the propriety of its action in terminating a contract for default must not be overlooked. The government must shoulder the burden of proving that it perceived an unequivocal manifestation of the contractor's alleged anticipatory repudiation. This burden, in the sense of the "risk of nonpersuasion," is not satisfied merely by evidence of the reasonableness of inferences drawn by the government. *Fairchild Scientific Corp., supra.*

The term "abandonment" does not necessarily carry a pejorative connotation so as to equate it with "anticipatory repudiation" in all instances. A promisor may be justified in abandoning performance of its obligations when the other party has committed a material breach, such as by delaying performance or otherwise rendering performance commercially impossible. Similarly, failure or unreasonable delay in making payment has been held to constitute a material breach, justifying abandonment of performance by a contractor. Therefore, abandonment of performance does not in itself justify a default termination. Of course, an unjustified abandonment of performance, accompanied by manifestation to the promisee of the promisor's unequivocal refusal to complete the contract, amounts to an anticipatory repudiation and gives rise to an immediate right of action. *Fairchild Scientific Corp., supra.*

## FAILURE TO PERFORM OTHER PROVISIONS OF CONTRACT

The standard Default articles provide that the government may terminate a contract in whole or in part if the contractor fails to perform any other provision of the contract. *See* FAR § 52.249-8(a)(1)(iii). But the government's right to terminate the contract under this subdivision of the Default article may be exercised only if the contractor does not cure such failure within 10 days, or such longer period as may be authorized in writing by the Contracting Officer, after receipt of notice from the government, specifying the failure. In order to sustain a termination under this subdivision, the government must show that the provision relied on was a "material" requirement of the contract, and hence a breach.

A contractor's failure to comply with contract requirements as to the submission of wage-hour information was held not to be a basis for termination because the failure was not proven to have been willful. Nor was the use of a disproportionate number of apprentices a basis for termination where there was no showing as to the general employment practices of the contractor or of the industry. *Conway Electric Co.,* ASBCA No. 6256, 61-1 BCA 2991. On the other hand, a default termination was proper where the evidence showed that the contractor had violated the Davis-Bacon Act by paying employees performing carpentry and painting work at laborers' salaries, contrary to the prevailing area practice of paying such employees at the mechanic wage rate. *Edgar M. Williams,* ASBCA No. 16055, 72-2 BCA 9734.

## CRIMINAL CONVICTION

Where a trucking contractor was found guilty of endeavoring to influence, obstruct, and impede the due administration of justice in a U.S. district court, in violation of 18 U.S.C. § 1503, it was held that the government properly terminated a trucking contract for default on the basis that the contractor was convicted of a crime involving corruption. Such a conviction was a valid basis for the conclusion that the contractor was not reliable, trustworthy, or of good character, which warranted termination of the contract under the Default article. The contractor argued that the individual owner was convicted, and since his corporation was the entity that had contracted with the government, his guilt was improperly imputed to the corporation. It was held that while it is generally recognized that the corporate form of organization is not to be disregarded, special problems are created with respect to family or one-man corporations. The record demonstrated that this was a family corporation. In such cases, a body of law has developed, governing the instances in which the corporate form of organization may be disregarded. It is now well settled by the great weight of authority that upon a proper showing that a corporation is but an instrumentality through which its owner or substantial owners for convenience transacts or transact his or their business, both equity and law will look through the form to its substance and will hold such corporation bound as the owner might be bound or conversely hold the owner by acts that bind his corporation. There was evidence that the actual conduct of business was not always in the corporate form. The evidence supported the conclusion that the owner had conducted the business of the corporation bearing his name essentially as a sole proprietorship. Thus, if the Contracting Officer had a reasonable basis for finding the owner untrustworthy, he may also find the corporation untrustworthy. The contractor's organization was such that the owner's transgressions could be imputed to the corporation, warranting the default termination under the circumstances. *B. Tedesco Trucking,* PSBCA No. 820, 80-2 BCA 14,818.

## EXCESS REPROCUREMENT COSTS

The Default articles provide that where the contract is terminated, in whole or in part, the government may acquire, under the terms and in the manner the Contracting Officer deems appropriate, supplies or services similar to those terminated, and the contractor shall be liable for any excess costs for those supplies or services. *See* FAR § 52.249-8. When the supplies or services are still required after termination, the government is required to repurchase the same or similar supplies or services against the contractor's account as soon as practicable. The repurchase must be made at as reasonable a price as practicable, considering quality and delivery requirements. If the repurchase is for a quantity not over the undelivered quantity terminated for default, either sealed bidding or negotiation may be used to place the reprocurement contract. If repurchase is made at a price in excess of the price of the supplies or services terminated, the Contracting Officer shall, after completion and final payment of the repurchase contract, make a written demand on the contractor for the total amount of the excesses, giving consideration to increases in other costs, such as transportation.*See* FAR § 49.402-6.

The concept of repurchasing against a defaulted contractor's account is founded on the presumption that repurchase was necessary to place the government in the same position it would have been in had the contract been completed. As to the method of acquisition (e.g., sealed bidding or negotiation) to be used by the government, the standard provision gives broad discretion to the Contracting Officer. While such broad discretion may not be abused, there is nothing in the contract provisions that could be interpreted to require reprocurement to be accomplished by a particular method of acquisition. *H&H Mfg. Co. v. United States,* 168 Ct. Cl. 873 (1964).

The FAR requires that the Contracting Officer repurchase the "same or similar supplies or services." But it is not understood that the word "similar" must in all cases be treated as meaning "identical." A composite of the definition of the word *similar,* as given in Black's and Bouvier's law dictionaries, is to the effect that it means "nearly corresponding; resembling in many respects; somewhat alike; having a general likeness or sameness in all essential particulars." Rarely has it been held to be identical. *Associated Traders v. United States,* 144 Ct. Cl. 744, 169 F. Supp. 502 (1959).

The term "similar" has thus been defined as meaning "similar in physical and mechanical characteristics as well as functional purpose." Accordingly, where the reprocured items have the same functional purpose, but the physical and mechanical characteristics vary because of relaxed specifications, it has been held that the specifications used in reprocurement were substantially different from those of the original contract and that the reprocured item was not "similar" within the intended meaning of the word as used in the Default article. *Lome Electronics,* ASBCA Nos. 8642 & 8707, 1963 BCA 3833.

Substantial and material differences in the physical characteristics of the supplies or services repurchased, as contrasted with those specified in a defaulted contract, have been repeatedly held to be such a material deviation as to render the defaulting contractor not liable for excess reprocurement costs incurred in the repurchase of allegedly "similar" goods or services. But proof of specification changes after award of the reprocurement contract does not invalidate an excess cost assessment where the changes are corrections of errors, omissions, or normal updating of specifications as more production experience leads to simplifying manufacture or production improvement, so long as the specification changes do not go to the heart of the procurement by affecting function or repurchase cost. *Consolidated Airborne Systems v. United States,* 172 Ct. Cl. 588, 348 F.2d 941 (1965); *Marmac Industries,* ASBCA No. 12158, 72-1 BCA 9249.

A reduction in quantity will generally not bar recovery by the government if discretion was reasonably exercised. However, the government may be required to absorb some increase in cost, if there was in fact an increase, and if it can be shown that the increase was directly related to the decrease in quantity.*Consolidated Airborne Systems, supra.* Conversely, the Contracting Officer may repurchase a quantity in excess of the undelivered quantity terminated for default when the excess quantity is needed, but the excess cost may not be charged against the defaulting contractor's account for more than the undelivered quantity terminated for default. *See* FAR § 49.402-6.

The government has substantial rights in a reprocurement action against a defaulted contractor, as the excess cost provision suggests. It is thus vested with broad discretion, so long as its actions are reasonable, *Barnhart-Morrow Consolidated Mono Belting Division,* ENG BCA No. 3572, 78-1 BCA 12,692, to include manufacturing the terminated items in the government's own plants if need be, *R.A. Miller Industries,* ASBCA No. 16433, 72-1 BCA 9409. In the case of urgency, this may be the appropriate course. Under such circumstances, the government would be justified in assessing the contractor with the full measure of the difference between the defaulted contract price and the government's manufacturing costs. The fact that the government cost is considerably higher, standing alone, does not make such action unreasonable or unconscionable. *Collins Electronics,* ASBCA No. 16956, 72-2 BCA 9542.

The requirements for reasonableness of reprocurement price and mitigation of excess costs are closely related, and a number of factors are applied by the courts and Boards of Contract Appeals to determine whether the government has satisfied those requirements. Specifically, consideration is given to whether (1) give-and-take negotiations were conducted, (2) a cost breakdown was obtained, (3) the government conducted any cost or price analysis, and (4) the Government obtained a satisfactory explanation for any substantial increases over the reprocurement contractor's bid on the original contract. *Solar Laboratories*, ASBCA No. 19957, 76-2 BCA 12,115.

Therefore, the amount of the government's recovery has frequently been reduced when the government did not demonstrate that it had made adequate efforts to obtain the lowest reasonable prices on the repurchase, especially where the reprocurement contract is awarded on a sole source basis. In some cases, the Boards have simply relied on the absence of an explanation for increases in the reprocurement contractor's price over his bid on the defaulted contract, or bids on other contracts for the same supplies or services, to deny recovery. *Standard Engineering & Mfg. Co.*, ASBCA No. 3733, 57-2 BCA 1477. In other cases, the Boards have emphasized specific actions the government could or should have taken, but failed to take, to assure reasonableness or mitigate excess costs—sometimes in the face of substantial increases over previous prices, at other times without mention of such increases.

When a reprocurement action against a defaulted contractor's account has been found to be defective, it is proper for the Boards to find the defaulting contractor liable for what the reprocurement cost reasonably should have been if that can be determined from the record, rather than excusing him from excess cost liability altogether. *Cable Systems Assembly Co.*, ASBCA No. 17844, 73-2 BCA 10,172. In the absence of a better measure, where the reprocurement contractor was the second low bidder contending for the defaulted contract, the Boards will frequently adopt his original bid as a means of assessing excess costs.

Before the government can collect excess costs from a defaulted contractor, it must show that final payment has been made under the reprocurement contract and that the excess cost assessment is made thereon. *Arjay Machine Co.*, ASBCA No. 16535, 73-2 BCA 10,179. Excess reprocurement costs are assessable only when the costs have in fact been incurred and are so shown by prima facie evidence. *Roflon Co. v. United States*, 7 Cl. Ct. 242 (1985).

While excess reprocurement costs have been challenged by defaulting contractors on a wide variety of grounds, the most common basis is to question the validity of the default termination itself. It is well established that the defaulting contractor may be exempted from the imposition of excess reprocurement costs if he proves by a preponderance of the evidence that the default was without his fault or negligence. *Roflon Co., supra.*

The government only has the right to assess excess repurchase costs following a valid default termination. *Coastal Bend Constr. Co.*, ASBCA No. 19628, 75-1 BCA 11,005; *Elgin National Watch Co.*, ASBCA No. 10421, 67-2 BCA 6400. If, on appeal, it is determined that the default termination was improper, the termination is treated as one for the convenience of the government. In the event the contractor failed to file a timely appeal with respect to the default termination, but did file a timely appeal with respect to the excess reprocurement costs, the question of the propriety of default itself may be raised at that time. *Clarke Enterprises,* ASBCA No. 24306, 80-2 BCA 14,548.

This decision follows the rule stated by the Armed Services Board in *Fulford Manufacturing Co.,* ASBCA Nos. 2143 & 2144, 6. Cont. Cas. Fed. (CCH) 61, 815 (1955), which has been followed by all Boards of Contract Appeals since 1955. The rationale in support of the use of the doctrine includes such factors as these: (1) a contractor may not be interested in contesting a termination for default until such time as excess reprocurement costs are assessed, (2) unnecessary litigation is avoided, and (3) the legality and propriety of a termination for default are necessarily in issue when excess reprocurement costs are in issue. Moreover, the Contract Disputes Act does not bar a contractor from contesting the propriety of a termination for default in a suit appealing a Contracting Officer's final decision, assessing excess reprocurement costs, if such a suit is filed within 12 months of that decision. *D.H. Moody & Co. v. United States,* 5 Cl. Ct. 70 (1984).

## GOVERNMENT'S RIGHT TO SET OFF

The government has the right to set off any claim it has against a contractor by refusing payment of funds that are otherwise due the contractor. In this regard, the Comptroller General has stated at Comp. Gen. B-163625 (1968) and Comp. Gen. B-176791 (1972) that:

> The right to set-off has been held to be inherent in the United States and to be grounded in the common law right of every creditor to apply the monies of his debtor in his hands to the extinguishment of the amounts due him from the debtor. *Gratiot v. United States,* 40 U.S. 336 (1941); *McKnight v. United States,* 98 U.S. 176 (1878); *Barry v. United States,* 229 U.S. 47 (1913). Thus, where a person is both a debtor and a creditor to the Government in any form, the accounting officers of the Government are required by law to consider both the debts and credits and to set off one indebtedness against the other, and certify only the balance. *Taggert v. United States,* 17 Ct. Cl. 322 (1881). The Government's right to set off a contractor's debts against contract proceeds extends to debts owed by the contractor as a result of separate and independent transactions. *United States v. Munsey Trust Co.,* 332 U.S. 234 (1947). Where the amount due the Government had not been finalized under the procedures provided by the contract, we sanctioned the unilateral deduction of the amount estimated by the Government to be due.

In both *Dale Ingram, Inc. v. United States,* 201 Ct. Cl. 56, 475 F.2d 1177 (1973), and *Project Map v. United States,* 203 Ct. Cl. 52, 486 F.2d 1375 (1973), the government withheld payment of a sum awarded by the Board of Contract Appeals on one contract because there were then pending before the Board disputes as to another of the respective contractor's agreements under which the Contracting Officer had held the contractors indebted to the government in a larger sum. Both plaintiffs argued that the failure to pay the conceded sums was a breach of contract, entitling the claimants to immediate judgment. The court rejected the arguments of both plaintiffs on the ground that the government has the right of offset with respect to the decision of the Contracting Officer on the other contract now pending before the Board, in which the Contracting Officer held that plaintiffs were indebted to the government for sums greater than the amount withheld. The decisions of the Contracting Officer in this regard are final and binding until and unless they are reversed or overturned on appeal.

## COMMON LAW BREACH DAMAGES

The Default articles specifically provided that the "rights and remedies of the government in this clause are in addition to any other rights and remedies provided by law or under this contract." *See* FAR, § 52.249-8(h). Under these provisions of the FAR, the government may elect to pursue other remedies available to it, instead of, or in addition to, assessing excess reprocurement costs.

Where it was found that the government had not made its reprocurement in a reasonable time, it lost its contractual right to assess excess reprocurement costs. Subsequently, the government set off the amount of excess costs incurred in the reprocurement against a later production contract. To ascertain the final position of the parties vis-à-vis one another, it had to be determined whether the government had a valid claim for common law breach of contract damages and, if so, how those damages were to be measured. The government, as any private party, has a common law right to damages for breach of contract, measured by the difference between the contract price and the reasonable replacement cost of the contract items, in addition to specific contract remedies. *Rumley v. United States,* 152 Ct. Cl. 166, 285 F.2d 773 (1961). Case law clearly supports the proposition that the government is entitled to common law damages in addition to other remedies in the contract. The government has a right, as a matter of law, to seek common law damages in the Claims Court, despite a loss of the express contractual right to excess costs. *Morley v. United States,* 152 Ct. Cl. 205, 423 F.2d 324 (1970).

More importantly, neither the *Rumley* nor the *Morley* decision suggests or even hints that the government must first exercise its contractual right to excess costs before resorting to its right to common law damages. Rather, the government can utilize in default termination situations either, or both, of the two remedy avenues available to it under the provisions of the contract. If, in a given situation, the government utilized the "excess cost" approach and recovered only the difference between the defaulted contract price and the reprocurement contract price, it would not be precluded from seeking in a judicial action additional costs it incurred as a result of a contractor's breach. The government may seek to recover all damages that are the foreseeable, direct, natural, and proximate results of the breach. Recovery may be had for all additional costs, to include properly established "administrative costs." *Tester Corp. v. United States,* 1 Cl. Ct. 370 (1982).

## DEFAULTED CONTRACTOR ELIGIBLE FOR AWARD OF REPURCHASE CONTRACT

Although the government need not, in all cases, consider a defaulted contractor for reprocurement, the defaulted contractor may be permitted to bid on the repurchase solicitation. If the defaulted contractor is found to be responsible and capable of performance, responsive to the solicitation, and the lowest bidder, he may receive the repurchase contract. If awarded the reprocurement contract, the defaulted contractor, notwithstanding his submission of the lowest bid, may not receive more than the initial contract price for his reprocurement performance. *Churchill Chemical Corp. v. United States,* 221 Ct. Cl. 284, 602 F.2d 358 (1979).

## NOTE

1. Carl L. Vaketta, "Litigating Contract Performance Problems Before Boards of Contract Appeals: Changes, Terminations for Contractor Default and Terminance for the Convenience of the Government," in *Government Contract Litigation: The Current Status* (Washington, D.C.: American Law Institute, American Bar Association, 1985), p. 169.

# 10

# Impossibility of Performance

## INTRODUCTION

Primary considerations in determining whether the contractor or the government should bear responsibility for unexpected performance difficulties are the nature of the contract and its specifications and the relative expertise of the parties. In this context, two bases for nonperformance will be explored. First, circumstances of extreme difficulty, traditionally referred to as "impossibility of performance," that prevent performance of a contractual obligation will be examined. Second, in limited circumstances, the government may have a duty to disclose its superior knowledge regarding the subject matter of the contract if such knowledge is vital to contract performance. Failure to fulfill this duty may be viewed as a breach of contract by the government.

## DOCTRINE OF IMPOSSIBILITY

A default termination is the government's way of telling the contractor that he has breached the contract. In a default termination, the government assumes the risk of having the termination converted to one for convenience if it is wrong and the contract so provides. When the government actually issues the termination notice, it runs that risk. It takes only one valid defense to void a default termination, and impossibility of performance is a classic defense to a breach of contract action. *Dynaelectron Corp. (Pacific Division) v. United States,* 207 Ct. Cl. 349, 518 F.2d 594 (1975). Although actual or economic impossibility may excuse nonperformance, mere performance difficulties will not provide a basis for relief for the contractor. If other contractors, manufacturers, or producers have demonstrated the capacity to accomplish the objective of the contract, a defaulting contractor's inability to perform is not a sufficient basis to establish impossibility.

Performance difficulties arising during the term of the contract present questions as to whether the contractor or the government should bear the responsibility for unanticipated burdens. Either the government or the contractor may assume a risk of performance under the contract, including the risk of impossibility of performance, and the relative expertise of the parties regarding the subject matter of the contract will typically suggest which party assumes a particular risk.

A contractor who suggests a method of performance that is accepted by the government is deemed responsible for its success in the absence of an express assumption of responsibility by the government. Similarly, performance specifications place responsibility on the contractor for establishing methods and procedures to accomplish the objectives of the contract. Performance requirements beyond the state of the art, however, may exceed the contractor's promise, unless he has expressly assumed that risk. The contractor is obligated to perform that which he has undertaken. Mere performance difficulties, short of actual or economic impossibility, will not excuse a contractor from performing his promise.

On the other hand, the risk of impossibility may have been assumed by the government if it provides detailed design specifications, under the theory that the government warrants that satisfactory performance is possible if the contractor complies fully with the specifications. When defective specifications are followed and satisfactory performance does not result, the contract may be considered impossible to perform. By insisting on its design specifications, particularly in the light of known deficiencies, the government accepts the responsibility for their impossibility. If the government requires performance by other than the specified means, the contractor may recover excess costs incurred in attempting to perform according to the change.

The doctrine of impossibility is concerned primarily with those situations where extra work is performed by the contractor because the requirements of the specifications could not be accomplished without an inordinate expenditure of resources. For the contractor to recover under such circumstances, it is not essential to demonstrate actual impossibility. Rather, a showing that it is practically impossible to produce the desired object of the contract will generally suffice.

Fundamentally, the doctrine of impossibility involves two essential elements: (1) that the work is not within the contractual objectives agreed to by the parties; and (2) that the costs and difficulty of the work render the work commercially senseless. Thus, in legal contemplation, something is impracticable when it can only be done at an excessive cost. *Hol-Gar Mfg. Corp. v. United States*, 175 Ct. Cl. 518, 360 F.2d 634 (1966); *United States v. Wegmatic*

*Corp.,* 360 F.2d 674 (2d Cir. 1966). The doctrine represents the ever-shifting line, drawn by courts hopefully responsive to commercial practices and mores, at which the community's interest in having contracts enforced according to their terms is outweighed by the commercial senselessness of requiring performance. *Transatlantic Financing Corp. v. United States,* 363 F.2d 312 (D.C. Cir. 1966). To establish commercial impossibility, the contractor must demonstrate that the work called for by the contract specifications was either absolutely or practically impossible to perform. In order to do this, the contractor must not only establish his own failure of performance, but also prove that no one else could have performed under such circumstances. *General Instrument Corp.,* DOTCAB No. 67-9A1, 72-1 BCA 9389. But if the contractor was aware of the impossibility of performance, having been forewarned, he is generally held to have assumed the risk of impossibility. *Canadian Commercial Corp.,* ASBCA No. 17187, 76-2 BCA 12,145.

Where a small business concern failed to meet the requirements of a performance-type specification, calling for the production of power supply units for use with Army radios, the Armed Services Board concluded that practical, legal impossibility of performance had been established by the contractor. This ruling took into consideration the lack of evidence indicating inadequate technical competence on the part of the contractor or its approach to the solution of design problems, as well as the fact that the precise unit had not previously been manufactured. In addition, it was found that the government had assumed—as reflected in the brevity of the schedule and the use of small business set-aside provisions in a sealed-bid procurement—that the contract work could be performed by a small business concern without the technical or financial capacity to carry out an extended design program. In reaching its decision, the Board thought it doubtful that the contractor had made out a case of literal impossibility of performance.

There may, however, be legal impossibility without literal impossibility. The Restatement of Contracts in Section 454 (1932) states that "impossibility means not only strict impossibility but impracticability because of extreme and unreasonable difficulty, expense, injury or loss involved." The first comment of that section of the Restatement limits the situation by explaining that "Mere unanticipated difficulty, however, not amounting to impracticability is not within the scope of the definition." It has been suggested that a workable definition of practical impossibility would be to say that it "means not possible within the basic objectives contemplated by the parties—as evidenced by the contract itself and surrounding circumstances." In this case, the contractor's efforts to perform the contract were far in excess of what it might have reasonably have expected from all the circumstances and made evident to it at the time of bidding for the contract. *Johnson Electronics,* ASBCA No. 9366, 65-1 BCA 4628.

Except so far as a seller may have assumed a greater obligation, delay in delivery or nondelivery is not a breach of his duty under a contract for sale if performance as agreed has been made impracticable by the occurrence of a contingency the nonoccurrence of which was a basic assumption on which the contract was made. U.C.C. § 2-615; *United States v. Wegmatic Corp., supra.* The case is different where the contractor draws up the specifications and thereby undertakes a firm obligation to perform thereunder. *Austin Co. v. United States,* 161 Ct. Cl. 76, 314 F.2d 518, *cert. denied,* 375 U.S. 830 (1963).

A thing is impossible in legal contemplation when it is not practicable; and a thing is impracticable when it can only be accomplished at an excessive and unreasonable cost. When the issue is raised, the court is asked to construct a condition of performance based on the changed circumstances, a process that involves at least three reasonably definable steps. First, a contingency—something unexpected—must have occurred. Second, the risk of the unexpected occurrence must not have been allocated either by agreement or by custom. Finally, occurrence of the contingency must have rendered performance commercially impracticable. Unless the court finds these three requirements satisfied, the plea of impossibility must fail. Moreover, when performance of a contract is deemed impossible, it is a nullity. *Foster Wheeler Corp. v. United States,* 206 Ct. Cl. 533, 513 F.2d 588 (1975); *Natus Corp. v. United States,* 178 Ct. Cl. 1, 371 F.2d 450 (1967); *Transatlantic Financing Corp. v. United States, supra.* The excuse of legal impossibility is only available where, under government specifications, failure to perform is due to the circumstance that no way is known in industry how to manufacture the supplies in question according to the specified design or performance characteristics. *J.A. Maurer Inc. v. United States,* 202 Ct. Cl. 813, 485 F.2d 588 (1973).

If a contractor proves the "impracticability" (i.e., "commercial impossibility") of performing a contract, he is entitled to recover his costs of attempting to perform the contract. *Foster Wheeler Corp. v. United States, supra; Stock & Grove v. United States,* 204 Ct. Cl. 103, 493 F.2d 629 (1974); *Tombigbee Constructors v. United States,* 190 Ct. Cl. 615, 420 F.2d 1037 (1970). However, as the Armed Services Board emphasized in *Patushin Aviation Co.,* ASBCA Nos. 21243 & 22960, 82-1 BCA 15,639, mere difficulty not amounting to commercial impracticability is not an excusable cause of default. *See Firestone Tire & Rubber Co. v. United States,* 214 Ct. Cl. 457, 558 F.2d 577 (1977); *Natus Corp. v. United States, supra.* Commercial impossibility, as a legal theory, is measured by objective rather than subjective standards. *ESB, Inc.,* ASBCA No. 22914, 81-1 BCA 15,012. Claims of impossibility are frequently rejected where another contractor has been shown to have produced the item under the identical specification. *Tech Power Co.,* ASBCA No. 16399, 72-2 BCA 9563.

Once commercial impracticability has been established, the courts and Boards of Contract Appeals will examine the contractual relationship of the parties and allocate the risk of impossibility to whichever party should bear responsibility for the failure of contract performance. Under section 456 of the Restatement of Contracts, the risk shifts to the government in those situations where neither party can foresee the event that creates the difficulties:

> Parties may bind themselves by contract to perform what is in fact impossible. It is only where the promissor has no reason to know of the facts to which the impossibility is due, and where he does not agree to bear the risk of their existence that the formation of a contract is prevented. Parties deal with reference to unknown existing facts in the same way that they do with supervening events and so does the law. Risk is not assumed by [the] promissor unless, on an interpretation of the contract in the light of accompanying circumstances and usages, an intention is manifested that it shall be assumed.

This doctrine was applied in *E.L. Cournand & Co.*, ASBCA No. 2955, 60-2 BCA, where the major issue in dispute was whether the contract was correctly terminated for default or whether, as the contractor contended, it should have been terminated for the convenience of the government on the basis that it was impossible to comply with the specifications. The contract called for the development and application of new metal and nonmetal substances for use in missile containers. The Board held that it had had occasions before to refer to the settled principle of law that in the absence of exceptional circumstances, a contractor has the right to rely on the government's specifications and can be charged with no responsibility for their inadequacy if such they prove to possess, with particular reference to the statement of this rule in *R.M. Hollingshead Corp. v. United States*, 124 Ct. Cl. 681, 111 F. Supp. 285 (1953). The plaintiff in *Cournand* urged that because of a mutual mistake as to a material fact, the parties made a contract that was impossible to perform. It argued that since the government prepared the contract, which specified that the liquid should be shipped in metal containers, it implicitly represented that if the specifications were complied with, satisfactory performance would result.

It is easy, of course, to imagine a situation where a person has in mind the manufacture of an object, but no special knowledge of the process of its manufacture, and he places an order with a factory to manufacture the specified article out of specified materials. If the manufacturer knows, or perhaps from his experience should know, that the desired article cannot be made from the specified materials, he has no right to make a useless thing and charge the customer for it. But when the government, through one of its important agencies, orders the production of a specified thing by specified means, it would be a rare instance when the supplier could reasonably be expected to investigate for himself whether compliance would in fact produce the desired result. In accord is *GTE Sylvania*, DOTCAB No. 78-57, 79-2 BCA 14,069, where a default termination of a contract to manufacture and supply halogen lamps was converted to one for the convenience of the government because the specifications were impossible to perform and the contractor had not assumed the risk of performing impossible specifications.

A contractor was entitled to recover all costs incurred in attempting to perform a contract for the first mass production of an electronic device, even though it was operating at a loss when the contract was terminated for the convenience of the government, because it was impossible to meet the contract's performance specifications. The contract was the production phase of a prior research and development effort, but the specification requirements for the production contract included some specific requirements that clearly exceeded those of the earlier undertaking. Principal problems encountered by the contractor pertained to the specification limitation on input power and the contractor's inability to locate a transistor in chip form from either commercial or government sources that met all the performance functions necessary to produce a successful module. *Scope Electronics,* ASBCA No. 20359, 77-1 BCA 12,404. Moreover, the fact that the product, built to government design, had to meet test specification performance requirements does not shift the risk of design inadequacies to the contractor. *Radionics,* ASBCA No. 22727, 81-1 BCA 15,011.

If the contractor knew, or should have known, from the nature and object of the contract that compliance with specifications might be impossible to attain, the contractor is generally held to assume the risk of that impossibility. This is particularly so if performance is based on the contractor's specifications, or if the contractor is deemed to have superior expertise. Under such a contract, the contractor's obligation goes beyond the mere duty to exercise the skill and competence of ordinary prudent and skillful craftsmen engaged in a similar field or enterprise; his obligation does not stop until performance is reached, and if the task is impossible, he must bear the cost attributable to nonperformance. *Austin Co.,* ASBCA No. 4255, 61-1 BCA 2927.

Additionally, once a contractor knows, or should reasonably know, of the deficiency, a requirement to place the government on notice exists. Such notification enables the government to determine whether to continue performance of the contract and whether continued performance is the most feasible and economic means of correction. *Vector Plastics Corp.,* ASBCA No. 9552, 65-2 BCA 5286. *See also Austin Co. v. United States,* 161 Ct. Cl. 76 (1963).

In those instances where the contractor represents that he possesses more than ordinary expertise and capability, assuring the government that he has developed novel and revolutionary technical processes, and the Government awards a contract to him in reliance on such assurances, the contractor must bear the responsibility for failure to perform. In *United States v. Wegmatic Corp.,* 360 F.2d 674 (2d Cir. 1966), the defaulting contractor was not excused from paying liquidated damages, excess reprocurement costs, and useless preparatory costs to the government because it encountered unexpected technical difficulties in manufacturing a new computer of its own design and in accordance with its own specifications.

The foregoing does not stand for the proposition that if a contractor specializes in a particular field or manufactures a certain product line, the consequences of impossibility will be imputed to him. Rather, it must be shown that the contractor possessed special knowledge that induced the government to award the contract to him. Applying this rule in *Ryan Aeronautical Co.*, ASBCA No. 13366, 70-1 BCA 8287, it was held that the Contracting Officer improperly issued a default termination upon the contractor's failure to meet contract requirements that were impossible of performance because the contractor did not assume the risk of impossibility. The government prescribed as a specification requirement the use of a specified guidance system, and with that system, the landing accuracy specified in the contract could not be met. The government contended that the contractor's past experience gave it superior knowledge on which the government relied in awarding the contract and that the contractor therefore assumed the risk of impossibility. The contractor had had no experience with the landing requirements, as none of its prior contracts had contained such a requirement. In accepting the contract, the contractor relied on the adequacy of the government-furnished guidance system without making any independent investigation. Despite the extensive experience of the contractor, the government, through the conduct of in-house effort, had superior specific knowledge of the circular error probability requirements of the precision drop glider in an automatic homing mode that was the object of the contract. Having acquired this knowledge, the government was under a duty to make full and effective disclosure thereof to the contractor and other prospective bidders so as to alert them to the proportions of the task that lay ahead, which otherwise they could not reasonably have anticipated. *Helene Curtis Industries v. United States,* 160 Ct. Cl. 437, 312 F.2d 774 (1963); *Johnson Electronics,* ASBCA No. 9366, 65-1 BCA 4628. The government's failure to do so at the time of negotiations is inconsistent with an assumption of the risk of impossibility by the contractor.

Conversely, the Court of Claims held that a contractor who attempted, but failed, to make a lineal survey of a rocket test track could not invoke the doctrine of practical impossibility to avoid a termination for default, despite its contention that contract specifications could not be met by using any available technology, because it had superior expertise in the field and had defined the methods for performing the contract. This constituted an implied warranty that it was able to overcome the technical difficulties inherent in the project. The excuse of legal impossibility is available only where, under government specifications, failure to perform is due to the circumstance that no way is known in industry to manufacture the supplies according to the specified design or performance characteristics. Under such circumstances, the government is held to an implied warranty. Here, the parties did not intend "limitations with reference to the state of the art." The contractor knew the work tasks to be performed had not been done before. No implied warranty could be imputed to the government, and, therefore, the conceptual underpinning for the impossibility defense was missing. *J.A. Maurer, Inc. v. United States,* 202 Ct. Cl. 813, 485 F.2d 588 (1973).

The reasoning of the court was generally in accord with its prior decisions and strongly supported by them. In *Austin Co. v. United States,* 161 Ct. Cl. 76, 314 F.2d 581, *cert. denied,* 375 U.S. 830 (1963), the court assumed that the contractor's failure to perform was due solely to the fact that it was impossible to do so under the specifications. However, the specifications were prepared by the contractor after it had reviewed those prepared by the government and found them to be unworkable. The court held that the contractor, having promised to perform under its own substituted specifications, fully assumed the risk of impossibility. As the government was responsible for losses due to its own specifications if they were defective, the converse should apply to the contractor. The court followed *Austin* in *Bethlehem Corp. v. United States,* 199 Ct. Cl. 247, 462 F.2d 1400 (1972), holding that the contractor was recognized to have superior expertise. Its technical proposal was made part of the contract, and the government modified its specification, pursuant to the contractor's advice. Bethlehem had thus assumed the risk of nonperformance notwithstanding impossibility.

The conceptual underpinning for the assertion of impossibility in connection with government specifications is a determination that the government expressly or impliedly warranted the adequacy of the specifications. *J.A. Maurer, Inc. v. United States, supra.* But where the government expressly and emphatically does not warrant its specifications to the contractor, there is no basis for concluding that the contractor, by following the specifications, either as they read at the time of award or as changed during the first article approval period, will produce a successful and acceptable end item. *PRB Uniforms,* ASBCA Nos. 21504, 21505, et al., 80-2 BCA 14, 602.

The invitation to an unexperienced contractor to entangle himself in this briar bush may be deemed morally reprehensible. But it cannot be and is not denied that the law allows the government to do it if it disclaims any warranty by clear and unambiguous language. This is particularly so where the contractor knew that the specification requirements were beyond the state of the art and commercially impracticable. *Rixon Electronics v. United States,* 210 Ct. Cl. 309, 536 F.2d 1345 (1976); *J.A. Maurer, Inc. v. United States, supra.* Even assuming arguendo that the contractor did not assume the risk of impossibility, he must prove that the specifications were beyond the state of the art or impossible. For relief to be granted for impossibility, the contractor must show that the nature of the performance he promised was commercially senseless, not only to himself, but also to other manufacturers. *Gulf & Western Industries,* ASBCA No. 21090, 80-1 BCA 14,304; *see also Special Electronics Corp.,* ASBCA Nos. 6378 & 6665, 1962 BCA 3280.

In *Jennie-O-Foods v. United States,* 217 Ct. Cl. 314, 580 F.2d 400 (1978), poultry disease, which allegedly reduced the number of turkeys available from a contractor's supplier, did not excuse the contractor's late performance or relieve it from liquidated damages assessment because the disease problem was of limited extent and the contractor did not exhaust alternative sources of supply that might have been available. The court held that the plaintiff's problem in obtaining sufficient numbers of high-grade turkeys to satisfy the delivery schedule was a case of economic hardship, rather than legal impossibility of performance. The latter term, in its modern usage, is a "coat of many colors," encompassing much more than literal or actual impossibility. *Natus Corp. v. United States,* 178 Ct. Cl. 1, 371 F.2d 450 (1967). Within its scope is included performance that is excused because the attendant costs would be excessive and unreasonable. *Foster Wheeler Corp. v. United States,* 207 Ct. Cl. 533, 513 F.2d 588 (1975); *J.A. Maurer, Inc. v. United States,* 202 Ct. Cl. 813, 485 F.2d 588 (1973).

The commercial impracticability standard can be easily abused. Thus, the courts have not applied it with frequency or enthusiasm. It is not invoked merely because costs have become more extensive than originally contemplated. *Natus Corp., supra; Anthony P. Miller Inc. v. United States,* 161 Ct. Cl. 455, *cert. denied,* 375 U.S. 879 (1963). There are other judicially imposed limits to the doctrine of commercial impracticability that suggest the correctness of labeling a case one of economic hardship. The doctrine may be utilized only when the promissor has exhausted all his alternatives, when in fact he is determined that all means of performance are commercially senseless. *Natus Corp., supra.* There can be little sympathy for contractors who seek refuge behind the label of commercial senselessness (impracticability) without proof that they have made an effort to obtain performance in an alternative fashion.

When a contractor complains that he is unable to obtain a supply of a particular commodity called for by the contract, he must show that the product was unavailable within the boundaries of a reasonable area in order to have a creditable excuse. *See Mitchell Canneries v. United States,* 111 Ct. Cl. 228, 77 F. Supp. 498 (1948), where the court excused performance after adverse weather conditions destroyed a blackberry crop, preventing the contractor from completing contract deliveries. The contractor sought unsuccessfully to locate a substitute crop within a 600-mile area. In excusing performance, the court pointed out that regardless of whether or not a contract provides for findings, there must be some reasonable limit to the area from which a contractor can be expected to acquire raw materials in performance of a contract. If the doctrine that a contractor may not be excused when materials are available anywhere, at any price, were carried to its logical conclusion, it would follow that there would have to be a crop failure over the entire surface of the earth before a contractor could be relieved from damages. If some small quantity of materials had been available in some distant country, a contractor could not be excused. It would be an unconscionable result to hold the contractor liable for damages for failure to complete the contract when the raw material was actually unobtainable.

The elimination or reduction of the contractor's own supply without proof of more widespread calamity, rendering performance truly senseless, will not suffice to excuse performance. A contractor's failure to exhaust alternative sources of performance highlights the difference between subjective impossibility (I cannot do X) and objective impossibility (X cannot be done). Only the latter is the basis for excusing performance. The contractor has the burden of proof that he explored and exhausted alternatives before concluding performance was commercially senseless. *Jennie-O-Foods v. United States, supra; Clark Grave Vault Co. v. United States,* 178 Ct. Cl. 52, 371 F.2d 459 (1967).

## DOCTRINE OF SUPERIOR KNOWLEDGE

When a contractor has no way of knowing essential information concerning the performance of his contract and the government has such information, the government has an affirmative duty to disclose such knowledge if that knowledge is vital to contract performance. Failure to fulfill that duty could constitute a breach of contract by the government. However, there is no obligation for the government to put a contractor on notice of every difficulty a procuring agency believes the contractor might encounter during contract performance or for it to share every bit of information it has, whether or not the contractor requests such information. To sustain an allegation that the government has violated its duty of disclosure by withholding superior knowledge, the contractor must show that the government in fact possessed such knowledge and that it was vital to contract performance.

Where the government has made no misrepresentations, has no duty to disclose information, and does not improperly interfere with performance, a fixed-price contractor bears the burden of unanticipated increases in costs. *Rolin v. United States,* 142 Ct. Cl. 73, 169 F. Supp. 264 (1958). The government can rightly rely on him to fulfill the agreement he chose to make. In the same manner, an end-product specification leaves it to the contractor to perform as best as he can. *John Thomson Press & Mfg. Co. v. United States,* 57 Ct. Cl. 200 (1922). There are many contracts—where the contract generally relates to known or standard products, or where the ratio of actual and potential knowledge definitely favors the contractor, or where a contractor can reasonably be expected to seek the facts for himself—in which the government may be under no duty to volunteer information in its files. *Shayne Brothers v. United States,* 134 Ct. Cl. 154, 137 F. Supp. 433 (1956).

There are other instances in which the government is clearly under an affirmative obligation and cannot remain silent. The government is not excused from liability if it breaches an independent duty to reveal data, or if the end product embodies a material misrepresentation misleading the contractor. Where the government possesses vital information that it was aware that bidders need, but would not have, it cannot properly let them flounder on their own. Although it is not a fiduciary toward its contractors, the government—where the balance of knowledge is so clearly on its side—can no more betray a contractor into a ruinous course of action by silence than by the written or spoken word. *Globe Woolen Co. v. Utica Gas & Electric Co.*, 224 N.Y. 483, 121 N.E. 378 (1918).

The sorting out of duties arising from a conflict between the contractor's assumption of risk in bidding on a contract without thorough inquiry and the obligation of the government to disclose factors of substantial influence on contract performance depends on three general situations producing the problem; the government (1) may know, but conceal; (2) may not know, and not be charged with knowing; or (3) may not know, yet be legally charged with the knowledge because of its superior opportunity (or other factors warranting a bidder's reasonable expectation). The earned consequences in the first and second instances are predictable, but in the third, the responsibility should be determined on the basis of the balance of fault and reasonable expectations, with the outcome dependent on the circumstances of the individual case. *Aerodex v. United States*, 189 Ct. Cl. 344, 417 F.2d 1361 (1979).

Where the manufacturer contracts to meet a performance specification, he assumes the risk that he may be unable to do so. *Aerodex*, ASBCA No. 7121, 1962 BCA 3492. That risk can be shifted to the government where the government has some superior knowledge that it knew, or should have known, that the contractor did not possess, which would have aided performance, and that the government failed to disclose to the contractor. *Helene Curtis Industries v. United States*, 160 Ct. Cl. 437, 312 F.2d 774 (1963). The government violates its contractual obligations if it permits the contractor to bid for a project and subsequently undertakes a course of action in pursuance thereof that the government knows to be defective, provided that the government possesses knowledge that is vital to the successful completion of the contract, and provided further that it is unreasonable to expect the contractor to obtain that vital information from any other accessible source. *Continental Rubber Works*, ASBCA No. 22447, 80-2 BCA 14,754; *Santa Fe Engineers*, ASBCA No. 17235, 75-1 BCA 11,570. Of course, the corollary of the *Curtis* rule is that the government is under no duty to volunteer information in its files if the contractor can reasonably be expected to seek and obtain the facts elsewhere. *Ambrose-Augusterfer Corp. v. United States*, 184 Ct. Cl. 18, 394 F.2d 536 (1968); *Piasecke Aircraft Corp.*, ASBCA No. 18783, 78-1 BCA 12,886.

In *Helene Curtis Industries v. United States,* 160 Ct. Cl. 437, 312 F.2d 774 (1963), the supplier contracted with the Army in 1951 and 1952 to supply large quantities of a disinfectant chlorine powder to be used by troops in Korea to disinfect eating utensils and fresh fruits and vegetables. The contractor encountered production problems directly attributable to the fact that while each batch of chlormelamine—a central ingredient of the disinfectant manufactured by a sole supplier—was uniform in itself, there were significant and obvious differences among batches. A succession of different batches could be handled appropriately, but blended batches caused grave problems such that the contractor had to grind blended batches of chlormelamine in order to reduce the particle size to meet required solubility standards. It was found by the court that (1) The Army knew that the grinding of separate batches would in all probability be necessary, not because the specifications required that process, but because the end product could not in fact be made without it; (2) On the basis of the data it had, or should be expected to obtain, the contractor reasonably expected that the job could be done by simple mixing, without grinding; (3) The Army was aware that the contractor (and most of the other bidders) expected to produce the disinfectant without grinding blended batches; and (4) The Army did not otherwise inform the contractor as to the probable need for grinding blended batches. The disinfectant was novel and had never been mass-produced; the government had sponsored the research and knew much more about the product than the bidders did or could. It knew, in particular, that the main ingredient, chlormelamine, was a recent invention, uncertain in reaction, and requiring extreme care in handling. It also knew that the more costly process of grinding blended batches would be necessary to meet the requirements of the specification, but that in their understandable ignorance, the bidders would consider simple mixing adequate, and that the urgency for the disinfectant was such that potential contractors could not expend much time learning about it before bidding. Specifications so susceptible of a misleading reading, or implication, subject the government to answer to a contractor who has actually been misled to his injury. *United States v. Spearin,* 248 U.S. 132 (1918); *Arcole Midwest Corp. v. United States,* 125 Ct. Cl. 818, 113 F. Supp. 278 (1953); *Railroad Waterproofing Corp. v. United States,* 133 Ct. Cl. 911, 137 F. Supp. 713 (1956).

It is clear that the same rules apply if the government deliberately misrepresents its requirements. In *Flores Drilling & Pump Co.,* AGBCA No. 82-204-3, 83-1 BCA 16,200, the government willfully misstated the depth of a well to be dug, as well as the diameter of the well casing, because of a shortage of funds. The contract called for the drilling of a well to an estimated depth of 150 feet, plus or minus 25 percent, and an 8-inch well casing, which would have been adequate for that depth, but not for a well 300 to 400 feet in depth. The Board found that a conscious decision was made by the government, for budgetary reasons, to specify a well of considerably lesser depth and that it did not advise bidders of the estimated depth of a successful well. This special knowledge, which bidders could not be expected to obtain from other sources, was vital to a contractor's estimate of costs and formulation of a competitive bid.

The contractor reasonably relied on the estimated depth in the bid schedule. Since an estimate is used for guidance to bidders when specific information is not readily available, the estimate should be based on such relevant information as is available to the author of the specification. The bidder is entitled to rely on government estimates as representing honest and informed conclusions. *Womack v. United States,* 182 Ct. Cl. 399, 389 F.2d 793 (1968). The contractor was misled by the government's failure to reveal its knowledge about the probable depth of a successful well, the probable nature of the material, and the formation to be encountered. Such information would have alerted the contractor that at the lower depths he would encounter lava flows (dense hard rock) imbedded with sand. The nature of the formation was an essential element in formulating his bid, and the courts and Boards take an uncompromising attitude toward the withholding of such information. *Hardeman-Monier-Hutchinson v. United States* 198 Ct. Cl. 492 (1972); *Helene Curtis Industries v. United States,* 160 Ct. Cl. 437, 312 F.2d 774 (1963); *John Murphy Construction Co.,* AGBCA No. 418, 79-1 BCA 13,836; *Power City Electric,* IBCA No. 950-1-72, 74-1 BCA 10,376.

In the context of a duty to disclose, superior knowledge on the part of the government is material only when it is specific as to some fact that a contractor needs to know in order to produce an item that meets the specification and when it either is exclusive or is not reasonably available elsewhere. However, it would impose an unreasonable burden on the government to hold that it is under an implied contractual duty to put a contractor on notice with respect to all the difficulties that might be encountered in the performance of the contract. *Industrial Electronics Hardware Corp.,* ASBCA Nos. 10201 & 11364, 68-1 BCA 6760. And if the superior knowledge is equally available to both government and industry, the government is not obligated to obtain such information and provide it to the contractor. *Prestex,* ASBCA Nos. 21284, 21372, et al., 81-1 BCA 14,882.

# 11

# Termination for the Convenience of the Government

## INTRODUCTION

The ebb and flow of international commitments, constant changes in requirements for goods and services, funding limitations, and continuing advances in science and technology demand that the government possess the flexibility to cancel contracts, in whole or in part, when it is in the public interest to do so. The concept of contract termination for the convenience of the government has evolved over time and is intended to protect the government from unneeded acceptance of equipment, material, or supplies that, through usage, no longer suit its needs or that have been made obsolete by advances in technology; it also applies where, for a variety of reasons, the government must have the ability to cancel contracts for goods or services that, though required at the time of contract award, became excess to the needs of the government prior to contract completion. Such a termination may be ordered when the Contracting Officer determines that, for reasons other than the default of the contractor, it is in the government's best interest to discontinue all, or some part, of the remaining work under the contract.

The Termination for Convenience articles permit the government to discontinue performance of a contract with only limited liability. If, in a private contract, a party attempts to terminate an agreement without a contractual right to do so, that party would be liable for breach of contract damages. The Termination for Convenience article in the government contract converts what would otherwise be a breach into an administrative claim cognizable under the contract. The fault concept is of only minor, if any, significance in termination for convenience actions. Although a small number of contractors have appealed from terminations for convenience, alleging bad faith or arbitrariness, they have been uniformly unsuccessful. Concepts of fault or improper actions usually are related indirectly to terminations for convenience, generally when a wrongful default termination is converted into one for the convenience of the government.

## METHODS OF INVOKING CONVENIENCE TERMINATIONS

A termination for the convenience of the government may be invoked by the Contracting Officer's delivering a formal notice of termination to the contractor or by operation of law. If the termination is directed by written notice, the notice must indicate (1) that the contract is being terminated for the convenience of the government pursuant to the contract provisions authorizing the termination, (2) the effective date of the termination, (3) the extent of the termination, (4) any special instructions applicable to the termination, and (5) steps that the contractor should take to minimize the impact on personnel if the termination, together with all outstanding terminations, will result in a significant reduction in the contractor's work force. *See* FAR § 49.102.

A termination for the convenience of the government may arise by operation of law in a number of ways. Whenever a termination for default is found to be improper, or whenever a constructive termination has occurred, the termination may be converted by regulation and the clause itself into one for convenience. If, after termination for default, it is found that the contractor was not in default or that the default was excusable, the rights and obligations of the parties are the same as if the termination had been for the convenience of the government. *See* FAR § 52.249-8(g).

The doctrine of constructive termination for the convenience of the government is relied on by the courts and Boards of Contract Appeals to obtain jurisdiction in those situations where the contract has either been erroneously canceled or not properly entered into. For example, the court has accepted the government's argument that cancellation of a contract was required, based on a Comptroller General ruling that the contract has been improperly solicited, and treated the cancellation as a constructive termination for convenience even though the Contracting Officer did not follow regulatory requirements. It cannot be contrary to the "best interests of the Government"—the controlling standard of the termination clause—to end a contract that the Comptroller General has branded as incorrectly advertised. *John Reiner & Co. v. United States*, 163 Ct. Cl. 381, 325 F.2d 438 (1963). The contractor is not entitled to recover anticipatory profits because the government could have invoked the termination for convenience provision regardless of whether the contract involved was of the "requirements" type or the "indefinite quantity" type. In comparable circumstances, it has been held that the failure of the government to invoke the convenience termination article makes no difference and that that clause nevertheless sets the limit for any possible recovery. *Nesbitt v. United States,* 179 Ct. Cl. 666, 345 F.2d 583 (1965).

The doctrine of constructive termination for convenience has also been relied on in those factual situations where the government is prevented by the application of equitable estoppel from repudiating a contractual arrangement. This is especially true if the government fails to comply with regulatory procedures governing the award of contracts by sealed bidding, particularly where a lower successful bid has been accepted after bid opening. If the government fails to timely notify the otherwise low bidder of a late lower acceptable bid, and if that contractor relies on the government's inaction to his detriment, an equitable adjustment will be authorized under the Termination for Convenience article. *Emeco Industries v. United States,* 202 Ct. Cl. 1006, 485 F.2d 652 (1973).

In those cases where the government attempts to invoke some other clause to terminate a contract and directs that performance cease, but fails or refuses to classify the termination as one for convenience, the contractor has no alternative but to appeal to the courts or Boards to establish his entitlement to a settlement. *TMC Systems & Power Corp.,* ASBCA No. 15211, 72-1 BCA, is typical of this line of cases. In *TMC,* the cost-plus-fixed-fee contract contained a pre-1966 Limitation of Cost article. As contract funds neared exhaustion, the contractor, in compliance with the provisions of the article, gave the government appropriate notice regarding the status of funds, to include projected expenditure schedules. The government took no action on those notices for 17 months, and it refused to direct the contractor as to how to close out the contract even though it maintained that the contract had expired. The contractor rightfully considered his contract to have been terminated for the convenience of the government even though the Contracting Officer would not act on his termination settlement claim. On appeal to the Armed Services Board, the contractor successfully argued that the Contracting Officer's failure to take appropriate action on timely notices mandated by the Limitation of Cost clause constituted a termination for the convenience of the government. The Board agreed, holding that because the government had delayed unreasonably in responding to overrun notices, the contract had not expired on its own terms.

## THE GOVERNMENT'S RIGHT TO TERMINATE

The authority of the Contracting Officer to enter into a contract includes the authority to terminate the contract when to do so would be in the public interest and the authority to make a binding agreement with the contractor in full and final settlement of his termination claim. *United States v. Corliss Steam Engine Co.,* 91 U.S. 321 (1875). Thus, a department or agency head who is authorized to execute contracts has inherent authority to enter into modifications of those contracts, to include termination either for the convenience of the government or for the default of the contractor. *Gene Peters v. United States,* 694 F.2d 687 (1982).

It is well settled that when the public interest requires such action, the government may terminate a contract notwithstanding the fact that the contract does not provide for termination thereof. It necessarily follows therefore that the government may also terminate or cancel any orders placed against a federal supply schedule contract when such action is determined to be in the best interest of the government; in that event, the government may agree with the contractor on an amount to compensate the contractor for expenses incurred as a result of the cancellation. 19 Comp. Gen. 36 (1939).

Limitations on the government's right to terminate a contract for its convenience are prescribed in neither the standard termination clauses nor the FAR. The convenience termination clauses provide for termination "whenever the Contracting Officer shall determine that such termination is in the best interest of the Government." They are designed to provide a mechanism whereby the government may end its obligations on a contract and yet limit its liability for the contractor's costs and profit on the preparations made and the work done. It may well be that the government does not promote confidence when it terminates a contract and deprives the contractor of the profits of the bargain. But the determination of the interest and convenience of the government is by the contract clause left to the Contracting Officer. Absent bad faith, or some other wrong to the contractor, or illegal conduct, the government alone is the judge of its best interests in terminating a contract for convenience, pursuant to the discretionary power reserved to the government by the clause. *Colonial Metals Co. v. United States,* 204 Ct. Cl. 320, 494 F.2d 1355 (1974).

The government, accordingly, has virtually unrestricted rights to cancel a contract, providing that the cancellation is in its best interests and was made in "good faith." Bad faith or arbitrariness is significantly more difficult to establish in a government contract environment than under commercial standards. Nevertheless, the courts have acknowledged that, under appropriate circumstances, the contractor may be able to overcome the limitations of the Termination for Convenience articles by showing that the termination was in fact made in bad faith. *Jacobs Instrument Co. v. United States,* 147 Ct. Cl. 605, 239 F.2d 459 (1957).

In the absence of clear evidence to the contrary, it is presumed that the public officials involved in the termination of the contractor's agreement were acting conscientiously in the discharge of their duties when the contract was terminated for the purported convenience of the government. *Librach & Cutler v. United States,* 147 Ct. Cl. 605 (1959). The courts have always been loath to find to the contrary, and it requires "well-nigh irrefragable proof" to induce the courts to abandon the presumption of good faith dealing. In cases where the courts have considered allegations of bad faith, the necessary irrefragable proof has been equated with evidence of some specific intent to injure the plaintiff. Bad faith, in many respects, is comparable to actions that are motivated by malice alone (i.e., the court has found bad faith in a civilian pay suit only in view of a proven "conspiracy to get rid of the plaintiff" or conduct that was "designedly oppressive"). Applying this standard, bad faith does not exist in such cases where (1) the Contracting Officer awards a contract to another company after terminating a plaintiff's contract, or (2) there is an incorrect reading of the contract by the government, which is not tantamount to bad faith. *Kalvar Corp. v. United States,* 211 Ct. Cl. 192, 543 F.2d 1298 (1976).

If the contractor does allege bad faith on the part of the government, he must be given an opportunity to introduce such evidence into the record so as to permit the court to reach an appropriate determination. At least one case has been returned to the trial judge with instructions to allow the contractor to introduce into evidence all findings of the Board that showed or tended to prove—directly, indirectly, or circumstantially—bad faith acts on the part of the same Contracting Officer or Officers, or other employees of the same government agency, in handling, administering, and terminating the contracts involved at any time during their existence, and also acts of such government employees occurring after termination of the contract. The trial judge was also instructed to allow the contractor to introduce other available evidence, if any existed, of bad faith acts on the part of such government employees, in addition to the findings of the Board, if any. Inasmuch as the main issue in the contractor's breach of contract suit before the court was alleged bad faith, evidence bearing on that issue was relevant notwithstanding that the contracts contained a Termination for Convenience clause in favor of the government. The termination of a contract for the convenience of the government is valid only in the absence of bad faith. *National Factors v. United States,* 204 Ct. Cl. 98, 492 F.2d 1383 (1974).

A termination for the convenience of the government that was made in bad faith or that was a clear abuse of the Contracting Officer's discretion breaches the contract and renders the government liable for common law breach damages. For however sweeping its prerogative is to declare a contract terminated for convenience, the government cannot insulate itself from common law liability if it abuses its discretion or acts in bad faith. *Curtis L. Holt v. United States,* 226 Ct. Cl. 653 (1981). But where the Contracting Officer's decision to terminate the contract for convenience was motivated by an intent to prevent further cost overruns, bad faith was lacking. *Breed Corp. v. United States,* 233 Ct. Cl. 702 (1980). Moreover, a party to a contract may justify an asserted termination, rescission, or repudiation by proving that there was, at the time, an adequate cause, although it did not become known to him until later. *College Point Boat Corp. v. United States,* 267 U.S. 12 (1925).

The common law rule holding the government liable for breach of contract damages where there is an improper termination for convenience applies to requirements-type contracts, as well as to those having a fixed quantity. It is the very essence of a requirements contract that the buyer agrees to turn to the supplier for all of its needs. The government may not use the standard Termination for Convenience clause to dishonor, with impunity, its contractual obligations. Where a contract bound the Navy to place all of its pest control needs with the contractor, the Navy could not just walk away from this promise without making a mockery of the contract. It is nothing more than basic contract law that a power to terminate must be limited in some meaningful way, as measured by the requirement for consideration. Although the government may argue that there are no limits on its power to invoke termination for convenience, its unrestricted use of the clause cannot be correct. Any contract containing the clause, in the absence of something else to furnish consideration, would fail for the lack of any binding obligation. Termination based on knowledge of a lower cost when the knowledge preceded award of the contract cannot be condoned. *Torncello v. United States,* 204 Ct. Cl. 320, 494 F.2d 1355 (1982).

The court in *Torncello, supra,* suggested that there must be a "change in circumstances" before the Contracting Officer can invoke the Termination for Convenience clause. It followed this position in *Municipal Leasing Corp. v. United States,* 7 Cl. Ct. 43 (1984), where it held that a Termination for Convenience clause can appropriately be invoked only in the event of some kind of change in the circumstances of the bargain or in the expectations of the parties. The Termination for Convenience clause will not act as a constructive shield to protect the government from the consequences of its decision to follow an option considered, but rejected, before contracting with the contractor.

## DE FACTO DEBARMENT

A further restraint on the government's right to terminate a contract for convenience is that the termination cannot act as a de facto debarment. It is well settled that while no individual or corporation has a right to be awarded a specific government contract, one who has been dealing with the government on an ongoing basis may not be blacklisted from further contracting, except for valid reasons and in conformity with the procedural safeguards established by law. It is clear that due process of law requires that before a contractor may be blacklisted (whether by debarment or by suspension), he must be offered specific procedural safeguards, including inter alia a notice of the charges against him, an opportunity to rebut those charges, and, under most circumstances, a hearing. Absent a factual basis in the record, the courts will not allow the government to hide behind the cloak of such conclusory phrase as "termination for the convenience of the government" to justify its actions. *Art-Metal-USA v. Solomon* 473 F. Supp. 1 (D.C., DC Cir. 1978).

## LIMITATIONS ON RECOVERY

When a contract is terminated for the convenience of the government, either by the Contracting Officer's written notice or by operation of law, a settlement should compensate the contractor fairly for the work done and the preparations made for the terminated portions of the contract, including a reasonable allowance for profits. The contractor may generally recover the cost of performance up to the point of termination, certain continuing costs after termination, settlement expenses, and reasonable profit on costs recovered, provided that the contract was not in a loss position. Nevertheless, the Termination for Convenience articles operate as limitation of remedies clauses since they place restrictions on the amount of recovery that a contractor may be entitled to if his contract is cancelled.

Following termination, the contractor is required to submit a final termination settlement proposal to the Contracting Officer within one year of the effective date of the termination—unless the Contracting Officer grants an extension of time. If the contractor fails to submit a settlement proposal within the prescribed time, the Contracting Officer may determine, on the basis of available information, the amount, if any, due the contractor and pay that amount. See FAR § 52.249-2(d). If a settlement proposal is submitted, the contractor and the Contracting Officer may agree on the whole or any part of the amount to be paid. The amount agreed to may include a reasonable allowance for profit on work completed, but the agreed amount may not exceed the contract price less payments previously paid. *See* FAR § 52.249-1(e). If the parties fail to agree on the amount to be paid, the Contracting Officer may make a unilateral determination of the amount under the terms of the clause. The contractor has the right of appeal, under the Disputes clause, from any determination made by the Contracting Officer, except that if the contractor failed to submit a timely termination settlement proposal or to request a time extension, there is no right of appeal. *See* FAR § 52.249-2(i). Under no circumstances, however, are anticipatory profits or consequential damages allowable. FAR § 49.202(a).

In establishing a settlement limit based on contract price under an indefinite-quantity contract terminated for the convenience of the government, the contractor's recovery is limited to the minimum value of the supplies or services the government was obligated to order, plus the value of any supplies or services it had ordered in excess of that minimum. *Okaw Industries,* ASBCA Nos. 17863 & 17864, 77-2 BCA 12,793. It is well settled that termination claims based on loss of business or anticipated sales are not allowable, particularly when the contractor has not incurred costs in expectation of receiving the balance of the minimum order. *Unified Engineering,* ASBCA No. 21565, 81-1 BCA 14,940.

It is equally well settled that where the government has breached the contract, anticipatory profits are recoverable. This rule applies in those cases where the government's action to cancel a contract cannot be legally justified either by the terms of the contract or by the reasons given in support of cancellation. If the contractor was at all times ready, willing, and able to perform his obligation under the contract, but was prevented from doing so by the unauthorized act of cancellation on the part of the government, there is no question that the cancellation was a breach of contract by the government. It is settled law that an unqualified and positive refusal to complete performance of a contract, though the performance is not yet due, may be treated as a complete breach and entitle the injured party to bring his action at once and be compensated therefor. Under these circumstances, the measure of the contractor's damages is the amount of profit he would have earned had the contract not been cancelled. *David J. Joseph Co. v. United States,* 113 Ct. Cl. 3, 82 F. Supp. 345 (1949).

When the government enters into a contract, it has rights, and it ordinarily incurs responsibilities similar to those of a private person who is a party to a contract. If the government terminates a contract without justification, such termination is a breach of the contract, and the government becomes liable for all of the damages resulting from the wrongful act. The damages will include not only the injured party's expenditures and losses in partially performing the contract, but also, if properly proved, the profits that such party would have realized if he had been permitted to complete the contract. The object is to put the injured party in as good a position pecuniarily as he would have been in if the contract had been completely performed. *G.L. Christian & Assocs. v. United States,* 160 Ct. Cl. 1, 312 F.2d 418, *cert. denied,* 375 U.S. 954 (1963).

Thus, after the government terminated a contract for the production of Veri pistols for its convenience at the end of World War I, the court held that where there was a termination clause in the contract, there could be no recovery for loss of profits. The right to terminate contemplates the possibility of not being allowed to complete the contract, with the attendant loss of profits, and the contractor's bid includes this risk. It also includes the possibility of termination before any of the articles contracted for are completed. Hence, the right to recover prospective profits is negatived by the very insertion of the termination clause in the contract. *North Star Aviation Corp. v. United States,* 198 Ct. Cl. 178, 458 F.2d 64 (1972); *Davis Sewing Machine Co. v. United States,* 60 Cl. Ct. 201 (1925).

If the government has reserved the right to terminate a contract for convenience and then does so, there is no breach, and normally there can be no recovery for the profits that would have been made if the government had not exercised its reserved right. The termination clause limits profit to work actually done and prohibits the recovery of anticipated, but unearned, profits. That limitation is a deeply ingrained strand of public procurement policy. Regularly, since World War I, it has been a major government principle, in times of stress or increased military procurement, to provide for the cancellation of contracts when they are no longer needed, as well as for the reimbursement of costs actually incurred before cancellation, plus a reasonable profit on that work. Since World War II, the standard termination article promulgated by the Defense Department has taken the same tack. Literally thousands of defense contracts and subcontracts have been settled on that basis in the past decades. The Defense Department and the Congress would be loath to sanction a large contract that did not provide for power to terminate and, at the same time, guard against a common law measure of recovery that had been disallowed for so many years in military procurement. *G.L. Christian & Assocs. v. United States, supra.*

Moreover, anticipatory profits are not allowed in those cases where a default termination has been converted into one for the convenience of the government even though the default articles provide for an "equitable adjustment" for wrongful default terminations. It has long been held that on cancellation of a contract under the power reserved to the government, just compensation does not include anticipatory profits. A major reason for the initiation and use of Termination for Convenience articles has been to allow the government to avoid paying unearned profits. Thus, any recovery of profits on a terminated contract is limited to profits on work actually performed prior to the termination. *General Builders Supply Co. v. United States,* 187 Ct. Cl. 477, 409 F.2d 246 (1969). *Accord Dairy Sales Corp. v. United States,* 593 F.2d 1002 (1976).

## RECOVERY OF PRE-CONTRACT COSTS

Periodically a contractor will incur performance costs prior to the effective date of the contract. In the case of a properly priced fixed-price contract, the contractor will recover all performance costs if the contract is fully performed. If the contract is terminated for the convenience of the government, the contractor will be required to justify all costs incurred and, in the absence of an advance agreement with the Contracting Officer, may not be allowed recovery of pre-contract costs. Pre-contract costs are defined as those costs incurred before the effective date of the contract directly pursuant to the negotiations and in anticipation of the contract award when such incurrence is necessary to comply with the proposed contract delivery schedule. FAR §§ 31.205-32, 31.109.

An electronic communications contractor's claim for $76,523 was disallowed in his settlement proposal because, even though the costs were incurred in the development and production of contract items, they were incurred prior to the effective date of the contract. They were not incurred in the performance of work terminated, nor was such incurrence necessary to comply with the proposed delivery schedule since at the time they were incurred there was no proposed contract and no proposed delivery schedule. *Codex Corp.,* ASBCA No. 17983, 74-2 BCA 10,827.

In order to recover pre-contract costs, the contractor must establish that time was of the essence. Because it is often difficult to determine after a convenience termination if the contractor would have been capable of meeting the contract's schedule without resorting to pre-contract expenditures, the courts and Boards have adopted a test of good faith and the exercise of reasonable judgment in determining whether the incurrence of such costs were necessary. Thus, costs incurred by a contractor in connection with the production of a B–1 bomber weapons system before the contract was executed by the government were reimbursable because they met all the tests set out in the procurement regulations concerning the allowability of preperformance costs. The contractor believed the work to be necessary and undertook it in good faith. Furthermore, the government authorized pre-contract costs, although from a date subsequent to the date on which the contractor began to incur the costs, and the government was unable to offer any reasonable explanation to differentiate the earlier costs from the pre-contract costs it had authorized. *North American Rockwell Corp.,* ASBCA No. 15863, 72-2 BCA 9490.

On the other hand, it has been held that a contractor was not entitled to compensation for research performed during the interim after completing one contract and while awaiting award of a second related contract. The contractor continued to perform after completion of the phase one contract and asserted that the work was essential to proper continuance of the program, despite the lack of specific authorization to do so. The pre-contract cost authorization was expressly limited to a period not including the time in which the interim research work was completed. *National Committee on International Trade Documentation,* DOTCAB No. 76-28, 77-1 BCA 12,368. See *Universal Match Corp. v. United States,* 161 Ct. Cl. 418 (1963), where it was held that "No costs were properly incurred under the contract, and the United States is not liable under the termination clause for costs improperly incurred."

## POST-TERMINATION COSTS

The Termination for Convenience clauses require that the contractor stop work immediately on the terminated portion of the contract and that all subcontracts related to the terminated portion of the work be terminated. The main purpose of these requirements is to have the contractor cease incurring costs under the contract. Nevertheless, the government realizes that a contractor cannot immediately cease to incur some costs on receipt of a termination notice. Certain post-termination costs will, of necessity, be incurred by the contractor in complying with the termination notice and in presenting a settlement claim to the Contracting Officer. Costs that cannot be discontinued immediately after the effective date of the termination are generally allowable if the contractor made a reasonable effort to discontinue their incurrence. Any costs continuing after the effective date of the termination due to the negligent or willful failure of the contractor to discontinue the costs are not allowable. *See* FAR § 31.205-42.

Applying the test of reasonableness, the Engineer Board of Contract Appeals allowed the contractor to recover costs incurred by reason of a judgment against it in a Miller Act suit, even though the judgment represented a compromise of the claim of the discharged contractor. Payment on the judgment was required after the termination, but the costs it represented were for materials and services supplied and rendered prior to the termination. The Board also allowed, as a settlement expense, a judgment for breach of contract in favor of a subcontractor. The discharging of the subcontractor was a reasonably prudent business decision under the circumstances, despite the possibility of a breach of contract action, and, therefore, the payment of the judgment was an allowable expense. *Nolan Brothers,* ENG BCA No. 2688, 67-1 BCA 6095.

Severance pay for terminated employees may be allowable as a direct cost if required by law, an existing employer-employee agreement, or an established policy that constitutes an implied agreement. And, under certain circumstances, a contractor's established policy may properly provide for severance pay beyond a normal two-week period. *Trustees of Columbia University in the City of New York,* ASBCA No. 15578, 73-1 BCA 9777; *Systems Development Corp.,* ASBCA No. 16947, 73-1 BCA 9788; *Telecomputing Service,* ASBCA No. 10644, 68-1 BCA 7023.

# 12

# Inspection and Acceptance

## INTRODUCTION

The government has the right to obtain, and the contractor has a duty to furnish, the precise goods or services called for in its contracts in a timely manner. It assures that these conditions are met through some form of inspection prior to acceptance. The government may rely on the contractor's internal controls, hold him responsible for inspection and testing before he tenders delivery, or require that he maintain an acceptable quality control system. In addition, the government may conduct its own inspection and testing prior to acceptance. To these ends the FAR mandates that procuring agencies include inspection and other quality control requirements in every contract awarded to the private sector and that all goods or services tendered to the government meet established requirements. *See* FAR § 46.102. The FAR clauses governing inspection and acceptance differ significantly from the rights and obligations normally included in contracts between private parties, which generally do not provide for in-process inspection or the absolute right to require correction of defects except in unusual circumstances. Acceptance is generally conclusive on the government, and the government normally cannot recover for defects discovered after acceptance, except for defects that result from the contractor's fraud or gross mistake amounting to fraud or for latent defects not discoverable during a reasonable inspection.

## INSPECTION

The primary means available to the government to ensure contractor compliance with its contract specifications are set out in the various inspection clauses prescribed by the FAR. Inspection, from the government's perspective, means the examination and testing of goods or services (including, when appropriate, raw materials, components, and intermediate assemblies) to determine whether they conform to contract requirements. Inspection may be conducted at the contractor's facility, during manufacture or process, or in the finished state, and may be performed by the Contracting Officer or by government personnel designated by the Contracting Officer. Because of the sheer volume of contracts with the private sector and the limitation of resources to devote to inspection functions, the government relies extensively on its contractors and their quality control measures to assure contract compliance.

Under the Inspection articles prescribed for fixed-price supply contracts, the government has the right to inspect and test all supplies called for by the contract to the extent practicable at all times and places, including the period of manufacture and, in any event, before acceptance. This right extends to subcontracts, if any, as may be necessary to determine whether the supplies or services furnished by subcontractors conform to the requirements of the contract. The government also has the right to accept goods conforming to its requirements or to reject or require correction of nonconforming supplies or services. Goods or services are nonconforming when they are defective in material or workmanship or are otherwise not in conformity with contract requirements. The government may reject nonconforming supplies with or without disposition instructions as to the goods. *See* FAR § 52.246-2. With respect to services that do not conform to contractual requirements, the government may either require the contractor to perform the services again, at no increase in contract price, or, in those cases where defects in services cannot be corrected by reperformance, the government may require the contractor to take appropriate steps to ensure future contract performance compliance and reduce the contract price to reflect the value of the reduced services. *See* FAR § 52.246-2.

Inspection is required prior to acceptance unless the contract, by express agreement, permits acceptance before inspection through the use of a certificate of conformance or some other mechanism that preserves the government's rights to reject any defective supplies at a later date. A certificate of conformance may be utilized in certain instances in lieu of a source inspection when it is in the government's interests, and small losses would be incurred in the event of a default; or, based on the contractor's reputation or past performance, when it is likely that the supplies or services furnished would be acceptable and that any defective work would be replaced, corrected, or repaired without contest. Use of the certificate of conformance does not prejudice the government's right to inspect supplies under the provisions of the contract. *See* FAR §§ 45.604, 52.246-15.

Although the Inspection articles give the government broad powers, they obligate the government to perform its inspections and tests so as not to unnecessarily delay the work in progress. *Forsberg & Gregory, Inc.*, ASBCA No. 17598, 75-1 BCA 11,176. They also do not permit the government to directly supervise the work of the contractor. Thus, where the government's representative served in the dual capacity of resident engineer and chief inspector on a paving contract and attempted to directly supervise all aspects of the work in progress, the court held that the government's domination and control of the work was a breach of contract. There was nothing in the language of the contract that authorized the government's representative to supervise the work to the extent of authorizing complete control and dominion over the performance of the contract. Despite his conviction of the necessity therefore, such acts by the government's representative constituted a breach of its implied obligation neither to hinder the contractor in the discharge of his obligations nor to increase his cost of performance. *Joseph H. Roberts v. United States*, 174 Ct. Cl. 940, 357 F.2d 938 (1966).

The government must be consistent in its inspection techniques, and its representatives are not permitted to establish stricter standards than those prescribed by the contract. Thus, by refusing to allow a contractor and its cabinet subcontractor reasonable tolerances as to the squareness of cabinet frames and the levelness of doors, the government's resident engineer and its inspector on a Capehart Act housing project caused a breach of contract by the government. By their actions, they forced the contractor's cabinet subcontractor to attempt to perform to a "zero tolerance" standard. In the opinion of the court, absent contract provisions prescribing a stricter standard, it was reasonable for the contractor, in entering into the contract, to believe that the standards as to squareness of frames and levelness of doors customarily applied in the building industry would be applied in passing on the acceptability of cabinets under the contract. The government imposed unjustifiably stricter standards of perfection on the contractor, and since the Changes clause of the Capehart Act contract did not authorize unilateral changes, this amounted to an unwarranted interference with the contractor in the performance of the contract. The government thereby breached its implied contractual obligation not to impede the contractor's performance of the work. Furthermore, the contractor was subjected to multiple inspections of the same framing work by different inspectors, where items approved on a previous inspection would subsequently be disapproved. These inconsistent inspections amounted to an unreasonable interference with the contractor in its attempt to perform the contract. *WRB Corp. v. United States*, 183 Ct. Cl. 409 (1968).

Contracts awarded by the government specify that inspection will be conducted at the point of origin, at destination, or at some intermediate point, and such provisions are strictly construed on review by the courts and Boards of Contract Appeals. In *Dittmore-Freimuth Corp. v. United States*, 182 Ct. Cl. 507, 390 F.2d 664 (1968), the contract provided that the end items to be procured would be "inspected at the contractor's plant or elsewhere as directed" by the Contracting Officer. The contract also expressly provided that preproduction and production samples would be inspected by a Navy activity to be designated by the Bureau of Aeronautics and that the contractor would not conduct such tests. When the contract ended in dispute, the contractor included costs of testing and retesting in its settlement claim. The contractor contended that all inspection and testing would be accomplished at its plant and that the trips and travel expenses arising out of testing at an off-site facility involved extra compensation since such testing amounted to a change under the contract. The contractor's claim was denied on the grounds that the contract specifically provided that the contractor was not to conduct the tests and that the contract's specifications, by their terms, permitted testing at a facility to be designated by the government—which provisions were not in conflict with any others found in the contract.

When the contract provides that inspection will be performed at a specific location, the contractor may be entitled to recover increased performance costs if the government subsequently changes the location for such inspection. For example, the inspection clause of a contract specified that inspection on nine rigid frame columns would be performed at the factory prior to their being shipped to the job site. The contract's specifications provided that continuous inspection by a qualified welding inspector would be conducted at all times when welding was being accomplished—together with x-ray inspection of welds to aid in performing the continuous visual inspection. In bidding on the job, the contractor had a right to assume that it could rely on the government to accomplish the type of inspections that the specifications provided that it would furnish; and, therefore, it could safely exclude from its bid price the expense of having to duplicate any inspection and testing services that the specifications stated would be furnished by the government. Because the government failed to perform x-ray inspection as part of factory inspection and released the nine rigid columns for shipment to the job site, it subsequently required the contractor to provide facilities for on-site x-ray inspection and to repair and replace welds in the nine columns that had been identified by the government. While it may be true that the specification provisions for x-ray inspection were for the benefit of the government and could be waived by the government, it does not follow that the government had a right under the contract to subject the contractor to increased performance costs by deferring x-ray inspection to a later time in the performance sequence than that specified in the contract, instead of simply waiving x-ray inspection. *Gordon H. Ball, Inc.*, ASBCA No. 8316, 1963 BCA 3925.

In *Southwest Welding & Manufacturing Co. v. United States*, 188 Ct. Cl. 925, 413 F.2d 1167 (1969), the contract's specifications provided that inspection of materials and finished articles to be incorporated into the work at the job site would be made at the place of production, manufacture, or shipment and that such inspection or other formal acceptance would be final. The Contracting Officer ordered the contractor to remove and replace all welds accomplished in the fabrication shop by using a single pass technique with twin arc automatic welding machines. The welds had been examined radiographically in the fabricating shop and passed by the government's inspectors. The contractor protested the order, but performed the work as directed, after giving notice to the Contracting Officer that it would be considered extra work. The government clearly had ordered extra work above and beyond the requirements of the contract, which it had drafted, and was therefore responsible for increased costs incurred by the contractor in complying with its orders.

Conversely, where the specifications as to final examination and acceptance contemplated a single acceptance upon overall completion of the work, there could be no final acceptance of component parts fabricated at plant locations until installed at the job site and there inspected and accepted. Nor did "acceptance" of the material at the fabrication plant relieve the contractor of responsibility for defects discovered before final acceptance at the job site. Under the specifications, the plant inspector was not authorized to make final inspections and did not purport to do so. *Merrit-Chapman & Scott Corp. v. United States,* 178 Ct. Cl. 883 (1967).

If the government performs inspections or tests on the premises of a contractor or subcontractor, the contractor is required to furnish and to have its subcontractors furnish, without additional charge to the government, all reasonable facilities and assistance for the safe and convenient performance of these duties. *See* FAR § 52.246-2. But when the government insists on more than reasonable facilities and assistance, the contractor may be entitled to recover increased performance costs incurred, if any. Thus, where shallow observation wells, constructed at the direction of the government, were in purpose and effect special inspection devices ordered by the government to aid its own function of inspecting the work and related subsurface conditions, the contractor was entitled to compensation therefor. *Corbetta Constr. Co.,* ASBCA No. 5045, 60-1 BCA 2613.

If the demands for inspection assistance are not unreasonable, the contractor has no basis for complaint. Where the contractor was ordered to furnish labor and equipment for taking soil samples required in trioxial tests to determine the strength of compacted impervious material, recovery was denied because the applicable contract clause, a standard clause that had been in use for some time, clearly contemplated that the Contracting Officer could make reasonable demands on the contractor for the use of men and equipment. *Tecon-Green,* ENG BCA No. 2667, 67-1 BCA 6147. But it is well established that the government cannot charge the contractor for the cost of employing an outside firm for the purpose of conducting, or assisting in, the conduct of government inspections. *S.S. Silverblatt, Inc.,* PODBCA No. 243, 74-2 BCA 10, 770.

When supplies are not ready at the time specified by the contractor for inspection or test, the Contracting Officer may charge the contractor for the additional cost of inspection or testing. *See* FAR §§ 52.246-2, 52.246-12. Under these rules, the contractor may be liable for the cost of "reinspection" of his work if he was not prepared for the "final" inspection at the time he had indicated that he would be or at the time specified in the contract.

Inspection of materials and workmanship under a construction contract may be broadly classified into three separate undertakings, none of which, because of their nature, can be clearly delineated as to when inspection begins or ends. The first type are those that are conducted either periodically or on a continuing basis during progress of the work by a government representative. The second type of inspection are those conducted for the purpose of determining substantial completion. The third type is the "final" inspection, which requires that the contractor signify that he is ready for final inspection and essentially declare that all work has been "fully completed." A contractor should not frivolously request final inspection because the government is obligated, under the terms of the contract, to conduct a final inspection within a reasonable or stated period after receipt of a request to do so. If the project is not accepted by the government as being fully completed, a list of deficiencies and omissions will be prepared and presented to the contractor. The contractor, of course, is required to diligently work toward completion of the contract. When the contractor requests a final inspection, but is not prepared for such, construction contract clauses generally permit the government to charge the contractor for costs incurred in preparing for or actually conducting "final reinspection" because the project was not fully completed, as the contractor represented that it would be. *Oakland Constr. Co.*, GSBCA No. 3557, 72-2 BCA 9675.

When the Contracting Officer seeks to impose a cost reduction on a contractor based on a defective government inspection, the contractor may be entitled to an equitable adjustment in the contract price. For example, the inspection clause of a custodial services contract provided that no payment would be made for services that were not performed according to the contract's specifications and that the work was to be performed, and inspected, during normal duty hours (i.e., 8:00 A.M. to 5:00 P.M.). The government inspector assigned to the contract conducted his inspections at odd hours of the day or night, sometimes before duty hours and sometimes as late as 11:00 P.M. at night. The inspector had no set time for his daily inspections of the contractor's work, but conducted it when he felt like it. Based on deficiencies found during the course of these inspections, deductions were made from amounts payable to the contractor. On appeal, the Board held for the contractor because the inspector did not comply with the contract specifications in performing his assigned inspection duties. This failure of the government's representative was fatal to the government's position, and the contractor was entitled to recover all monies withheld under the contract. *Contract Maintenance,* ASBCA No. 19603, 75-1 BCA 11,097. Similarly, a services contractor was entitled to an equitable adjustment because the standards of cleanliness imposed by the Navy's inspectors were confusing and unreasonable. *G.B. International,* ASBCA No. 18743, 74-2 BCA 10,776.

The government may perform tests that are not specified in the contract to assure contract compliance, provided that the tests are reasonable in relation to the goods or services being acquired. Where a contract for the production of canteen covers specified a test for mildew resistance, this in no way precluded the government from making whatever tests were necessary to determine whether the felt that was lining the canteen covers complied with another element of the specifications—a prescribed mildew inhibitor content. It would have been meaningless for the contract to provide a specific chemical content for the felt, while at the same time precluding the making of such tests as were necessary to determine if that content was actually present. *Crown Coat Front Co. v. United States,* 154 Ct. Cl. 613, 292 F.2d 290 (1961).

If the government deviates from contract specifications in the conduct of its inspections, or if it fails to advise the contractor of its intended method of inspection after obligating itself to do so, thereby delaying the contractor's performance, the government may be liable for the delay. In *Adams Manufacturing Co. v. United States,* 175 Ct. Cl. 986 (1966), for example, the contractor's obligation was to produce wooden tent pins according to the contract's specifications. The contract prescribed that an acceptable quality level (AQL) would be used to determine when the number of defects found in sample lots warranted rejection of the entire lot, but the government failed to advise the contractor of the applicable AQL. Accordingly, since he was not advised of the number of major and minor defects that would be allowed in the sample size lot, the contractor could not anticipate in advance the number of defective pins he could produce without having an entire lot rejected. Moreover, a supplement to the defects classification procedure in effect altered the basic specifications of the contract by classifying certain defects as minor even though they were not prohibited by the contract. The government did not provide the contractor with a copy of that document, nor was the contractor advised of its contents.

Furthermore, the contractor received instructions from the government that stated that the inspector would work closely with the contractor and keep him advised of the method of inspection to be used. Although the contractor repeatedly requested the inspection procedures, the inspector refused to comply with his request. Such failure was deemed to have been arbitrary and unwarranted. There was also proof that the arbitrariness of the government's inspectors in deviating from the contract specifications caused the contractor a substantial increase in cost, for which he was entitled to recover.

Where performance is delayed by either improper or unreasonable inspection procedures, it is an excusable delay. For instance, the government's review procedures of a contractor's work in designing displays for a visitor's center, which specified four separate stages of review, were determined to have been so ponderous that they endangered performance. Termination of the contract for the contractor's failure to make progress on account of such onerous procedures was therefore converted into one for the convenience of the government. *Rogow & Bernstein,* ENG BCA No. 4421, 80-2 BCA 14,643.

Similarly, it was found to be improper to terminate a contract to clean aircraft engine coolers when the government had caused the default, in part, by imposing a standard of inspection in excess of contract requirements. Instead of accepting coolers that produced as many as 10 particles on a mesh screen used in inspection—as specified in the contract—the government rejected coolers that produced as few as one particle. *Texas Trinity Mfg. & Supply Co.,* ASBCA No. 10465, 75-1 BCA 11,151. And the GSA Board likewise overturned a termination for default after it found that the alleged default was caused by the contractor's failure to meet an inspection standard exceeding the standard previously established by acceptance of the contractor's work sample. *Ventilation & Cleaning Engineers,* GSBCA No. 3705, 74-1 BCA 10,390.

In *Gardiner Displays Co. v. United States,* 171 Ct. Cl. 497 (1967), the contract required the government to make inspections and tests in "such a manner as not to unduly delay the work." In failing to expeditiously instruct the contractor as to precisely what it wanted and in carrying out dilatory and inconclusive inspection and approval procedures, the government exceeded reason. It is settled that the government is liable for breach of its contract if it unreasonably delays or disrupts the contractor's work. *F.H. McGraw & Co. v. United States,* 131 Ct. Cl. 501, 130 F. Supp. 394 (1955).

If the Contracting Officer insists that the contractor perform to a level of quality or subject the contractor to a system of inspection not particularized by the contract and its specifications, the contractor is nevertheless obligated under the Changes and Disputes articles to comply strictly with the contract as changed and may not abandon the contract with impunity. The government has broad discretion in determining the number and types of inspections that it will perform to assure compliance with its contracts. Thus, a test not specified in the contract may be performed by the government and used as the basis for rejection of work tendered by the contractor, so long as the government does not impose a higher standard of quality than that called for by the contract.

An early case before the Court of Claims addressed the problem of the duty to proceed in the context of a default termination involving the delivery of hay to Fort Sam Houston, Texas, for the feeding of Army horses. Routinely, inspections were requested by contractors at the point of origin of the hay to avoid the expense incident to possible rejection, as well as to assure that hay of an inferior grade would not be tendered for acceptance under a contract. Where a complete inspection was made of hay by a federal civilian employee prior to its delivery to an Army post, Army regulations provided for its acceptance at the grade fixed by the civilian hay inspector, unless there was an obvious error in the prior grading. Reinspection was permitted at the destination, but the inspector could only change the grade if there were some obvious and outstanding error in the grade fixed at origin. In *Thomas C. Edwards v. United States,* 80 Ct. Cl. 118 (1934), the contractor's hay was rejected by an Army officer conducting a destination inspection. The contractor sold the hay to another contractor, who transferred it to other railcars and tendered it to the Army. The hay was then accepted in the same grade fixed at origin when the defaulted contractor initially had had the hay inspected, by the same Army officer who had first rejected it. The contractor's complaint revealed arbitrary and capricious action on the part of the government's representatives. The whole record led to the conclusion that the act in rejecting much of the hay submitted by the contractor was so arbitrary and capricious that performance was impossible.

In such cases, however, the contractor must also prove that it took all reasonable steps to perform the contract notwithstanding the occurrence of the excuse. *Jennie-O-Foods v. United States,* 580 F.2d 400 (1978).

But the duty to proceed when inspection methods and procedures are in dispute is not absolute. For example, a contractor may be excused from a duty to proceed where the government fails to establish firm objective requirements for changed inspection criteria and where the government refuses, after inquiry, to provide the contractor with definite inspection criteria even though it has established those criteria for its own use in directing the efforts of its quality assurance representatives. *Puma Chemical Co.,* GSBCA No. 5254, 81-1 BCA 14,844.

If a contractor employs more stringent inspection standards than those imposed by the contract, he generally will not be allowed to recover any increased costs of performance. A contractor has no contractual right to reject a buyer's engineering solution to a problem that the buyer is willing to accept and pay for as satisfactory performance without recourse. *Ramsey Silk & Woolens,* ASBCA No. 10035, 65-2 BCA 5107. If the item has passed the inspection and tests set forth in the contract, and if the contractor has been directed to ship the item, but refuses to do so because he wishes to conduct additional tests, the contractor thus arrogates to himself the responsibility for determining the needs of the government and has volunteered additional work to satisfy that for which the government was satisfied already. It is clear that the government is not responsible for that volunteered work. *Sancolmar Industries,* ASBCA No. 16193, 74-1 BCA 10,246. But those tasks performed to satisfy the inspector may be valid, if reasonable. There are many cases where the contract makes the satisfaction of one of the parties with respect to compliance the condition precedent to fulfillment, and good faith is all that is required to justify rejection of the work or product tendered. *Goltra v. Weeks,* 271 U.S. 536 (1926).

Under the Inspection articles, the government has the right to require the contractor to correct all nonconforming supplies. The articles do not prohibit a reinspection by the government, nor do they prohibit requiring the contractor to correct all defects found as a result of the reinspection. *See* FAR § 52.246-2.

In a contract calling for the manufacture of cyrogenic vessels for use in the propellant loading system of a Titan I intercontinental ballistic missile site, it was critical that all surfaces to be exposed to oxygen be free of particles more than 150 microns (six thousandths of an inch) in diameter. A government inspection was performed at the contractor's plant prior to shipment, and a reinspection was performed at destination. As a consequence of the reinspection, the contractor was required to reclean the vessels. When the Contracting Officer denied the contractor's claim for recleaning, the contractor took an appeal to the Armed Services Board. Here the Board held:

It is clearly established by the evidence that the cyrogenic vessels manufactured by appellant had not been cleaned so as to meet the cleanliness requirements of the specifications at the time they were delivered at the missile site. The cleaning which appellant performed at the missile site was not in excess of what was necessary to meet the applicable specifications. The recleaning at the missile site was rendered necessary, not by the Government's reinspection at the site, but by appellant's failure to meet the cleanliness requirements when it cleaned the vessels at the factory. Appellant was not required to do any additional cleaning at the site on those vessels shown by the site reinspection to have been cleaned at the factory in accordance with the specification requirements. Obviously cleaning that was necessary to comply with the specifications cannot be paid for as extra work, unless it can be established that prior to the time appellant was required to do such cleaning the Government had finally accepted the vessels so as to be barred by the terms of the contract from making any subsequent claim against appellant based on noncompliance with the specifications. We say "barred by the terms of the contract," because there is no principle of the law of contracts and sales which bars a buyer from asserting a claim against a seller for nonconformance with specifications after the buyer has inspected and accepted the supplies. Hence, if the Government is barred from asserting noncompliance with the specifications after inspection and acceptance of delivery at destination, it must be because of the terms of the contract. The alternative to acceptance of supplies is rejection. This appeal does not raise any question as to any right of the Government to reject the vessels, as the Government did in fact accept and retain the vessels and pay the contractor the full contract price for them. Thus, the crucial question in this appeal is whether under the terms of the contract the Government's actions in inspecting the vessels at the place of manufacture, authorizing the contractor to ship them to the destination point, receiving them at the delivery point and retaining them for several months bars the Government from thereafter asserting a claim against the contractor for noncompliance with the cleaning specifications and requiring the contractor to do additional cleaning at its own expense to comply with the specification requirements. The Government had the right to inspect "at all times and places," including, but not limited to, during the time and at the place of manufacture. Under this clause the Government had the right to inspect the vessels either at the place of manufacture or at the missile site delivery point, to inspect the vessels as many times as it wanted to or not to inspect them at all if it chose to waive its contract right to inspect. The Government's right to inspect was for its own benefit, and its inspections were for its own protection to provide maximum assurance that critical equipment to be installed at missile sites was safe and fit for its intended purpose. The Government's decision to perform a cleanliness inspection at the place of manufacture was not made in the exercise of an election, as the Government had the contract right to perform a cleanliness inspection at both the place of manufacture and the missile site, if it chose to do so.

*Lox Equipment Co.*, ASBCA No. 8518, 1964 BCA 4469.

## ACCEPTANCE

Acceptance is defined as an act of an authorized representative of the government by which the government, for itself or as an agent of another, assumes ownership of existing identified supplies tendered or approves specific services rendered as partial or complete performance of the contract. FAR § 46.101. The act of assuming ownership constitutes acknowledgment that the supplies or services conform with applicable quality and quantity requirements and with other terms and conditions of the contract. Acceptance may take place before delivery, at the time of delivery, or after delivery, depending on specific provisions of the contract. Supplies or services ordinarily will not be accepted before completion of government quality assurance actions, unless a certificate of conformance is utilized. Moreover, acceptance is normally evidenced by execution of an acceptance certificate, an inspection or receiving report, or a commercial shipping document. FAR § 46.501.

Final acceptance can mean only one thing within the context of a government contract: conclusive and decisive action by which the government determines through its authorized agents that, on the basis of all the facts within its knowledge, the contractor has satisfactorily performed his obligations under the contract. *C.G. McQuagge v. United States*, 197 F. Supp. 460 (D.C. La. 1961). Further, inspection and acceptance of projects by phases or parts of the work comprise a recognized way of conducting construction projects. *L.A. Barton & Co.*, ASBCA No. 17547, 73-2 BCA 10,249. Supply contracts provide for acceptance either at the origin or at the destination. Normally, supplies accepted at a place other than the destination will not be reinspected at the destination for acceptance purposes, but are examined only for quantity, damage in transit, or possible product substitution or fraud.

Under ordinary circumstances, contractors tendering nonconforming goods or services are given the opportunity to replace or correct such goods or services and thus permit government acceptance, when this can be accomplished within the required delivery schedule. Unless the contract specifies otherwise, as may be the case with cost reimbursement contracts, replacement or correction is to be made without additional cost to the government. Otherwise, the Contracting Officer is ordinarily required to reject supplies or services when the nonconformance affects safety, health, reliability, durability, performance, interchangeability of parts or assemblies, weight, or appearance. *See* FAR § 46.407.

The government may, and often does, accept nonconforming supplies or services. There may be circumstances (i.e., reasons of economy or urgency) when acceptance of such supplies or services is determined to be in the government's best interest. The Contracting Officer's determination will normally take into consideration such factors as (1) the advice of technical specialists that the material is safe to use and will perform its intended purpose, (2) information regarding the nature and extent of the nonconformance, and (3) the contract price adjustment considered appropriate under the circumstances. As a matter of policy, Contracting Officers are required to discourage the repeated tender of nonconforming supplies or services, including those with only minor discrepancies, by appropriate action, such as rejecting the tender and documenting the contractor's performance record. *See* FAR § 46.607.

Where the work is accepted with knowledge that it has not been done according to the contract, or under such circumstances that knowledge of its imperfect performance may be imputed, the acceptance will generally be deemed a waiver of the defective performance. But this rule does not apply to latent defects. The acceptance of work that has been defectively done, the defects being unknown and not discoverable by inspection, does not amount to a waiver of the imperfect performance. This rule respecting final acceptance with knowledge of defects is the same in federal courts as in the *City of Seaside v. Randles,* 92 Or. 650, 180 P. 319 (1919). *C.H. McQuagge v. United States, supra.*

Acceptance of an initial delivery of nonconforming supplies or services does not prevent rejection of later deliveries for failure to meet the contract's specifications. The government will not be estopped to refuse to grant waivers, unless it has a consistent practice of granting waivers in every case. *Doyle Shirt Mfg. Corp. v. United States,* 199 Ct. Cl. 150, 462 F.2d 1150 (1972). But in some cases, government conduct could result in a waiver of nonconformity. If there exists a valid agreement between the contractor and a duly authorized government representative to omit certain production tests and to accomplish the same function by increased visual and mechanical inspections, the courts have held that a waiver of nonconformity has been granted. *Northbridge Electronics v. United States,* 175 Ct. Cl. 426 (1966).

Thus, the government may alter the original terms of a contract by subsequent action or conduct imputing acceptance of irregular performance. It is a familiar principle of equity that long-continued acquiescence in a course of conduct by one interested in it, especially when the rights of others are affected thereby, will induce the court to refuse him relief upon his subsequent complaint of it. It would be contrary to equity and good conscience to enforce such rights when a contractor has been led to suppose by the word, silence, or conduct of government representatives that there was no objection to his operations. *See Ucello v. Golden Foods,* 325 Mass. 319, 90 N.E. 250 (1950).

Under the Uniform Commercial Code, an acceptance of goods occurs when the buyer does any act inconsistent with the seller's ownership. U.C.C. § 2–606. Thus, government promptness in giving notice of rejection of goods or services tendered by a contractor is essential because if timely notice of rejection is not furnished, acceptance may in certain cases be implied as a matter of law. *See* FAR § 46.407.

The most common act resulting in a finding of implied acceptance is the retention and use of the seller's goods by the buyer. Thus, a construction contractor was entitled to recover the cost of repairing a boiler it had installed that exploded prior to acceptance, while being operated by government employees, because it had been under control of the government for three months at the time of the explosion. This was so even though the government had not formally inspected and accepted the boiler. The acts of taking possession of and operating the boiler constituted an implied acceptance. No provision of the contract authorized the government either to take possession of or to operate the boiler prior to the written notification from the contractor that the boiler was ready for final inspection and acceptance. To the extent that notice was a condition precedent to acceptance of the boiler, it was equally a condition precedent to the government's possessing and operating it. Yet the government did take possession and did operate the boiler for an extended period. By placing the boiler in operation, it rendered unnecessary a written notice from the contractor that work on the boiler was complete and that the boiler was ready for inspection.

No useful purpose would have been served by the contractor's advising the government of what it was already well aware. In short, the failure of the government to await a written notice from the contractor before taking possession of the boiler constituted a waiver of the notice provision of the contract. Nor having waived the notice requirement could the government revive it and assert it as an impediment to acceptance. The final inspection was the government's responsibility, and since it did take possession of the boiler and place it in operation, it was in no position to complain that it did not make a final inspection. The government was deemed to have accepted the boiler because during the period in which its representatives operated it, the contractor had no control over the boiler or the employees operating it. *John C. Kohler Co. v. United States,* 204 Ct. C1. 777, 498 F.2d 1360 (1974).

Where the government, or a prime contractor, installs equipment or a component, it must pay the contract rate for any such goods deemed to have been accepted. *Fram Corp. v. Crawford,* 443 F.2d 611 (5th Cir. 1971). If the government accepts supplies and subsequently pays for them, with knowledge that the contract had been terminated for default, it has been estopped to rescind the acceptance. Controlling were the facts that the government, with full knowledge of the default and questionable acceptance, paid the contractor in full 13 days after acceptance and that it then waited another 23 days before initiating rescission action. Because of its delay, the government lost the right to rescind its acceptance. *Norwood Precision Products,* ASBCA No. 24083, 80-1 BCA 14,405.

In *Makoor Products Manufacturing Co.,* GSBCA No. 5779, 81-1 BCA 15,135, the government was found to have improperly terminated contracts for the supply of hand cleaner for default based on leakage found after a reinspection because the containers for the cleaner had previously been inspected and accepted by the government. Absent latent defects, fraud, or gross mistake amounting to fraud, there was no basis for revoking the acceptance to restore the status quo ante. The government attempted to revoke its prior acceptance of supplies, which, at the time of the attempted revocation, consisted in a significant, but undetermined, part of quite acceptable units notwithstanding that the contract did not contain any methodology for rejection on a lot basis for failures of the product to meet the shelf life requirements of the contract after acceptance. There was no post-acceptance right on the part of the government to reject the supplies.

Acceptance is conclusive on the government, except for latent defects, fraud, or gross mistake amounting to fraud. *See* FAR § 52.246-2(k). The effect of a latent defect is to remove the finality of the final acceptance, thereby entitling the government to the same remedies it would have had if acceptance had not occurred (e.g., correction of defects, the cost of which would be borne by the contractor, or rejection). *United States v. Franklin Steel Products,* 482 F.2d 400 (9th Cir. 1973).

As to fraud, the government must prove that the contractor, with an intent to deceive the government, knowingly or in reckless and wanton disregard of the truth, misrepresented or concealed a material fact on which the government relied in making acceptance. Fraudulent practices could include the submission of false certifications or false inspection or laboratory reports, or the substitution of products not in conformance with the government's specifications after inspection.

With respect to a gross mistake amounting to fraud, the government has the burden of proving (1) that its acceptance was induced by its reliance on (2) a misrepresentation of fact, actual or implied, or the concealment of a material fact, (3) made with knowledge of its falsity or in reckless and wanton disregard of the facts, (4) with intent to mislead the government into relying on the misrepresentation, (5) as a consequence of which the government has suffered injury. Gross mistake connotes a mistake so serious or uncalled for as not to be reasonably expected, or justifiable, in the case of a responsible contractor for the items concerned. It must also be so palpable or flagrant, or so irreconcilable with good faith, as to constitute a gross mistake amounting to fraud. It is essential to demonstrate that the gross mistake complained of actually induced the final acceptance that was sought to be set aside. *Stewart Avionics,* ASBCA No. 15512, 75-1 BCA 11,253.

# 13

# Government Audit Rights

## INTRODUCTION

Audits of government contracts are performed for disparate purposes by different agencies. The General Accounting Office (GAO) performs independent audits in order to ascertain whether government agencies are making acquisitions in the most effective, economical, and efficient manner and to advise Congress of the GAO's recommendations for administrative or legislative actions needed to improve agency contracting practices and procedures. Additionally, the GAO may review individual contracts to determine whether excessive or unreasonable payments have been made to contractors. The Contracting Officer, through the Defense Contract Audit Agency (DCAA) or agency audit resources, performs pre-award audits to verify the validity of costs and prices included in offers submitted to the agency in response to a given solicitation. In conducting post-award audits, the Contracting Officer seeks to assure that the contract is being performed according to its terms, conditions, and legal requirements and to determine the propriety of contract payments.

## AUDITS BY THE GENERAL ACCOUNTING OFFICE

Audits conducted by the GAO, during or after contract performance, are made primarily for the purpose of informing Congress of the manner in which procuring agencies are administering appropriated funds. The authority of the GAO to conduct audits in negotiated acquisitions is statutory. The Armed Services Procurement Act and the Federal Property and Administrative Services Act, as amended, reserve the right for the Comptroller

General and his representatives to examine any book, document, paper, or record of the contractor, or of his first-tier subcontractors, that pertains to and involves transactions relating to the contract or first-tier subcontract for a period of three years after final payment has been made. 10 U.S.C. § 2313(b) & (c); 41 U.S.C. § 254(c); FAR § 15.106-1. The requirement for including the Examination of Records clause (FAR § 52.215-1) in negotiated contracts grew out of congressional concern over the pricing of such contracts and is intended as an additional safeguard in the expenditure of public funds.

The purpose of statutory audits was reemphasized by the Comptroller General in hearings before the Military Operations Subcommittee of the House Committee on Government Operations:

> The language of the Act and the legislative history clearly establish that the basic purpose of the statutory provision was to make possible the close supervision and control over negotiated procurements, which the Congress regarded as necessary in the interest of the Government. This purpose requires that the Act be interpreted to permit detailed examination of a contractor's records to ensure the necessary degree of supervision and control.

89th Cong., 1st Sess. 44–46 (1965). The clear intent of the statutes is to provide for the examination by the GAO of such records of a contractor to such an extent as will permit a meaningful examination of the prices charged to the government.

As early as 1952, the Comptroller General had stated that the purpose of the examination of records statute was, among other things, to afford a means whereby Congress would be informed of any excessive or unreasonable payments to contractors holding negotiated contracts and to serve as a deterrent to the making of contracts providing for unreasonable profits to government contractors. 32 Comp. Gen. 277, 278 (1952).

The statutory audit right of the Comptroller General has been broadly interpreted by the courts. In *Hewlett-Packard v. United States,* 385 F.2d 1013 (9th Cir. 1967), *cert. denied* 390 U.S. 988 (1968), the contractor refused to permit the GAO to examine certain documents on the basis that cost or production information was not directly pertinent to the contracts under review. The trial court disagreed and declared that the company's direct material, direct labor, and overhead costs in producing the items furnished under the contracts directly pertain to, and involve transactions relating to, these contracts. The court further declared that the Comptroller General and his representatives have the right to examine the books, documents, papers, and records of the company relating to or otherwise disclosing these production costs and ordered the contractor to make this information available to the government.

On appeal, Hewlett-Packard argued that the decision of the district court gave no effect to the words of limitation contained in 10 U.S.C. § 2313(b) and reflected in clause 10 of the contracts under review. The appellate court found that it was clear that the district court had sought to give effect to such words of limitation and held that:

The question is whether it gave full effect to those words. This depends upon the meaning to be attached to those words. The key word in the limitation clause is "contract." If that word is used in section 2313(b) only with reference to the terms and conditions of an agreement and the procedures whereby those terms and conditions were formulated, then the district court failed to give full effect to the limitation clause. As Hewlett-Packard correctly points out, production costs were not taken into consideration in arriving at the terms and conditions of the contracts in question. Thus data pertaining to production costs could be said to directly pertain to, and involve transactions relating to, the contracts, as defined. In our opinion, the word "contract," as used in this statute is intended to have a broader meaning, embracing not only the specific terms and conditions of the agreement, but also the general subject matter. The subject matter of these four contracts is the procurement of described property by the Government. Production costs directly pertain to that subject matter, because if out of line with the contract price, the contract may have been an inappropriate means of meeting this particular procurement need of the Government. While this appraisal could not affect these particular contracts, it could lead to the use of other methods of meeting future procurement needs. Production costs involve transactions relating to the contract, because they encompass business arrangements made by the contractor in obtaining the materials, labor, facilities, and the like required by it in fulfilling its commitment with reference to the subject matter of the contract.

In *Bowsher v. Merck & Co.*, 460 U.S. 824 (1984), the Supreme Court held that 10 U.S.C. § 2313(b), as applied to fixed-price contracts for standard commercial items, established the GAO's right to inspect the contractor's record of direct costs, but not of indirect costs: The focal point of the controversy is the meaning of the statutory phrase "directly pertain to and involve transactions relating to the contract." It is plain from the face of the provisions that these are words of limitation designed to restrict the class of records to which access is sought by requiring some close connection between the type of records sought and the particular contract.

The legislative history of the access provisions underscores what the language reflects: the intention of Congress to limit to some degree the Comptroller General's access powers. Therefore, we must be mindful of Congress' aim to protect contractors from broad-ranging government intrusion into their private business affairs. The legislative history also reveals that Congress sought, in granting the GAO this access authority, to equip that agency with a tool to detect fraud, waste, inefficiency, and extravagance in government contracting generally. It is clear that Congress envisioned use of the access authority as an adjunct to the Comptroller General's statutory responsibility to "investigate all matters relating to the receipt, disbursement, and application of public funds" and to "make recommendations looking to greater economy in public contracting."

The appropriate accommodation of the competing goals reflected in the legislative history counsels us to draw the line precisely where lower courts have drawn it. Thus, under the four fixed-price contracts in question, the Comptroller General should be permitted access to records of direct costs. He should be barred, however, from inspecting records of costs incurred in the areas of research and development, marketing and promotion, distribution, and administration, except to the extent the contractor has allocated these costs as attributable to the particular contract.

Direct costs pertain directly to even a fixed-price contract, for direct costs are, by definition, readily identifiable as attributable to the specific product supplied under the contract. Consequently, as a rational businessman, the contractor will have some regard for these in setting even a catalog price in order to avoid a loss on the product. Because these costs therefore have a very direct influence on the price charged the government, the GAO would have need to examine records of these costs to determine whether the contractor is making an excessively high profit or whether the government is getting a "fair deal" under the contract.

Presumably, indirect costs also influence in some manner the setting of a catalog price, although to what extent is unclear, given the somewhat arbitrary accounting allocations that must be made to determine what portion of indirect costs may be attributed to a specific product. Nevertheless, the degree of intrusion into the contractor's private business affairs occasioned by GAO scrutiny of indirect cost records is far greater, particularly where pure fixed-price contracts are involved. Such an inspection would entail exposure to the GAO of many of the contractor's nongovernmental transactions. We therefore conclude that the appropriate balance of public and private interests in this situation weighs in favor of access to direct cost records, but against access to Merck's indirect cost records.

But where the contract that serves as the predicate for the GAO's access demand is a cost reimbursement contract, the contractor is in no position to complain of the intrusiveness of GAO inspection of indirect cost records. By claiming from the government full reimbursement for these costs under the cost-based contract, the contractor represents that these costs are justified as attributable to the performance of the government contract, and not to any nongovernmental transactions. Therefore, the public interest served by permitting the GAO to inspect records supporting these claims clearly outweighs any privacy interests the contractor possesses in those records. *Bowsher v. Merck & Co., supra.*

## AUDITS BY THE DEFENSE CONTRACT AUDIT AGENCY

Of all the controls exercised over a defense contractor's business affairs, the Defense Contract Audit Agency (DCAA) is the one that most challenges the contractor's entrepreneurial management. The purpose of contract auditing, as performed by the DCAA, is to assist in achieving the objective of prudent contracting by providing those responsible for procurement and contract administration with financial information and advice on proposed or existing contracts and contractors. Under the provisions of the directive establishing the audit agency, DoD acquisition and contract administration agencies are required to utilize the audit services of the DCAA to the extent appropriate in connection with the negotiation, administration, and settlement of contract prices or payments that are based on costs (incurred or estimated) or on cost analysis.

Section 15.805-5 of the FAR requires that, when cost or pricing data are required, Contracting Officers request a field pricing report (which may include an audit review by the cognizant audit activity) before negotiating any contract or contract modification resulting from a proposal in excess of $500,000, unless information available to the Contracting Officer is considered adequate to determine the reasonableness of the proposed cost or price.

The DCAA's responsibilities include performing necessary audits for DoD and its procuring agencies, and for other government agencies as appropriate, as well as providing accounting and financial advisory services regarding contracts and subcontracts to all DoD components responsible for acquisition and contract administration. The DCAA's principal functions provide for it to

1. Audit, examine, and/or review contractors' and subcontractors' accounts, records, documents, and other evidence; systems of internal control; and accounting, costing, and general business practices and procedures; and
2. Examine reimbursement vouchers received directly from contractors and subcontractors, under cost-type contracts, transmitting those vouchers for payment to the cognizant issuing office or, alternatively, issuing DCAA Form 1, "Notice of Costs Suspended and/or Disapproved," with a copy to the cognizant Contracting Officer, with respect to costs claimed, but not considered allowable.

The DCAA's access rights to a contractor's books and records are set forth in standard FAR clauses. Section 52.214-26 applies to the pricing of modifications to sealed-bid contracts when the contract amount is expected to exceed $100,000. By its terms, if the contractor has submitted cost or pricing data in connection with the pricing of any modification to the contract—unless the pricing was based on adequate competition or on established catalog or market prices of commercial items sold in substantial quantities to the general public or was set by law or regulation—the Contracting Officer or a representative who is an employee of the government shall have the right to examine and audit all books, records, documents, and other data of the contractor (including computations and projections) related to negotiating, pricing, or performing the modification in order to evaluate the accuracy, completeness, and currency of the cost or pricing data.

Section 52.215-2 of the FAR applies to negotiated cost reimbursement, incentive, labor hour, time and materials, and price redeterminable contracts, or any combination of these, and provides that the contractor shall maintain—and the Contracting Officer or representative of the Contracting Officer shall have the right to examine and audit—books, documents, records, and other evidence and accounting procedures and practices sufficient to reflect properly all costs claimed to have been incurred in performing the contract. Both clauses require the retention of records, papers, documents, and associated material for a period of three years following final payment under the contract.

With the establishment of the DoD Inspector General, the DCAA has been assigned new responsibilities, with corresponding authority, with respect to fraud, waste, and abuse cases in federal contracting. At the minimum, it is required to report irregularities to the Inspector General. As a practical matter, the DCAA has become deeply involved in the fraud, waste, and abuse campaign. Indeed, it is responsible for detecting many of the irregularities that have been uncovered in recent years. On February 12, 1983, in a speech in New Orleans, before the Public Contract Law Section of the American Bar Association, Charles O. Starrett, Jr., Director, Defense Contract Audit Agency, indicated that his agency had reported 150 irregularity cases to the Inspector General. Of these reports, 75 percent were "audit-detected," and 40 percent were related to timekeeping problems.[1]

During the past several years, the DCAA has aggressively sought to perform "floor audits" in the facilities of many government contractors. During such audits, the DCAA auditors interview individual employees of the contractor to determine the work being performed by the employee, the work order being charged, any instructions concerning time charging given by supervisors, and the employee's view of the accuracy of the time card. In view of the new role of the DCAA, prudent contractors should establish an access management program for DCAA floor audits. As a minimum, the program should provide for (1) obtaining advance notification of the DCAA's intention to conduct a floor audit, (2) designating a company official to escort the DCAA auditor, (3) reviewing and approving the DCAA questionnaires, and (4) restricting the questions to be asked by the DCAA to specific subject areas that relate to the contract(s) that the DCAA is in fact auditing.

As was the case with the GAO, and in spite of its broad authority, the DCAA's powers are not without limitation. If the government agrees to pay a contractor's cost of performance, it also reserves the right to satisfy itself with reasonable certainty what those costs truly are. When a contractor's obligation is to deliver to the government something for a competitively arrived at fixed price, he retains the right to keep his own counsel and strict privacy as to his costs of delivering that item. On the other hand, if a contractor enters into a contract in which the government agrees essentially to pay him what it costs him to perform, that contractor has also invited the government into his office to determine what those costs are. Thereafter, a government auditor looks over his shoulder.

The marriage of government auditor and contractor is not easily dissolved. That auditor certainly has no right to roam without restriction through all the contractor's business documents that have no connection with the government contract. But he has a right to satisfy himself as to items claimed to be part of the costs of performing the government contract. When the claim is as to an overhead or indirect cost, there may be some necessity to look at entries other than those for labor, material, and equipment used directly in the performance of the government contract. The courts and Boards conceive of the audit function, when it applies, as a broad rather than a narrow one. *Grumman Aircraft Engineering Corp.*, ASBCA No. 10309, 66-2 BCA 5846. *Accord American Business Systems*, GSBCA Nos. 5140 & 5141, 80-1 BCA 14,461; *Hayes International Corp.*, ASBCA No. 18447, 75-1 BCA 11,076.

The fundamental purpose of a government audit of a contractor's books and records is to assure that claimed costs were in fact incurred, or are to be incurred, and that they were reasonable. However, the government is not entitled to assume the role of management or to review records and books not associated with or directly related to the public contracts performed, or to be performed, by the contractor. The audit clauses contain broad authority for the government, but they also contain limitations. While the government's auditors have ready access to directly pertinent books, documents, papers, and records that reflect incurred costs on specific public contracts, they have no authority to review purely commercial transactions of the contractor.

## SUBPOENA POWER

The GAO, the DCAA, and agency Inspectors General have authority to subpoena contractors' records in connection with irregularities under a government contract. Under the Defense Authorization Act of 1986, Pub. L. No. 99-145, the Director of the DCAA was granted authority to subpoena contractors' books, documents, and related records. The DCAA's procedures require that, before a request for subpoena is made to the Director of the DCAA, auditors pursue access to the records in question by conventional means. After all such means have been exhausted, the regional

DCAA office will become involved by reviewing the case and recommending, if the circumstances warrant, that a subpoena be obtained from the DCAA's headquarters. The DCAA regulation specifies that the General Counsel of the DCAA will review each request to assure that it is within the scope of the law and to notify the Justice Department in the event the DCAA needs to enforce the subpoena with judicial assistance.

The subpoena power of the audit agencies and the Inspectors General is not without limitation. As government regulation of business has mushroomed in recent years, the need for effective investigative techniques to achieve the aims of such regulation has been the subject of substantial comment and legislation. It is now settled that when an administrative agency subpoenas corporate books or records, the fourth amendment requires that the subpoena be sufficiently limited in scope, relevant in purpose, and specific in directive so that compliance will not be unreasonably burdensome. *See v. City of Seattle,* 387 U.S. 541 (1967). Moreover, the investigation must be conducted for a legitimate purpose, and inquiry must be relevant to that purpose. *United States v. Richards,* 631 F.2d 341 (4th Cir. 1980). Each request by an agency for corporate records must be considered in light of the particular function assigned to that agency by Congress. Thus, in *CAB v. Frontier Airlines,* 686 F.2d 854 (10th Cir. 1982), the court rejected the agency's demand for all of the airline's board of directors' minutes for a one-year period. While the parties agreed that the specific minutes relating to matters relevant to a specific CAB inquiry should be produced, the court refused to allow plenary inspection by the government. Inspection of documents must be related to the purpose of the statute authorizing inspection. Inspection is therefore governed by a reasonable relationship to the purpose of the statute.

A government investigation into corporate matters may be of such a sweeping nature and so unrelated to the matter properly under inquiry as to exceed the investigatory power of the agency. But it is sufficient if the inquiry is within the authority of the agency, the demand is not too indefinite, and the information sought is reasonably relevant. Relevancy and adequacy or excess in the breadth of the subpoena are matters variable in relation to the nature, purposes, and scope of the inquiry. The breadth of a subpoena or of a search made in records may be excessive, but the test is relevance to the specific purpose, and the statement or purpose must be apparent from the order. *Montship Lines v. United States,* 295 F.2d 147 (D.C. Cir. 1961). The agency must disclose its purpose to enable a court to make a determination of relevance. Otherwise, no inquiry into the underlying reasons for the examination is possible. *CAB v. United Airlines,* 542 F.2d 394 (7th Cir. 1976).

The power of Congress to conduct investigations is inherent in the legislative process, *Watkins v. United States,* 354 U.S. 178 (1957), and is necessarily incident to the power to legislate wisely. *See Quinn v. United States,* 349

U.S. 155 (1955). The GAO serves as investigative and auditing arm of Congress and is responsible for investigating all matters relating to the receipt, disbursement, and use of public money and for making recommendations looking to greater economy or efficiency in public expenditures. 31 U.S.C. § 53 (recodified at 31 U.S.C. § 712); *Bowsher v. Merck & Co.*, 460 U.S. 824 (1983).

In the General Accounting Office Act of 1980, Congress gave the GAO effective tools for carrying out its investigative function—the power to subpoena records to which the GAO has access by law or by agreement, 31 U.S.C. § 54(c)(1) (Supp. IV 1980), and the power to initiate subpoena enforcement proceedings in district court, 31 U.S.C. § 54(c)(2) (Supp. IV 1980). Issuance of subpoenas has long been held to be a legitimate use by Congress of its power to investigate. *Eastland v. United Servicemen's Fund*, 421 U.S. 491 (1975), and Congress, in legislating section 54(c)(2), specifically entrusted the district courts with enforcement of subpoenas issued under the authority of section 54(c)(1). The power to enforce a subpoena necessarily carries with it the power to determine if enforcement is proper. In this regard, the district court must interpret the scope of the access clause of the contract to determine, among other things, whether the subpoena was issued for a lawful purpose. *Oklahoma Press Publishing Co. v. Walling*, 327 U.S. 208, 209 (1946).

The subpoena power of the GAO, and presumably that of the DCAA and the Inspectors General, extends to documents related to all government contracts where there is a suspected irregularity, as well as to foreign military sales contracts. *United States v. McDonnell Douglas Corp.*, 751 F.2d 220 (8th Cir. 1984).

Nonetheless, there are limitations to be observed by the audit agencies. The DCAA's statutory subpoena power extends to cost information related to government contracts. But it does not have unlimited power to demand access to all internal corporate materials of companies performing cost-type contracts for the government. Cost verification data, not the work product of internal auditors, is the proper subject of a DCAA subpoena. *United States v. Newport News Shipbuilding & Drydock Co.*, 862 F.2d 464 (4th Cir. 1988).

In contrast, the agency Inspectors General has the responsibility and the power to conduct, supervise, and coordinate audits and investigations relating to agency acquisitions in order to promote efficiency and to prevent fraud and abuse. And the mere likelihood or even an imminence of criminal proceedings does not bar enforcement of a subpoena sought by the Inspector General in connection with investigations of fraudulent practices on the part of government contractors, so long as the agency has not made a formal recommendation to the Department of Justice to prosecute. Once a legitimate fraud investigation is under way, the Inspector General's power to subpoena documents in support of that investigation is quite valid. *United States v. Art-Metal-*

*U.S.A.*, 484 F. Supp. 884 (D.N.J. 1980). If there has been merely an institutional (i.e., intra-agency) commitment to refer the matter to Justice, but no formal recommendation, then a summons may be enforced, unless the party opposing enforcement is able to show that there is no civil purpose for the summons. *United States v. Genser*, 602 F.2d 69 (3d Cir. 1979).

The language of 42 U.S.C. § 7138(g)(2) does not provide authority for the Inspector General in the exercise of his special subpoena power to compel an individual to appear to give testimony, however. There is no reference in this section to a subpoena requiring the attendance of a witness to give oral testimony. On the contrary, the section refers only to the "production of all information, documents, reports, answers, records, accounts, papers, and other data and documentary evidence." In short, the language is directed at the production of documentary evidence, as contrasted to oral testimony. The general word "information" is defined and limited by the language that follows, specifying written materials and documentary evidence. That language does not suggest that appearance to give oral testimony may be demanded.

That Congress in other statutes has explicitly provided for the power to subpoena the attendance and testimony of witnesses reinforces the conclusion that the subpoena authority under section 7138(g)(2) is restricted to documentary evidence. The most striking example of such an explicit grant of power is found in the Federal Energy Administration (FEA) Act, the predecessor of the Department of Energy Organization Act. In granting subpoena power to the Administrator, the FEA Act expressly included the power to subpoena "the attendance and testimony of witnesses," in addition to the production of "all information documents." 15 U.S.C. § 772(e)(1) (1976). This makes it plain that if Congress had intended to authorize the Inspector General to compel the attendance of witnesses, it would have specified that power in section 7138(g)(2). *United States v. Iannone*, 610 F.2d 943 (1979).

Contractors are not powerless to prevent unwarranted intrusion into their affairs. Established legal principles delineate the scope of administrative investigative powers, and the courts will intercede when agencies exceed their authority or fail to establish that document requests are reasonably relevant to a lawful investigative purpose. Any request by the GAO, the DCAA, or an agency Inspector General must be authorized by a specific statute or contract clause, and these provisions define and limit the purposes for which records may be sought.[2]

## NOTES

1. David Hirsch, "Counseling Clients in Connection with Defense Contract Audit Agency Dealings," in *Defense Procurement Enforcement* (New York: Law & Business/Harcourt, Brace, Jovanovich, 1983), p. 202.

2. Clarence T. Kipps, Jay L. Carlson, and Alan C. Brown, "Confronting the DoD 'Access to Records' Offensive," *Federal Contracts Report* 43 (1985): 1025–26.

# 14

# Bid Protests, Disputes, and Extraordinary Relief

## INTRODUCTION

Bid protests, the disputes process, and the equitable remedy of extraordinary relief are statutorily based remedies available to the contractor, or prospective contractor, doing business with the government. Each remedy has its application during a specific phase of the acquisition process. Bid protests are associated with the award phase and are generally concerned with some irregularity in the selection of a bidder or offeror for contract award or with allegations of defective specifications or terms and conditions of the proposed contract. Contract disputes arise during the performance phase, whereas extraordinary relief is only available to certain defense contractors when all other means have been exhausted.

## BID PROTESTS

The bid protest process is based on the implied contract theory. The issuance of a solicitation instrument and the submission of a bid or offer in response thereto result in the creation of an implied contract that the government will fairly and honestly consider each bid or offer received in accordance with the express criteria set forth in the solicitation, the agency's rules and regulations, the FAR, and appropriate statutes. Failure on the part of the agency to abide by these criteria is generally viewed as a breach of an implied contract. The bid protest process is also an avenue through which interested bidders or offerors can bring irregularities in the specifications or the terms and conditions of the proposed contract to the attention of the procuring agency. Thus, protests may be filed in either the pre-award of post-award phase of the acquisition process.

The Comptroller General has jurisdiction to consider the legality of bidding procedures, as well as bid protests and claims of illegal awards, under statutory authority to settle all claims and demands against the government. 31 U.S.C. § 71. The Competition in Contracting Act (CICA) amended the Budget and Accounting Act to give the Comptroller General statutory authority to determine whether the solicitation, proposed award, or award complies with applicable statutes and regulations. 31 U.S.C. § 3554(b)(1).

The Comptroller General does not have exclusive jurisdiction over protests, however. CICA did not affect the rights of an interested party either to file a protest with the procuring agency or to seek injunctive relief in a federal district court or the Claims Court. 31 U.S.C. § 3556. Moreover, CICA amended section 111 of the Federal Property and Administrative Services Act of 1949 (40 U.S.C. § 759) to provide that an interested party may protest an automatic data processing acquisition by filing with the General Services Board of Contract Appeals (GSBCA). The GSBCA has the power to review any decision of a Contracting Officer alleged to violate a statute or regulation pertaining to the acquisition of automatic data processing equipment and may suspend acquisition authority, unless the agency establishes that compelling circumstances exist that significantly affect the interests of the United States. FAR § 33.105.

Section 33.102(b)(1) of the FAR encourages protesting contractors to seek resolution of their complaints with the procuring agency prior to filing a protest with the Comptroller General or with the GSBCA regarding the award of an automatic data processing equipment contract. When a protest is filed with an agency, an award cannot be made until the matter is resolved, unless the Contracting Officer or other designated official determines that (1) the supplies or services to be contracted for are urgently required, (2) delivery or performance will be unduly delayed by failure to make an award promptly, or (3) a prompt award will otherwise be advantageous to the government. FAR § 33.103(a).

Under the provisions of CICA, a protest filed with the Comptroller General by an interested party shall be decided by the Comptroller. 31 U.S.C. § 3552. "Protest" has been defined to mean a written objection by an interested party to a solicitation by an executive agency for bids or proposals for a proposed contract for the procurement of property or services or a written objection by an interested party to a proposed award or the award of such a contract. 31 U.S.C. § 3551(1). "Interested party" means an actual or prospective bidder or offeror whose direct economic interest would be affected by the award of the contract or by the failure to award. 31 U.S.C. § 3551(2).

Prior to the passage of CICA, a parents' association was permitted to protest the award of a contract for a model day-care center even though the association was not a bidder or offeror on the proposed contract. Since the parents' association showed a clear financial interest in the form of paying for 15 percent of the total operating costs of the center, it qualified as an interested party. Comp. Gen. B-183190 (1975). With the passage of CICA, there is no doubt that such association would continue to qualify on the basis that it had a direct economic interest that would be affected by the proposed award or the failure to award.

Conversely, a protest by a "concerned citizen" who argued that only one bidder on a challenged procurement provided an appropriate response to the solicitation could not be considered by the Comptroller General because the protestor did not qualify as an interested party. The requirement that a party be interested is designed to assure his diligent participation in the protest process so that the issues are sharply presented and the record is made complete, as well as to avoid frivolous protests. In making the determination as to what "interests" entails, the Comptroller General will consider the nature of the issues raised and the direct or indirect benefits to the protestor. Comp. Gen. B-184852 (1975). The Comptroller General has also held that the protest of a nonresponsible contractor cannot be considered because the party is not an interested party. *Therm-Air Mfg. Co.,* Comp. Gen. B-191540.2 (1978). The same rule applies to contractors who are debarred or suspended.

If a protest is filed with the Comptroller General, the protestor is required to furnish a copy of its complete protest to the official designated in the solicitation or, in the absence of such a designation, to the Contracting Officer no later than one day after the protest has been filed. Failure to furnish a complete copy of the protest within one day may result in the dismissal of the protest by the GAO. FAR § 33.104. Moreover, the Comptroller General is required to notify the procuring agency involved of the protest within one working day of receipt of such protest. 31 U.S.C. § 3553(b)(1).

Except as provided below, a contract may not be awarded in any acquisition where the procuring agency has received notice of a protest regarding such acquisition from the Comptroller General, pending resolution of the protest. 31 U.S.C. § 3553(c)(1). This prohibition against making an award while a protest is under review has strengthened considerably the authority of the Comptroller General in the acquisition process and generally follows the position taken by the courts in recent years. In *Robert E. Derecktor of Rhode Island v. Goldschmidt,* 506 F. Supp. 1059 (DC R.I. 1980), for instance, Derecktor filed a protest with the GAO prior to the execution of a contract for the construction of nine Coast Guard cutters. Notwithstanding the protest, the Coast Guard executed the contract three days after it had been filed with the GAO. The court held that it was the duty of the court to hold unlawful and set aside agency action found to be (1) arbitrary, capricious, an abuse of discretion, or otherwise not in accordance with law; or (2) without observance of procedures required by law. 5 U.S.C. § 706(2). When a protest has been filed before award, the agency will not make an award prior to the resolution of the protest, except as provided in the applicable procurement regulations. 4 C.F.R. § 20.4 (1980). Regulations require that the notice of intent to make the award shall be furnished prior to making the award. Failure to comply with the regulations cannot be considered to be in accord with law or in observance of procedures required by law and is therefore a violation of 5 U.S.C. § 706(2)(A) & (D). Agency regulations have the force and effect of law. The Coast Guard's action in awarding the contract must be held to be unlawful and must be set aside.

The head of the acquiring agency responsible for award of a contract, on a nondelegable basis, may authorize the award of the contract while the protest is pending upon a written finding (1) that urgent and compelling circumstances that significantly affect interests of the United States will not permit waiting for the decision of the Comptroller General and (2) that award is likely to occur within 30 days of the finding. 31 U.S.C § 3553(c)(2) & (3); FAR § 33.104(b)(1) & (2).

If a procuring agency receives notice of a protest from the Comptroller General after the contract has been awarded, but within 10 days of the date of the contract award, the agency is required to immediately suspend performance or terminate the contract. Performance of the contract may not be resumed while the protest is pending, unless the head of the procuring activity responsible for contract award, on a nondelegable basis, authorizes continuance notwithstanding the protest. The head of the procuring activity is required to issue a written finding (1) that contract performance is in the best interests of the United States or (2) that urgent and compelling circumstances that significantly affect the interests of the United States will not permit waiting for the Comptroller General's decision. Contract performance cannot be authorized, however, until the agency has notified the Comptroller General of its findings. 31 U.S.C. § 3553(d); FAR § 33.104(c).

The GAO is required to issue a final decision on a protest within 90 working days from the date of the protest, or within 45 working days under the express option, unless the GAO establishes a longer period of time within which to process the protest. It may dismiss a protest that is frivolous or that, on its face, does not state a valid basis for protest.

The Comptroller General is statutorily authorized to determine whether the solicitation, proposed award, or award complies with statutes and regulations governing the procurement process. If it is determined that the solicitation, proposed award, or award does not comply with appropriate statutes and regulations, it is statutorily required to recommend that the procuring agency (1) refrain from exercising any of its options under the contract, (2) recompete the contract immediately, (3) issue a new solicitation, (4) terminate the contract, (5) award a contract that is consistent with such statutes or regulations, or (6) perform any combination of the foregoing. If the head of the procuring agency makes a finding either to award the contract or to continue contract performance where the protest has been received after contract award, the Comptroller General is required to make recommendations without regard to any cost or disruption from termination, recompeting, or reawarding the contract. 31 U.S.C. § 3554(b)(2).

Under CICA, the head of the procuring activity responsible for the solicitation, proposed award, or award of a contract that is the subject of a protest is required to notify the Comptroller General within 60 days if the agency does not implement the Comptroller General's recommendations. To assure control over the protest procedures, Congress requires the Comptroller to report annually by January 31 as to each instance in which a procuring agency did not implement its recommendations during the preceding year. 31 U.S.C. § 3554(e)(2).

When the Comptroller General determines that a solicitation, proposed award, or award of a contract does not comply with a statute or regulation, he may find the protestor to be entitled to the costs of filing and pursuing the protest, to include reasonable attorney's fees and bid and proposal costs. 31 U.S.C. § 3554(c)(1).

Actions by the Comptroller General with respect to protests are injunctive in nature. Accordingly, the importance of timely filing by an interested party cannot be overemphasized. In case after case, the Comptroller General has refused to consider valid protests that were not filed in a timely manner. As a general rule, an alleged impropriety or ambiguity in a solicitation instrument that is apparent on the face of the solicitation should be protested before the time set for bid opening or the closing date set for the receipt of proposals. The protest gives the government an opportunity to correct such defect, and failure to protest could constitute acceptance of the defect once the award has been made. Otherwise, a protest must be filed within 10 days of establishing a basis for adverse agency action.

A protest alleging that a solicitation for a 100 percent small business set-aside containing a $2 million size standard was unduly restrictive of competition was dismissed because, after bid opening, but prior to contract award, the size standard was increased to $4.5 million by publication in the *Federal Register.* The protestor failed to file the protest within 10 working days of publication of the new size standard. The Comptroller General ruled that all parties are held to be on constructive notice of materials published in the *Federal Register,* and, therefore, the protest was untimely. Comp. Gen. B-192188 (1978).

A protestor's allegation that he should have been given additional time to submit a revised proposal was untimely because it was not filed within 10 working days after the agency first notified him that his earlier letter, making the same request, was rejected. After being informed that his proposal was unacceptable, the offeror submitted a letter requesting a time extension in order that he could prepare and submit another proposal. The agency met with the offeror and denied his request. This denial constituted initial adverse agency action, from which time the protestor was required to file his protest. Since he did not file within 10 working days from that date, the GAO had no alternative but to dismiss the protest. Comp. Gen. B-193308 (1978).

The Comptroller General will not attempt to determine the technical competence of a prospective contractor. He has consistently denied consideration of protests concerning the rejection of proposals for technical reasons, which have been made without giving offerors an opportunity to modify their proposals. It is not the function of the Comptroller General to technically evaluate proposals or to decide the degree of effort required to render an unacceptable proposal acceptable. If such rejections are accomplished by the procuring agencies through established evaluation procedures, in accordance with the criteria set forth in the solicitation, and if there is no evidence of arbitrary or capricious action on the part of the agency, the Comptroller General will not intervene. Comp. Gen. B-157534 (1965).

Similarly, the Comptroller General has no authority to award contracts regardless of his findings in response to a protest. The Comptroller General's statutory authority is limited to ensuring that no contract is awarded if it does not conform to applicable statutes and regulations. He has no authority to establish the requirements of the executive branch or to direct that an award be made when, in the view of the procuring agency, the award should be delayed or that no award be made at all. Comp. Gen. B-160172 (1966).

## DISPUTES

Vestiges of a Disputes article have existed since the Civil War era, and a close equivalent of the current Disputes article came into use in 1926. That clause provided that in the event the Contracting Officer and the contractor were unable to resolve a dispute that arose under the contract, the Contracting Officer was required to issue a final decision, which could be appealed to the secretary of the department or the head of the agency concerned. The contractor was required to perform as directed following the final decision of the Contracting Officer, and if he failed to appeal within the allotted time, the decision of the Contracting Officer was final and conclusive upon him. Moreover, the legality of enforcing the Disputes clause, and of vesting appellate authority in the department secretary or agency head, has long been established. *United States v. Wunderlich,* 342 U.S. 98 (1951); *United States v. Moorman,* 338 U.S. 457 (1950); *United States v. Adams,* 74 U.S. (7 Wall.) 463 (1868).

There was a lack of consistency between the clauses used by the various departments and agencies, however, and there was no clear-cut statutory authority on which to base the processing of claims related to contract disputes. Hence, the Contract Disputes Act of 1978, Pub. L. No. 95-563, 41

U.S.C. §§ 601–609, was one of the most important procurement statutes enacted in recent years. With its passage, a new era in the resolution of government contract disputes emerged.

The Act mandates governmentwide uniformity for asserting and resolving claims arising under or in relation to a contract. It broadened and clarified the authority of agency Boards of Contact Appeals, mandated that all claims be submitted in writing to the Contracting Officer for final decision, made a final decision of the Contracting Officer a mandatory prerequisite to review by the Claims Court or a Board of Contract Appeals, provided a choice of forums to which the contractor could appeal, and established procedures whereby either the government or the contractor may appeal an adverse decision of the Claims Court or Board of Contract Appeals to the U.S. Court of Appeals for the Federal Circuit.

The Act also provides for the payment of interest on amounts found due to contractors on claims, for a civil penalty for the submission of fraudulent claims, and for contractor certification of all claims exceeding $50,000. Further, the Act specifies statutory time limits within which a contractor must file his claim.

One of the most significant provisions of the Act is that which gives the contractor an option as to the forum to which to take an appeal from a Contracting Officer's final decision. Prior to the passage of the Act, a contractor could appeal an adverse final decision only to the appropriate Board of Contract Appeals. The Act authorizes the contractor to appeal a final decision to the appropriate Board, 41 U.S.C. § 606; or, in lieu thereof, the contractor may appeal the final decision of the Contracting Officer in the Claims Court, notwithstanding any contract provision, regulation, or rule of law to the contrary, 41 U.S.C. § 609(a).

### Jurisdiction

Congressional concern with the independence, impartiality, and professionalism of Boards of Contract Appeals led, in part, to the passage of the Contract Disputes Act. Under the Act, Board jurisdiction does not depend on a delegation of authority from the department or agency. Rather, jurisdiction is derived from section 8(d), which provides that each agency Board shall have jurisdiction to decide any appeal from a decision from the Contracting Officer (1) relative to a contract made by the agency and (2) relative to a contract made by any other agency when such agency or the Administrator of the Office of Federal Procurement Policy has designated the agency Board to decide the appeal.

In exercising its jurisdiction, the agency Board is authorized to grant any relief that would be available to a litigant asserting a contract claim in the U.S. Claims Court. 41 U.S.C. § 607(d). Thus, the Boards and Claims Court may grant similar relief, and both forums have similar subpoena, discovery, and deposition powers. Further, the Act provides that both Board awards and Claims Court judgments be paid in the same manner, and from the same fund, 41 U.S.C. §§ 612(a) *et seq.;* and both forums pay interest on amounts found due to contractors on claims from the date the Contracting Officer receives the claim until payment thereof, 41 U.S.C. § 611.

But there are certain fundamental differences between the two forums that a contractor should take into consideration in making the forum selection decision. The Boards can act on a claim in less time than the Claims Court can dispose of a case, and litigation in court is considerably more expensive. Under the Act, the Boards are required to provide, to the fullest extent practicable, informal, expeditious, and inexpensive resolution of disputes. 41 U.S.C. § 607(e).

Rules of agency Boards are required to include a procedure for accelerated disposition of any appeal from a contractor where the amount of the dispute is $50,000 or less. The accelerated procedure is applicable at the sole election of the contractor, and appeals under the accelerated procedure require resolution, whenever possible, within 180 days from the date the contractor elects to rely on such procedure. 41 U.S.C. § 607(f). The Act also provides for the resolution of small claims of $10,000 or less in 120 days, at the sole election of the contractor. 41 U.S.C. § 608.

The Boards of Contract Appeals have authority to grant any relief under the Act that would be available to a litigant asserting a claim in the Claims Court. 41 U.S.C. § 607(d). Prior to the passage of the Act, it was well established that the Boards lacked the jurisdiction to consider the defense of mutual mistake. *National Linen Co.,* ASBCA No. 18739, 75-2 BCA 11,400. The Contract Disputes Act granted the Boards rescission and reformation authority for appeals subject to the Act. The Act also expanded the jurisdiction of the the Boards. *Paragon Energy Corp. v. United States,* 277 Ct. Cl. 176, 645 F.2d 966 (1981); *Applied Devices Corp. v. United States,* 219 Ct. Cl. 109, 591 F.2d 635, 640 (1979); *Pavco,* ASBCA No. 23738, 80-1 BCA 14,407. See also *Bromley Contracting Co. v. United States,* 219 Ct. Cl. 109, 596 F.2d 448 (1979). It is too clear to require citation of authority that Contracting Officers and Boards of Contract Appeals have authority under the Contracts Disputes Act to decide breach and reformation claims notwithstanding the fact that prior to the Act such claims were cognizable within the executive departments only as extraordinary relief under Pub. L. No. 85-804. *Gentex Corp.,* ASBCA No. 24040, 79-2 BCA 14,007.

As to bid and proposal costs, the contract under consideration is the implied contract that arose between the parties by virtue of a solicitation of bids or offers on a proposed contract and the submission by the contractor of a bid or offer in response to that solicitation. The government's duty under that implied contract is not to make an award to the low responsible offeror whose offer is responsive to the terms of the solicitation. Rather, the government's duty is only to give fair and honest consideration to all offers submitted in response to its solicitation. If an offeror can show that, had his bid or proposal been fairly and honestly considered, there was a substantial chance he would have received award of the proposed contract, then he may recover his bid preparation expenses.

A government breach of the implied contract of fair consideration occurs when the solicitation is but a ruse, the prospective contractor having been previously selected; when the government harbors an active prejudice against one of the offerors; or when the government knows that the contract to be awarded cannot be performed at the price a competitor has offered, but nonetheless proceeds with an award. The government's duty under the implied contract of fair consideration goes beyond the bad faith test. Where a decision is made to reject an offer, or to award a contract to a competing offeror, the government must make that decision without arbitrariness or caprice. If a disappointed offeror is able to show that such a decision was arbitrary or capricious, he is entitled to recover the costs incurred in preparing and submitting his offer. *L.A. Anderson Constr. Co.*, GSBCA No. 6235, 81-2 BCA 15,507. The Boards of Contract Appeals are authorized to grant any relief that would be available to a litigant asserting a claim in the Claims Court. The Claims Court has long accepted jurisdiction in situations where the contractor sought bid and proposal costs, and so, too, can the Boards. *Master Mechanic*, GSBCA No. 5535, 80-2 BCA 14, 854.

The Act provides that if two or more suits arising from one contract are filed in the Claims Court and with one or more agency Boards, the Claims Court may order the consolidation of such suits in that court or transfer any suits to or among the agency Boards for the convenience of the parties or witnesses or in the interest of justice. 41 U.S.C. § 609(d). Although the contractor has an election to appeal to either an agency Board or the Claims Court, it is clear that an appeal involving the same contract and issues cannot be filed in both forums simultaneously. See *David J. Tierney, Jr., Inc. v. United States*, 226 Ct. Cl. 513 (1981).

In order for the Boards or the Claims Court to obtain jurisdiction under the Contract Disputes Act, the contractor must (1) present a written and properly certified claim to the Contracting Officer and (2) obtain a final decision from the Contracting Officer on that claim. 41 U.S.C. § 605(a) & (c); *T.J.D. Services v. United States*, 6 Cl. Ct. 357 (1984).

This statutory requirement is intended to prohibit contractors from changing their claim, once a final decision has been reached by the Contracting Officer, on appeal to either a Board or the Claims Court. The prior practice under the contract Disputes clause turned on the premise that proceedings before an agency Board were de novo, and, as it often turned out, claims presented to, or decided by, an agency Board were quite different from those considered and denied by the Contracting Officer.

In many minds, that practice was abused by contractors who presented largely unsubstantiated claims that were properly denied by the Contracting Officer and who then fleshed out the claim, so to speak, during proceedings before agency Boards. In recognition of this concern, amendments to the Senate Bill renumbered section 5 as section 6 and revised the former section 5(a), which had read "all contract claims submitted by a contractor against the Government or by the Government against a contractor shall be in writing" to read "all claims by a contractor shall be in writing and shall be submitted to the Contracting Officer for decision." This amendment makes it clear that Congress intended that the term "claim" be narrowly construed in the sense that contractors were to present to the Contracting Officer the entirety of their claims and not wait for further proceedings to set forth all of the details. *Rubin & Janeiro, Inc.*, GSBCA No. 6042, 82-1 BCA 15,802.

A major purpose of the Disputes Act was to "induce resolution of contract disputes with the Government by negotiation rather than litigation." *Great Lakes Educ. Consultants v. Federal Energy Management Agency,* 582 F. Supp. 193 (W.D. Mich. 1984). Since the Contracting Officer is the official responsible for negotiating settlements with the contractor, that official must be furnished the entirety of the claim, to include detailed justification supporting the contractor's position, before the Contracting Officer can reach an objective decision as to either entitlement or quantum.

It is thus clear that the Act requires (1) that all claims against the government be in writing and submitted to the Contracting Officer for a final decision and (2) that all claims by the government against a contractor be the subject of a final decision by the Contracting Officer before an agency Board or the Claims Court can acquire jurisdiction over the disputed claim. 41 U.S.C. § 605(a) & (c); FAR § 52.233-1(d)(1); *Paragon Energy Corp. v. United States,* 227 Ct. Cl. 176, 645 F.2d 966 (1981); *Tilbury, Inc.,* ASBCA No. 25792, 82-1 BCA 15,644; *Modular Devices,* ASBCA No. 24198, 82-1 BCA 15,536.

Under the Act, the Contracting Officer is required to issue a written decision, stating the reasons for the decision reached, within 60 days from his receipt of a written request from the contractor that a decision be rendered within that period with respect to all submitted claims of $50,000 or less. If the claim exceeds $50,000, the Contracting Officer is required, within 60 days, to either issue a decision or notify the contractor of the time within which a decision will be issued. In the latter case, the decision is to be issued within a reasonable time, taking into consideration such factors as the size and complexity of the claim and the adequacy of the information in support of the claim furnished by the contractor. In the event of undue delay by the Contracting Officer, the contractor may request the agency Board of Contract Appeals to issue a decision. Any failure by the Contracting Officer to issue a decision within the period will be deemed to be a decision by the Contracting Officer denying the claim and will therefore authorize the commencement of an appeal or a suit under the Act. However, in the event an appeal or suit is commenced in the absence of a prior decision of the Contracting Officer, the tribunal may, at its option, stay the proceedings to obtain a decision on the claim by the Contracting Officer. 41 U.S.C. § 605. Accordingly, and until a final decision has been rendered by the Contracting Officer or is deemed to have been rendered, the contractor has not exhausted his administrative remedies. The linchpin for appealing claims under the Contract Disputes Act is the Contracting Officer's final decision. *Straga v. United States,* 8 Cl. Ct. 61 (1985).

By authorizing the contractor to file suit, the plain language of section 6(c)(5) provides that the contractor has the legal option or permission to go forward, when the government has not issued a timely decision, by filing a direct access suit in the U.S. Claims Court. *Vemo Co. v. United States,* 9 Cl. Ct. 217 (1985). The provision is designed to enable the contractor to obtain a judicial determination of its claim (or a determination by a Board of Contract Appeals, if the contractor follows that procedure) without awaiting the decision of a Contracting Officer who has failed to render a decision within the specified time limits. The contractor's right to institute suit under the "deemed denied" provision is permissive, not mandatory. *Pathman Constr. Co. v. United States,* CAFC No. 86-1537 (1987).

## Claim

The Contract Disputes Act does not define the term "claim." Claim, as used in the Act, is limited to those situations arising under or related to the contract where the contractor's alleged entitlement to monies due, recovery, or other relief is disputed by the government. Nonetheless, there are statutory requirements that must be met in order for the contractor's claim to be treated as such.

The FAR definition of claim is based on these statutory requirements and defines "claim" as meaning a written demand or written assertion by one of the contracting parties seeking, as a matter of right, the payment of money in a sum certain, the adjustment or interpretation of contract terms, or other relief arising under or related to the contract. A claim arising under a contract, unlike a claim relating to that contract, is a claim that can be resolved under a contract clause that provides for the relief sought by the claimant. A written demand or written assertion by the contractor seeking the payment of money exceeding $50,000 is not a claim under the Contract Disputes Act until certified. A voucher, invoice, or other routine request for payment that is not in dispute when submitted is not a claim under the Act. The submission may be converted under the Act by complying with the submission and certification requirements of the Disputes article if it is either disputed as to liability or amount or not acted on in a reasonable time. FAR § 52.233-1(c). See also *Z.A.N. Co. v. United States,* 6 Cl. Ct. 298 (1984).

Virtually all claims are submitted for negotiation and settlement. It is the government's policy to attempt to resolve all contractual issues by mutual agreement, at the Contracting Officer level, without resorting to litigation. FAR § 33.004. The concern of Congress with unsupported claims and improvident settlement agreements by government representatives must be kept in mind in interpreting the general purposes of the Act, as stated in Senate Report No. 95-1118: "The Contract Disputes Act of 1978 provides a fair, balanced, and comprehensive statutory system of legal and administrative remedies in resolving Government contract claims. The Act's provisions help to induce resolution of more contract disputes by negotiation prior to litigation." It is clear that Congress wanted to encourage fair and equitable settlements of money claims so as to avoid litigation of those claims before an agency Board or the Claims Court. *Newell Clothing Co.,* ASBCA No. 24482, 80-2 BCA 14,774.

## Certification

Section 6(c)(1) of the Act and section 33.007(a) of FAR require that the contractor certify that claims in excess of $50,000 are made in good faith, that the supporting data are accurate and complete to the best of his knowledge and belief, and that the amount requested accurately reflects the contract adjustment for which the contractor believes the government is liable. Moreover, the aggregate amount of both the increased and the decreased costs shall be used in determining when the dollar threshold requiring claim certification is reached. FAR § 33.004(b). If the contractor is an individual, the certificate must be executed by that individual. If the contractor is not an individual, the certification must be executed by a senior company official in charge at the contractor's plant or location involved or by an officer or general partner of the contractor having overall responsibility for the conduct of the contractor's affairs. FAR § 33.007(c).

It is clear that, without certification where appropriate and required, the Contracting Officer has no duty to issue a final decision on a claim submitted to him for review and a determination as to its merits. Certification is a condition precedent to the Contracting Officer's obligation to issue a decision. The Contracting Officer's duty to issue a decision on claims over $50,000 is made subject to prior certification by section 6(c)(2), which states the obligation in terms of time of receipt of a "submitted certified claim over $50,000." *Allied Machinery & Equipment Co.,* ASBCA No. 24373, 80-1 BCA 14,340. In cases where the Act requires certification and certification has not been made, the Contracting Officer has no authority to issue a decision. Written certification in simultaneous, literal compliance with the assertion set forth in 41 U.S.C. § 605(c)(1), made by the prime contractor and submitted with the claim, is necessary for there to be a valid claim under the Act. *Albers Constr. Co.,* GSBCA No. 6150, 83-1 BCA 16,171. Thus, the Boards will deny jurisdiction if the statutory requirements have not been complied with.

Certification is likewise a prerequisite for the Claims Court to acquire direct access jurisdiction under the Act. The requirement for certification of claims of more than $50,000 is an important part of the new procedures Congress provided in the Act for the handling of claims by government contractors. The purposes of the certification requirements are to discourage the submission of unwarranted claims and to encourage settlements. The statute thus provides that, to be valid, a claim must be properly certified. Until that requirement is met, there is simply no claim that the Claims Court may review under the Act. The Contracting Officer, in reviewing an uncertified claim of more than $50,000, has no authority to waive a statutory requirement that Congress has imposed. *Paul E. Lehman, Inc. v. United States,* 230 Ct. Cl. 142, 673 F.2d 352 (1982). The Claims Court has consistently interpreted 41 U.S.C. § 605(c)(1) as requiring the furnishing of such a certificate, by the contractor, in order to acquire direct access jurisdiction of a claim exceeding $50,000. *T.J.D. Services v. United States,* 6 Cl. Ct. 257 (1984).

To properly certify a claim, the contractor must make a statement that simultaneously makes all of the assertions required by 41 U.S.C. § 605(c)(1). The determination of the adequacy of the certification is not discretionary on the Contracting Officer's part. The statute requires that the contractor certify that (1) the claim is made in good faith, (2) the supporting data are accurate and complete to the best of his knowledge and belief, and (3) the amount requested accurately reflects the contract adjustment for which the contractor believes the government is liable. *Arlington Alliance v. United States,* 231 Ct. Cl. 347, 685 F.2d 1353 (1982); *W.H. Moseley Co. v. United States,* 230 Ct. Cl. 405, 677 F.2d 859 (1982).

The $50,000 certification threshold applies to each claim submitted under a contract. If multiple claims of less than $50,000 each are filed as a consequence of independent disputes, the government may not consolidate them for purposes of requiring certification. Where each of the items for which the contractor seeks relief meets the definition of "claim," each item is an independent dispute concerning contractual rights and is not intertwined in the merits of any other request for equitable adjustment. Therefore, each of the claims must exceed $50,000 before certification is required for that claim. The contractor should not be permitted to divide claims to avoid the certification requirements, as well as the requirements for cost and pricing data. While such a practice would contravene these requirements, if the record reflects that the areas of dispute involve different substantive matters and that the contractor has attempted to bring each of the matters to the government as soon as possible, there is no abuse of these requirements. On the other hand, certification requirements of the Act can be abused where the government, either intentionally or by inaction, allows individual claims to accumulate without a Contracting Officer's final decision until the aggregate exceeds the $50,000 threshold, at which time certification is required. *B.D. Click Co.*, ASBCA No. 25609, 81-2 BCA 15, 394.

A contractor will not be allowed to escape or circumvent the Act's certification requirements by splintering what is in actuality a single, unitary claim into multiple claims. Such a fragmented submission of a single claim violates the legislative purpose designed to ensure the integrity of the certification requirements by precluding the use of fragmented or multiple claims as a method of emasculating the certification requirement. Fragmented and individual descriptions of categories of incurred costs do not constitute separate claims, but rather serve as supporting data, justifying what is essentially a single claim for the total amount of the extra costs incurred. *Warchol Constr. Co. v. United States,* 2 Cl. Ct. 384 (1983).

The provision of the Act requiring certification and its background show a concern with and requirements for accurate, complete, and certified data in support of entitlement and amount. The certification requirement, in conjunction with section 5, Fraudulent Claims, of the Act was intended by Congress to discourage the unwarranted submission of undocumented contractor claims. Problems that arise from unsupported claims include the following:

1. The submission of an unsupported claim may lead the government to enter settlements independent of their legal merits.
2. Because such claims lack specificity, the burden shifts to the government to disprove them.
3. The government has limited resources that can be devoted to the resolution of claims disputes. 1978 U.S. Code Cong. & Admin. News, 5242.

Properly administered, the certification allows the Contracting Officer intelligently and confidently to evaluate all aspects of the claim in weighing settlement proposals and balancing the amount sought against the risk of litigation. Moreover, quantum data are likely to be an excellent measure of the seriousness of the claim. Thus, the Contracting Officer may consider quantum data before making his final determination of whether a claim should be paid in whole or in part or should be denied. Likewise, a reasonable businessman or his attorney probably will consider whether a claim can be supported and documented before making a final settlement offer.

The legislative history stresses the firm purpose of Congress to eliminate the negotiation tactics of claiming an amount beyond that which can be legitimately claimed and to assure that "disputes encompass only that amount which is truly contested." It is manifest from section 6(c)(2) of the Act that until the contractor submits the section 6(c)(1) certification, the Contracting Officer is not obliged to issue a final decision; nor does the clock start running on the period for issuing a final decision. See *Allied Machinery & Equipment Co.*, ASBCA No. 24373, 80-1 BCA 14, 340. Even after certification has been submitted, a contractor is not precluded from changing the amount of the claim or producing additional data. The only requirements are that the contractor certify to the amount he then honestly believes is due and that the data furnished at the time be accurate and complete to the best of his knowledge and belief. Contracting Officers can now demand that substantial contractor claims be fleshed out and supported before they decide whether the claims can be settled or should be contested. *Newell Clothing Co.*, ASBCA No. 24482, 80-2 BCA 14,774.

Section 6(c)(1) of the Act calls for certification to the Contracting Officer of claims in excess of $50,000 with respect to entitlement, amount, and supporting data. Absent a specific dollar claim, it is not possible to determine whether certification is required. This is intended to give a Contracting Officer the opportunity to consider all the facts and decide whether the claim should be paid, negotiated, or denied. *Sea Con Corp.*, AGBCA No. 81-204-1, 81-2 BCA 15,316.

The Contract Disputes Act requires that the claim be made in good faith and, if quantum is in issue, that the amount of the claim be stated as a sum certain. A finite amount cannot, of course, lend itself to qualifications or conditions. Any attempt to predicate the amount of the claim on a condition subsequent (i.e., "as amended according to proof at time of trial") effectively precludes any meaningful consideration of the claim by the Contracting Officer. In practical effect, the statutory function of the Contracting Officer would then be usurped by the Board.

Submission of a quantum claim in an undetermined amount does not accord with the legislative history of the purpose of this section of the Contract Disputes Act. Although the legislative history of the Act is not entirely clear in all respects, the purpose of this certification provision was to prevent the assertion of inflated claims against the government. The intent of Congress is clear that the certification be unqualified. If every contractor could emasculate the certification by adding material qualifications, the requirement for certification would be meaningless. The certification is a statement made in good faith to the best of the contractor's knowledge and belief. It does not preclude proof of a higher amount at hearing, nor does it have anything to do with liability under section 5 of the Act, a liability that exists whether or not there is a certification, but only where there is a misrepresentation of fact or fraud. *Hernischfeger Corp.*, ASBCA Nos. 23918 & 24733, 80-2 BCA 14,540.

### Timeliness in Appealing to Boards

The Contract Disputes Act provides that the contractor may appeal the final decision of the Contracting Officer to the appropriate agency Board of

Contract Appeals, providing that the appeal is filed within 90 days of receipt of such decision. 41 U.S.C. § 606. The statutory limit thus supersedes any shorter period that may be specified in the contract. The unambiguous language of the statute created a statutory right to appeal the Contracting Officer's decision within 90 days of its receipt. *University of Wisconsin Institute for Research on Poverty,* LBCA No. 81-BCA-1, 81-1 BCA 14,975.

In the event there is a dispute over when the contractor received the Contracting Officer's final decision, a presumption of receipt may arise. In order to satisfy such presumption, three elements must be established: (1) proper address, (2) sufficient postage, and (3) placement in the appropriate receptacle. The mere fact that a letter was written is insufficient to establish a presumption of mailing. *Cozzolino Constr. Co.,* PSBCA No. 103, 81-1 BCA 14,899.

If the appeal is mailed to a Board of Contract Appeals, the envelope must be postmarked within the 90-day period since it is the date of posting vis-à-vis the date of preparation that determines timeliness of filing. *Bardeen Mfg. Co.,* ASBCA No. 17724, 73-1 BCA 11,130. Where the date of mailing becomes a subject of proof, it is well recognized that a postmark is generally considered to be a reliable indication of the time of mailing. The degree of reliability differs depending on whether a postmark was affixed by a post office (a government agency) in its regular course of business or by a postage meter, which can be adjusted to reflect any desired date. A postmark affixed by a post office raised a strong presumption, if not an almost conclusive presumption, that the piece of mail was in the mail system at the time a postmark was affixed, while a postmark imprinted by a postage meter carries with it no such probative value. *Chicago Iron Works,* GSBCA No. 3169, 70-2 BCA 8525.

Boards of Contract Appeals are interpreting the Act, as it applies to timeliness of filing a claim, as being jurisdictional and not a mere procedural action. *Sofarelli Assocs.,* ASBCA No. 24580, 80-2 BCA 14,472. The Boards must consider the Act, which sets limits on the time for entertaining appeals, as removing their discretion to waive the late filing of appeals. *Avon C. Brown, Inc.,* DOTCAB No. 1082, 80-1 BCA 14,399. The Act does not contain specific language allowing for discretionary waiver considerations that would lend itself to such an interpretation. *Parkdale Building Maintenance,* ENG BCA No. 134-8-80, 81-1 BCA 15,105.

Accordingly, the 90-day time limitation set by section 7 of the Act is jurisdictional and precludes the Board's authority to entertain any appeal not taken within 90 days from the date a contractor receives the Contracting Officer's decision. The Act established a new statutory framework for the resolution of disputes related to government contracts. It amends the Tucker Act, 28 U.S.C. § 1491, with respect to actions in the Claims Court and provides for administrative adjudication of claims relating to contracts by agency Boards without regard to the presence of a Disputes clause or any other provision in such contracts. This "new statutory framework" is not simply an instruction to the administrative branch of the government to amend the Disputes clause and substitute 90 days for 30 days. Rather, it is a comprehensive legislative approach, providing for resolution of claims and disputes relating to government contracts awarded by the executive agencies. The Act represents an exclusive statutory scheme whereby the United States has consented to entertain litigation with respect to all claims relating to contracts to which the Act applies. Thus, failure of a contractor to comply with the notice requirements of section 7 acts as a statutory bar to any consideration of an appeal by the Boards. *Policy Research,* ASBCA No. 26144, 82-1 BCA 15,618.

Where a contractor has an option to appeal a Contracting Officer's decision to an agency Board of Contract Appeals within a finite time frame—but fails to do so within the prescribed period—the option ceases to exist. An untimely appeal to a Board is an absolute nullity, if not a contradiction in terms. If a contractor fails to take a timely appeal, there is no right of election, no valid means of invoking the jurisdiction of the Board, and no real choice of forums; rather, there is only a choice between a direct access suit and abandonment of his claim. *Cosmic Constr. Co. v. United States,* 5 Cl. Ct. 237 (1984).

### Timeliness in Appealing to the Claims Court

In lieu of appealing the Contracting Officer's final decision to an agency Board, the contractor may bring action on the claim directly to the Claims Court, provided that the action is filed within 12 months from the date of receipt by the contractor of the decision from the Contracting Officer regarding the claim. 41 U.S.C. § 609(a)(1) & (3). This section operates as a safety valve for the contractor. If he fails to file an appeal with the agency Board within the statutory 90-day time limit, he can still bring a direct access suit to the Claims Court. Failure to comply with the time limits for filing with the Claims Court operates as a statutory bar, precluding the court from deciding the case.

Hence, where the Contracting Officer's final decision was signed on November 6, 1979, and suit was not filed until March 9, 1981, the suit was time barred even though the contractor had sought review by an agency Board during the interim. The statutory limitation was not tolled by the contractor's efforts to seek review of the Contracting Officer's decision by the agency Board. Under the "direct access" provision of the Act, such administrative review was clearly not a mandatory prerequisite. Indeed, it was not a prerequisite at all; the presupposition of a "direct access" system is that suit may be commenced immediately after the Contracting Officer's decision. Congress set the 12-month limit, and the courts should not read into it exceptions and tolling provisions Congress did not contemplate or authorize. *Gregory Lumber Co. v. United States,* 229 Ct. Cl. 762 (1982).

The receipt of the Contracting Officer's decision by the contractor is the critical event that starts the running of the limitations period. The importance of this receipt is shown by the requirements in section 6(a) of the Act that the Contracting Officer's decision must be in writing, that the Contracting Officer must mail or otherwise furnish a copy of the decision to the contractor, and that the decision shall inform the contractor of his rights as provided in the Act. 41 U.S.C. § 605(a). A Contracting Officer's final decision that does not give the contractor adequate notice of his appeal rights is defective and therefore does not trigger the running of the limitations period. *Pathman Constr. Co. v. United States, supra.*

## Subcontractor Appeals

It is well established that subcontractors are not in privity with the government and therefore may not directly sue the government on their own initiative. They nevertheless may do so under the sponsorship rule. Under this rule, the subcontractor either (1) has the permission of the prime contractor to appeal or sue in the prime contractor's name or (2) has the prime contractor appeal or bring suit. See 41 U.S.C. § 601(4), which states that the term "contractor" means a party to a government contract other than the government, reflecting this longstanding rule of law.

Because the term "contractor" means a party to a government contract other than the government, it specifically excludes subcontractors under the provisions of the Act. It was expected that the sponsorship rules would remain in effect, which present a number of advantages. From the government's point of view, the sponsorship approach is the best method of administering complex procurements. By administering its procurement through a single point of contact, the government's job is made both simpler and cheaper. The single point of contact approach also helps suppress frivolous claims. If direct access were allowed to all government subcontractors, a Contracting Officer might, without appropriate safeguards, be presented with numerous frivolous claims that the prime contractor would not have sponsored.

By forcing the prime contractor to administer its subcontractor network, the government permits prime contractors and subcontractors at all tiers to use to some extent their familiar commercial procedures in contract award and administration. This advantage should not be underestimated since the considerable variation between government and commercial contract administration often requires extensive revisions in the administrative procedures of government prime contractors and considerable reeducation of contract personnel.

Finally, by denying the subcontractors direct access to administrative remedies, the government forces the prime contractor and the subcontractor to negotiate their disputes. Allowing direct access would eliminate some incentive to negotiate a settlement. This might result in additional time-consuming and expensive litigation. The forced negotiations under the present system can create a psychological familiarity between the prime contractor and subcontractor, resulting in greater likelihood of successful negotiation in future dealings.

On balance, although some inequities presently exist with respect to the treatment of subcontractor claims, these inequities are best handled by improved subcontract administration by the prime contractor with appropriate supervision by the government. The additional problems of contract administration and program management that would arise if subcontractors were given direct access to the government in disputes and claims outweigh the benefit to be gained. However, government contracting agencies must remain alert to problems associated with subcontractor claims and assure that those arising from government actions are decided fairly. S. Rep. No. 118, 95th Cong., 2d Sess. 16–17.

It is therefore clear that, unless the subcontractor can provide evidence of some type of contract between it and the United States, it cannot, as a subcontractor, sue the United States directly under the Contract Disputes Act. There is simply no privity of contract between the government and a subcontractor. The no-privity rule is synonomous with a finding that there is no express or implied contract between the government and a subcontractor. This concept of privity is reflected in the Act. According to 41 U.S.C. § 602(a), "this Act applies to an express or implied contract entered into by an executive agency." *United States v. Johnson Controls,* 713 F.2d 1541 (CAFC 1983).

Moreover, a dispute between a subcontractor and the government, when presented in compliance with the disputes procedure, will not be jurisdictionally barred by the apparent agreement of the prime contractor with the government's position. But a prime contractor's agreement with the government's position in a dispute with its subcontractor and the government can be used as evidence as to the reasonableness of the government's interpretation. *Hoffman Constr. Co.,* GSBCA No. 4036, 78-1 BCA 13,565.

## Fraudulent Claims

Section 5 of the Act provides that if a contractor is unable to support any part of his claim and it is determined that such inability is attributable to misrepresentation of fact or fraud, he shall be liable to the government for an amount equal to such unsupported part of his claim, in addition to all costs to the government attributable to the cost of reviewing that part of his claim. Liability under this subsection shall be determined within six years of such misrepresentation of fact or fraud. 41 U.S.C. § 604. The phrase "misrepresentation of fact" means a false statement of substantive fact, or any conduct that leads to a belief of a substantive fact material to proper understanding of the matter in hand, made with intent to deceive or mislead. 41 U.S.C. § 601(7).

This subsection was included out of concern that the submission of baseless claims contributes to the so-called "horse trading" theory where an amount beyond that which can be legitimately claimed is submitted merely as a negotiating tactic. Hence, payment of such a claim by the government would constitute a windfall to the contractor. It was Congress' view that to the extent that this practice is utilized, it should be eliminated so that disputes encompass only the amount that is truly contested. S. Rep. No. 96-118, 95th Cong., 2d Sess. 20. Claims of fraud are not intended to be the standard government response, however. The *Senate Explanation of Amendments* makes it clear that "this provision will in no way limit the right of contractors to make claims for recovery of legitimate costs. It will have no effect on the vast majority of contractors." 124 Cong. Rec. S18369 (daily ed. Oct. 12, 1978).

### Duty to Continue Performance

In 41 U.S.C. § 605(b), it is provided that "nothing in this Act shall prohibit executive agencies from including a clause in Government contracts requiring that pending final decision of an appeal, action, or final settlement, a contractor shall proceed diligently with performance of the contract in accordance with the Contracting Officer's decision." This requirement has been implemented in sections 33.013(a) and 52.233-1 of the FAR. It is similar to the requirements of the Changes article and need not be reiterated here.

## EXTRAORDINARY RELIEF

Public Law No. 85-804 granted the President broad powers to authorize those departments concerned with national defense to enter into contracts, or to make modifications or amendments to existing contracts, without regard to any other provision of law relative to contracting with the government, whenever he deems that such action will facilitate the national defense.

By Executive Order 10,789, November 14, 1958, the President authorized the heads of certain agencies to exercise the broad powers set forth in Public Law No. 85-804 and to delegate those powers to other officials within the agency. The importance of Public Law No. 85-804 and Executive Order 10,789 to the contractor performing in areas related to national security lies in the fact that they provide a mechanism whereby a contractor may obtain relief after all other remedies have been exhausted. The authority conferred by the statute and the executive order may not be used in a manner that encourages carelessness and laxity on the part of contractors engaged in the defense effort, and it cannot be relied on by the contractor as a means of relief when other adequate legal authority exists within the procuring agency. FAR § 50.102.

There are three broad areas in which a contractor might obtain relief under the statute, providing that he has exhausted all other remedies available under the contract and at law. The first provides that a contract may be amended without consideration where actual or threatened loss under a defense contract, however caused, will impair the productive capability of a contractor whose continued performance on any defense contract, or continued operation as a source of supply, is found to be essential to the national defense of the United States. The contract may be adjusted, but only to the extent necessary to avoid impairment of the contractor's productive ability. A contract may also be amended where the contractor suffers an actual loss on a defense contract as a result of some government action directed primarily toward that contractor in his contractual capacity, if equity and fairness so require. Though such actions by the government do not generally create any legal liability on its part, but do increase the cost of performance, considerations of fairness make such adjustments appropriate under the statute. The critical test of this authority is whether the contractor is essential to the national defense, either as a source of supply or for the performance of a given contract. It appears that few requests for relief have been approved under the source of supply criterion.

A substantial number of requests have been approved under the requirement that a particular contractor be essential to the performance of a contract. Under such authority, the government had determined that the product or service cannot be obtained elsewhere without delay and has often found that it would be more costly to obtain the item from another source. Relief for essentiality of continued performance has been denied, however, where other companies are capable of producing the product. *Edmonds & Sons Machine & Tool,* ACAB 1056, October 30, 1963.

In granting relief for essentiality of contract performance, the Boards of Contract Adjustment grant only enough relief to assure contract completion and will normally attach conditions for use of the funds allotted to assure completion. Conditions used include performance bonds, *Atlantic Diesel Mfg. Co.,* ACAB 215, February 26, 1957, and controlled bank accounts, *General Communications Co.,* NCAB, August 11, 1961.

The second avenue of relief under Public Law No. 85-804 involves mistakes consisting of a failure to clearly express the written agreement of the parties. These include a unilateral contractor mistake that was so obvious that it should have been apparent to the Contracting Officer and a mutual mistake regarding a material fact. Certain kinds of relief previously available only under Public Law No. 85-804, such as rescission and reformation for mutual mistake, are now available under the Contract Disputes Act of 1978. Thus, since the Disputes Act provides a remedy at law under the contract, it must be followed in order of precedence before relief can be had under Public Law No. 85-804. FAR § 50.102(c). The authority granted by Public Law No. 85-804 to correct mistakes rests on the presumption that amendments to correct mistakes with the least possible delay will facilitate the national defense by expediting the procurement program and by giving contractors proper assurances that such mistakes will be corrected expeditiously and fairly. If the contractor notifies the Contracting Officer of a mistake, either orally or in writing, (1) before the award of a contract under sealed-bid competitive procedures, (2) before the award of a contract under the competitive proposal procedure not requiring execution by both parties, or (3) before execution of contracts negotiated under the competitive proposal procedures, he is ineligible for relief under this authority.

Examples of correction of mistakes to make the contract express the intent of the parties are the deletion of a Patent Indemnity clause that was inserted in the contract by mistake, *Evans Reamer & Machine Co.*, ACAB 1003, March 31, 1959, and the revision of a contract to clearly state that general research and development costs were allowable costs, *Western Electric Corp.*, ACAB 1010, February 16, 1961.

There are numerous cases involving the correction of a mistake based on constructive knowledge of the Contracting Officer that the contractor's bid or proposal is based on a mistake. These cases arise after the contract has been awarded and include the submission of a low proposal together with a bill of materials that contained a major error, *Philco Corp.*, ACAB 1005, October 6, 1960, and the submission of a low bid and inability to verify complex prices prior to award, *Blaw-Know Co.*, ACAB 1019, April 19, 1960. Invariably, relief will be denied in those cases where it is found the contractor had ample warning of a potential mistake, but failed to protect his own interests. *Myers Corrugated Box Co.*, ACAB 1035, February 21, 1952.

The third avenue of relief lies in the formalization of informal commitments to permit payment to persons who have taken action without the benefit of a formal contract. Thus, where a person, responding to an agency official's written or oral instructions and relying in good faith on the official's apparent authority to issue them, has furnished or arranged to furnish supplies or services to the agency or to a defense contractor or subcontractor without formal contract coverage, relief may be granted. The formalizing of commitments under such circumstances facilitates the national defense by assuring such persons that they will be treated fairly and paid expeditiously. FAR § 50.302-2.

Normally, informal commitments will be formalized only in those situations where the need is compelling and of an unusual nature, such as when the national defense would have been seriously impaired or impeded if the supplies or services had not been furnished before the government had had an opportunity to prepare the necessary contractual documentation. The most difficult problem with respect to this remedy is that of meeting the statutory test that informal commitments cannot be formalized unless it is found that it was impracticable to use normal procurement procedures.

The determination of whether the use of normal procurement procedures was impracticable at the time the informal commitment is made depends on the circumstances surrounding the particular case. The Army Contract Adjustment Board has stated that one of the most important considerations in making this determination necessarily must be whether there is any evidence to indicate that the informal commitment was used as matter of convenience to circumvent or evade unnecessarily the statutory or administrative provisions involving military procurement. It has also been stated that a finding of impracticability could be made in the event the informal commitment resulted from a mistake of fact or error on the part of government personnel. Of course, a finding of impracticability may be made where normal procurement procedures cannot be complied with due to time limitations. *General Steam Navigation Co.*, ACAB 1007, February 26, 1960.

In *Radio Corp. of America*, ACAB 11039, April 12, 1962, the informal commitment arose initially as a result of the short period of time between the apportionment of contractual and governmental functions in relation to the Tiros II project and the scheduled launching date of the satellite. In addition, the Contracting Officer, although it later appeared that he was in error in the matter, was of the opinion that RCA could be paid for past services on the basis of anticipatory costs under a cost-plus-fixed-fee contract and later a fixed-price contract, to be executed with the subject firm. Under all the facts and circumstances, there was no evidence that government personnel utilized the informal commitment as a convenience or to avoid or circumvent normal procurement procedures. The evidence instead indicated that every effort was made to comply with normal procurement procedures, which efforts, however, were thwarted by the limitations of time and the subsequent discovery by the Contracting Officer that he could not execute a cost reimbursement or a fixed-price contract to cover the services rendered by RCA. In this situation, the policy of contracting through authorized procedures will not be prejudiced, and formalization of an informal commitment will be consistent with according the applicant fair treatment. *University of Alabama*, ACAB 1024, November 6, 1961; *Santini Brothers*, ACAB 1026, March 10, 1961.

Requests for relief under Public Law No. 85-804 are not claims within the purview of the Contract Disputes Act. But relief formerly available only under Public Law No. 85-804 (i.e., legal entitlement to rescission or reformation for mutual mistake) is now available within the authority of the Contracting Officer. FAR § 33.005(a); *Paragon Energy Corp. v. United States*, 227 Ct. Cl. 176, 645 F.2d 966 (1981). Accordingly, a contractor's allegation that he is entitled to rescission or reformation of his contract in order to correct or mitigate the effect of a mistake shall be treated as a claim under the Disputes Act. A contract may be reformed or rescinded by the Contracting Officer if the contractor would be entitled to such remedy or relief under the law of federal contracts. A claim that is either denied or not approved in its entirety under section 33.005(b) of the FAR may be cognizable as a request for relief under Public Law No. 85-804. However, the claim must first be submitted to the Contracting Officer for consideration under the Disputes Act because the claim is not cognizable under Public Law No. 85-804 unless other legal authority in the agency concerned is determined to be lacking or inadequate. FAR § 33.005(c).

Congress could not have expressed itself more clearly to the effect that all contractual claims based on a valid contractual theory fall within the procuring agency's jurisdiction under the Contract Disputes Act. This was essential to the congressional intent that all contract disputes be resolved according to the same set of procedures, beginning with the decision of the Contracting Officer. By implication—and also by express statement—equitable reformation to rectify bid mistakes is covered. There is no inconsistency here because while procuring agencies will be affording a remedy previously available only under Public Law No. 85-804, they will be proceeding not under the broadly discretionary "national defense" criterion of that law, but under the far more confining set of rules and principles that the Claims Court has evolved over a long string of reformation cases. Procuring agencies have authority under the Contract Disputes Act to reform contracts (and award proper monetary relief) to mitigate the effect of a unilateral bid mistake. A reformation claim for this purpose is cognizable before the Contracting Officer (and, by extension, agency Boards of Contract Appeals). *Paragon Energy Corp. v. United States, supra.*

# 15

# Debarment and Suspension

## INTRODUCTION

It is the policy of the government to award contracts to, and consent to subcontracts with, responsible contractors only. Debarment and suspension are discretionary actions that are appropriate means to effectuate this policy. The serious nature of these sanctions requires that they be imposed only in the public interest for the government's protection, and not for purposes of punishment. From the government's perspective, debarment and suspension are among the most effective administrative remedies available to a procuring agency to protect the government's interest. From the contractor's perspective, they are the most serious form of sanction that can be imposed because they bar a contractor from doing business with the government either for a specified period in the case of debarment or temporarily in the case of suspension. Debarment is authorized by statute as well as by regulation, whereas suspension is provided for only by regulation, but the validity of both measures is well established. *See Schlesinger v. Gates,* 249 F.2d 111 (D.C. Cir. 1957). In the case of both statutory and administrative debarment, it has been held that such are not penalties, but, if the procedures leading thereto are reasonable, proper regulatory measures for protecting the interests of the government. *Copper Plumbing & Heating Co. v. Campbell,* 290 F.2d 368 (D.C. Cir. 1961). Debarment and suspension, although harsh measures from the contractor's perspective, are the essential administrative mechanisms whereby the procuring agencies and departments maintain the integrity of the acquisition system.

## SUSPENSION

Suspension is generally imposed as a preliminary step to debarment and immediately precludes the contractor from participating in acquisition activities. Suspension is normally for a temporary period not to exceed 12 months (18 months, if requested by an Assistant Attorney General) or, if legal proceedings have commenced during that period, until the completion of such proceedings.

The government may suspend a firm or individual upon evidence of, inter alia, commission of fraud or a criminal offense in connection with obtaining, attempting to obtain, or performing a public contract or subcontract. FAR § 9.407-3(c). Under this criterion, a contractor may be suspended upon indictment for fraud.

For an agency to suspend a contractor, there must be adequate evidence, which has been defined as information sufficient to support the reasonable belief that a particular act or omission has occurred. FAR § 9.403. Evidence required to sustain a suspension is less than that which must be shown to convict the contractor of fraud, but is more than uncorroborated suspicion or accusation.

In *Horne Brothers v. Laird,* 463 F.2d 1268 (D.C. Cir. 1972), the court examined what it described as the serious and fundamental questions regarding the fairness of procedures utilized by the government in suspending contractors. It stated as a general proposition that an action that suspends a contractor and contemplates that he may dangle in suspension for a period of one year or more is such as to require the government to ensure fundamental fairness to the contractor whose economic life may depend on his ability to bid on government contracts. Fairness requires that the bidder be given specific notice as to at least some charges alleged against him and be given, in the usual case, an opportunity to rebut those charges. It suggests that generally a temporary suspension for a short period, not to exceed 30 days, without notice and opportunity to rebut charges may be acceptable. It also suggests that given the kind of evidence the government may be required to produce to comply with due process and the requirements of the regulation, whether there is adequate evidence to support the suspension is a question of judgment. On the one hand, such judgment may take into account the government's interest in national security and possible prejudice to prosecutorial action against the contractor; but on the other hand, it may not simply ignore the possibility of a legitimate interest in an opportunity for the contractor to be heard. *Accord Old Dominion Dairy v. Secretary of Defense,* 631 F.2d 953 (D.C. Cir. 1980).

## DEBARMENT

A contractor may be debarred following conviction of, or civil judgment for,

1. Commission of fraud or a criminal offense in connection with obtaining, attempting to obtain, or performing a public contract;
2. Violation of federal or state antitrust statutes relating to the submission of offers;
3. Commission of embezzlement, theft, bribery, falsification or destruction of records, false statements, or receipt of stolen property; or
4. Commission of any other offense indicating a lack of business integrity or business honesty that seriously and directly affects his present responsibility as a government contractor or subcontractor.

A contractor may also be debarred for violating the terms of a government contract or subcontract, but the violation must be of such a serious nature that debarment is fully justified. Such violations include (1) willful failure to perform in accordance with the terms of one or more contracts or (2) a history of failure to perform, or of unsatisfactory performance of, one or more contracts. *See* FAR § 9.406-2.

The Armed Services Procurement Act, 10 U.S.C. § 2305(c), and the Federal Property and Administrative Services Act, 41 U.S.C. § 252(b), provide the basic authority for procuring agencies to debar a contractor. Numerous other statutes also provide authority for debarment. Principal among these are the Davis-Bacon Act, the Services Contract Act, the Walsh-Healy Public Contracts Act, the Buy American Act, the Contract Work Hours and Safety Standards Act, the Clean Air Act, and the Federal Water Pollution Control Act. Debarment is likewise authorized for violation of the labor standards provisions of the statutes listed in the Labor Department's regulations at 29 C.F.R. § 5.1, as well as for noncompliance with the provisions of Executive Order 11,246, as amended, requiring equal opportunity in employment with respect to government contracts. Moreover, statutory debarments are effective governmentwide.

Administrative debarments, though effective throughout the executive branch of the government, may be waived under certain circumstances. Section 9.405(a) of the FAR provides that debarred or suspended contractors are excluded from receiving contracts, and agencies are prohibited from soliciting offers from, awarding contracts to, or consenting to subcontracts with these contractors, unless the head of the acquiring agency or his designee determines that there is a compelling reason for such action. Similar provisions are applicable to suspended contractors. FAR § 9.407-1(d). In order to waive the prohibitions of section 9.405(a), the agency head must state in writing the compelling reasons justifying continued business dealings between the agency and the contractor.

Under the provisions of sections 9.406-3 and 9.407-3 of the FAR, acquiring agencies are required to establish procedures governing the debarment and suspension decision-making processes so that they are as informed as is practicable, consistent with principles of fundamental fairness. In actions not based on a conviction or a judgment, if it is found that the contractor's submission in opposition to the proceeding raises a genuine dispute over facts material to the proposed debarment, acquiring agencies are required to afford the contractor an opportunity to appear with counsel, submit documentary evidence, present witnesses, and confront any person the agency presents; and the cause for debarment must be established by a preponderance of the evidence. FAR § 9.406-3(b) & (d).

These provisions are designed to assure that the due process requirements of the Constitution are not violated. The due process clauses of the fifth and fourteenth amendments require that a determination by a government authority stigmatizing a person as so lacking in integrity that he is to be deprived of property or the liberty to enjoy rights that he would otherwise enjoy must be preceded by written notice of the facts on which the charge is based and a reasonable opportunity to submit facts in response. *Perry v. Sindermann*, 408 U.S. 593 (1972); *Board of Regents v. Roth*, 408 U.S. 564 (1972); *Old Dominion Dairy Products v. Secretary of Defense*, 621 F.2d 953 (D.C. Cir. 1980); *Myers & Myers, Inc. v. United States Postal Service*, 527 F.2d 1252 (2d Cir. 1975); *ATL Inc. v. United States*, 3 Cl. Ct. 259 (1983).

That a person whose business or livelihood is largely dependent upon government contracts is entitled to procedural due process, including the rights to notice of specific charges and to an opportunity to present evidence before he can be blacklisted or barred from securing such contracts for actions demonstrating lack of integrity, is well established. The government cannot act arbitrarily, either substantively or procedurally, against a person. That person is entitled to challenge the processes and the evidence before he is officially declared ineligible for government contracts. Disqualification from bidding or contracting directs the power and prestige of government at a particular person and may have a serious economic impact on that person. Such debarment cannot be left to administrative improvisation on a case-by-case basis. The government power must be exercised in accordance with accepted basic legal norms. Considerations of basic fairness require administrative regulations establishing standards for debarment and procedures that will include notice of specific charges, and opportunities to present evidence and cross-examine adverse witnesses, all culminating in administrative findings and conclusions based on the records so made. Conceivably a temporary suspension for a reasonable period, pending investigation prior to a hearing, might be constitutionally permissible in some circumstances when procedural safeguards are accorded before a final decision is reached, but how long a temporary suspension could be sustained would depend on the need and other circumstances. *Gonzales v. Freeman*, 334 F.2d 570 (D.C. Cir. 1964).

Due process includes the right to be notified of the specific charge concerning the contractor's lack of integrity so as to afford the contractor an opportunity to respond to and attempt to persuade the government, in whatever time is available, that the allegations are without merit. Since a determination that a contractor lacks integrity may not be made without reference to specific charges or allegations, it will impose no burden on the government to notify the contractor of those charges. In so doing, the contractor will at least have the opportunity to explain his actions before adverse action is taken. In this way, a simple misunderstanding or mistake may be clarified before significant injury is done to both the government and the contractor. *Myers & Myers, Inc. v. United States Postal Serv., supra; ATL Inc. v. United States, supra.*

Under the provisions of section 9.406-4 of the FAR, contractors are debarred for a period commensurate with the cause. Generally, a debarment should not exceed three years. If a suspension was involved, the suspension period is to be taken into account in determining the debarment period. And if debarment was based on a statute, the resulting contract is void ab initio. *Paisner v. United States,* 138 Ct. Cl. 420, 150 F. Supp. 835 (1957), *cert. denied,* 355 U.S. 941 (1958). If the contractor was suspended or debarred in accordance with agency regulations, the contract is voidable at the government's option. *P.E.C. Corp.,* ASBCA No. 14241, 69-2 BCA 8056.

# Appendix: Federal Cases

*Aero Corp. v. Department of the Navy*, 504 F. Supp. 180 (D.C. Cir. 1982).

*American Electronic Laboratories v. United States*, CAFC 85–7080, 31 CCF 73,973 (1985).

*Aragona Construction Co. v. United States*, 165 Ct. Cl. 382 (1985).

*Armstrong v. United States*, 144 Ct. Cl. 441, 169 F. Supp. 259 (1959).

*W.H. Armstrong v. United States*, 98 Ct. Cl. 519 (1943).

*Bateson-Stolte, Inc. v. United States*, 158 Ct. Cl. 455, 305 F.2d 386 (1982).

*Bowsher v. Mercke & Co.*, 460 U.S. 824 (1984).

*Bruce Construction Corp. v. United States*, 163 Ct. Cl. 97, 324 F.2d 516 (1963).

*Allen M. Campbell Co. v. Lloyd Wood Construction Co.*, 446 F.2d 261 (5th Cir. 1971).

*Carrier Corp. v. United States*, 6 Cl. Ct. 169 (1984).

*G.L. Christian & Associates v. United States*, 160 Ct. Cl. 1, 312 F.2d 418 (1963).

*Clark Mechanical Contractors v. United States*, 5 Cl. Ct. 84 (1984).

*Condec Corp. v. United States*, 177 Ct. Cl. 958, 369 F.2d 753 (1966).

*Connelly Containers v. United States*, 7 Cl. Ct. 423 (1985).

*Cooke v. United States*, 91 U.S. 389 (1875).

*Helene Curtis Industries v. United States*, 160 Ct. Cl. 437, 312 F.2d 774 (1963).

*Cutler-Hammer Inc. v. United States*, 189 Ct. Cl. 76 (1969).

*Electro-Methods v. United States*, 7 Cl. Ct. 755 (1985).

*Foster Wheeler Corp. v. United States*, 206 Ct. Cl. 533 (1975).

*Fox Valley Engineering v. United States*, 151 Ct. Cl. 228 (1960).

*Freund v. United States*, 260 U.S. 60 (1922).

*General Casualty Co. v. United States,* 130 Ct. Cl. 520 (1955).

*Gulf & Western Industries v. United States,* 384 Ct. Cl. 77 (1980).

*Narva Harris Construction Co. v. United States,* 216 Ct. Cl. 238 (1978).

*J.D. Hedin Construction Co. v. United States,* 171 Ct. Cl. 70 (1965).

*Hewlett-Packard v. United States,* 385 F.2d 1013 (9th Cir. 1967), *cert. denied,* 390 U.S. 988 (1968).

*HLC & Associates Construction Co. v. United States,* 168 Ct. Cl. 873 (1964).

*Dale Ingram, Inc. v. United States,* 201 Ct. Cl. 56 (1973).

*Peter Kiewit's Sons Co. v. United States,* 138 Ct. Cl. 668 (1957).

*Laburnum Construction Corp. v. United States,* 163 Ct. Cl. 339 (1963).

*Law v. United States,* 195 Ct. Cl. 370 (1971).

*Len Co. & Associates v. United States,* 181 Ct. Cl. 29, 385 F.2d 438 (1967).

*Lockheed Aircraft Corp. v. United States,* 193 Ct. Cl. 86 (1970).

C.G. *McQuagge v. United States,* 179 F. Supp. 460 (D.C. La. 1961).

*Merritt-Chapman & Scott Corp. v. United States,* 192 Ct. Cl. 848 (1970).

*Midland Land & Improvement Co. v. United States,* 192 Ct. Cl. 848 (1970).

*M–R–S Manufacturing Co. v. United States,* 203 Ct. Cl. 551, 492 F.2d 835 (1974).

*Norair Engineering Corp. v. United States,* 229 Ct. Cl. 160, 666 F.2d 546 (1981).

*Olin Matheson Chemical Corp. v. United States,* 179 Ct. Cl. 368 (1967).

*Penn-Ohio Steel Corp. v. United States,* 173 Ct. Cl. 1064 (1965).

*Perkins v. Lukens Steel Co.,* 310 U.S. 113 (1940).

*Prestex v. United States,* 162 Ct. Cl. 620, 320 F.2d 367 (1963).

*Putnam Mills Corp. v. United States,* 202 Ct. Cl. 1 (1973).

*Radiation Technology v. United States,* 177 Ct. Cl. 227 (1966).

*Reeside v. Walker,* 52 U.S. (11 How.) 272 (1880).

*J.A. Ross & Co. v. United States,* 126 Ct. Cl. 323 (1953).

*Rumley v. United States,* 152 Ct. Cl. 166 (1961).

*Saddler v. United States,* 152 Ct. Cl. 557 (1961).

*Scherr v. United States,* 5 Cl. Ct. 249 (1984).

*Scott v. United States,* 44 Ct. Cl. 524 (1909).

*Singer Co., Librascope Division v. United States,* 217 Ct. Cl. 225, 576 F.2d 905 (1978).

*Space Age Engineering v. United States,* 212 Ct. Cl. 329 (1977).

*Max M. Stoeckert v. United States,* 183 Ct. Cl. 152 (1968).

*Sutton v. United States,* 256 U.S. 575 (1921).

*Tester Corp. v. United States,* 1 Cl. Ct. 370 (1982).

*Tibshraeny Brothers Construction v. United States,* 6 Cl. Ct. 463 (1984).

*Truong Xuan Truc v. United States,* 212 Ct. Cl. 51 (1976).

*United States v. Allegheny County,* 322 U.S. 174 (1944).

*United States v. Chichester,* 312 F.2d 275 (9th Cir. 1963).

*United States v. Corliss Steam Engine Co.,* 91 U.S. 321 (1875).

*United States v. Georgia-Pacific Co.,* 421 F.2d 92 (9th Cir. 1970).

*United States v. Maurice,* 26 F. Cas. 1211 (1823).

*United States v. Spearin,* 24 U.S. 132 (1918).

# Selected Bibliography


Cibinic, John, Jr., and Ralph C. Nash, Jr. *Federal Procurement Law: Volume I.* 3d ed. Washington, D.C.: George Washington University Press, 1977.

______.*Federal Procurement Law: Volume II.* 3d ed. Washington, D.C.: George Washington University Press, 1980.

______.*Government Contract Claims.* Washington, D.C.: George Washington University Press, 1981.

______.*Formation of Government Contracts.* Washington, D.C.: George Washington University Press, 1982.

______.*Administration of Government Contracts.* 2d ed. Washington, D.C.: George Washington University Press, 1985.

Coburn, George M. *The Contract Disputes Act of 1978.* New York: Practising Law Institute, 1982.

Grackle, Theo. W. *The Law of Government Defense Contracts.* New York: Baker, Vorhiss Co., 1941.

______.*The Law Governing War Contract Claims.* New York: Baker, Voorhiss Co., 1945.

Hearn, Emmett E. *Handbook on Government Contract Administration.* Los Altos, Calif.: Hearn Assoc., 1987.

Lether, Ivan J. *Government Procurement and Operations.* Cambridge, Mass.: Ballinger Co., 1977.

# Index

# About the Author

EUGENE W. MASSENGALE has served as a contracts manager in both government and private industry and, more recently, has lectured on the subject of contract law and procurement principles. In addition to writing a number of training courses on federal contracting for government agencies, he has contributed articles to *Worldview, The Review,* and *Military Review.*